Human Authors of the New Testament

Volume 1

MARK, MATTHEW, AND LUKE

Warren Dicharry, C.M.

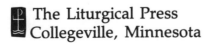
The Liturgical Press
Collegeville, Minnesota

Cover woodcut by Robert F. McGovern; design by Don Bruno.

1	2	3	4	5	6	7	8	9

Library of Congress Cataloging-in-Publication Data

Dicharry, Warren F.
    Human authors of the New Testament / Warren Dicharry.
        p.   cm.
    Includes bibliographical references and index.
    Contents: v. 1. Mark, Matthew, and Luke.
    ISBN 0-8146-1956-8 (v. 1)
    1. Evangelists (Bible)—Biography. 2. Paul, the Apostle, Saint.
    3. Bible. N.T.—Criticism, interpretation, etc. I. Title.
BS2441.D53 1990
225.9'22—dc20
[B]   90-45349
                                                             CIP

To the many wonderful people who are so hungry for the Word of God and so receptive to my biblical missions, retreats, and workshops, this labor of love is humbly, cordially, and gratefully dedicated.

ILLUSTRATIONS:

MAPS

CONTENTS

The ruins of ancient Byblos, from which the word Bible eventually is derived. It was the main port in Phoenicia (Northern Canaan) for importing papyrus from Egypt, where the papyrus plant grows.

Introduction

Unique among our world's vast and varied literature, there is a collection of writings, composed over a period of more than a thousand years, of whose authorship we can speak only in terms of mystery. I refer, of course, to Sacred Scripture, or the Holy Bible.[1] Most Christians and Jews commonly revere these writings as inspired, that is, as having God for their author in an absolutely singular way.[2] At the same time, however, we recognize that God did not simply drop them from heaven or dictate them verbatim. No, in his wisdom, he employed human authors as living instruments who, whether or not they were conscious of being inspired, wrote as people of flesh and blood, intelligence and free will, as members of a faith community living in a particular age and area of the world, thinking and writing according to their own cultural and personal characteristics.[3] How this could be done is certainly a mystery of God's unlimited wisdom, love, and power, but that it was done is a doctrine of our Judeo-Christian faith.[4]

In times past and still to a large extent today, devout Christians and Jews have tended to place the major emphasis on the divine rather than the human authorship of the Bible. This is quite understandable. After all, it is precisely the divine authorship that makes this marvelous literature unique, for all other writings in the world are the result of merely human authorship. Besides, in the belief of both Christians and Jews but in different degrees according to various traditions and affiliations, the divine authorship ensures inerrancy, which means that the Bible, when properly understood, is free from formal error, especially in matters pertaining to salvation.[5]

Why not, then, content ourselves with our traditional emphasis on the divine authorship? The answer, according to the true tradition of the Church as reflected in Jerome, Augustine, Chrysostom, Aquinas, and a host of other ancient, medieval, and modern sources, lies in those three words of the previous sentence, "when properly understood." Since God used human authors writing in a human way, albeit inspired, we can hardly expect to understand what they meant to say if we ignore their human authorship. No, we need to learn something about their times, their historical situation, their manner of thinking and writing, the languages they used in expressing themselves, the literary forms they employed, the people for whom they wrote, their purpose in writing, and anything else that can provide us with helpful insights into what they meant to tell their readers. For what they intended to say is, in a biblical sense, the literal meaning of Sacred Scripture.[6]

The human authors frequently couched their thought in highly imaginative language, but what they intended to express, whether figuratively or prosaically, is still the literal sense of the sacred text and the first meaning we are to search for in reading the Bible.[7] Any other approach does violence to the Bible as the Word of God in words of men.[8] We refer to this as the first meaning because, in addition to the literal sense which is always present, there may sometimes be a spiritual meaning[9] intended by the divine author beyond the awareness of the human author, a meaning which is clarified through later inspiration. This is particularly true of a number of texts in the Old Testament which become fully clear only in the New, or Christian, Testament. An outstanding example occurs in Isa 7:14 where the prophet Isaiah, in the context of his time, circumstances, and language, was apparently promising the continuation of the Davidic dynasty in the kingdom of Judah through the birth of a son, the remarkable Hezekiah, to King Ahaz and his young wife; but later this same text was reinterpreted in messianic and virginal terms in the Jews' own Septuagint Greek translation two centuries before Jesus Christ, and still later in the Infancy Gospels of "Matthew" and Luke.[10]

Thus the contributions of both the divine and human authors must always receive our fullest attention when we read the Bible, lest we run the risk of distorting or at least restricting its rich and salutary content. This is merely another way of saying that we must always read the Bible as it was written, namely by both divine and human authors. To neglect one or the other authorship results in just as unbalanced a picture as to ignore the divine or human nature of Jesus Christ himself. In the great encyclical of modern Catholic biblical studies, *Divino Afflante Spiritu* (1943), Pope Pius XII, following St. John Chrysostom and others, declares in effect, "Just as the incarnate Word of God is human in all things except sin, so is the inspired Word of God human in all things except error!"[11]

This approach to Scripture should not at all be understood as intended to discourage individual reading of the Bible with the help of the Holy Spirit, but rather as encouraging and urging readers of Sacred Scripture to keep their more personal and subjective reading of God's Word always within the context of the more communal and objective understanding of the Bible according to its dual authorship. In a sense, we could apply to the subjective and objective reading of Scripture what Jesus insists on with the scribes and Pharisees in Matt 23:23: "You ought to have done these things without omitting the others!"

The "error" spoken of in Pius XII's encyclical refers, of course, only to formal and not material error, as I have indicated earlier. That there can be material error in the Bible is simply the consequence of the limited knowledge of the human authors inspired by God. To them, science was no more than the observed present, history nothing more than the remembered past. And understandably, their observations of the world about them, as well as their remembrance and traditions of past happenings, left much to be desired when compared to our own knowledge of science and history. Nor were they intent on writing works of science or history in the first place, but rather works of religion, glorifying God in his creation and saving intervention in human events. The Bible is not a book or even a library of books about history as we normally understand it, still less about science, but about nothing less than salvation history, which is far more profitable for us and for the world.[12]

But did not God reveal to the human authors the scientific and historical information reflected in the Bible, thereby ensuring its accuracy? No, such a notion confuses revelation and inspiration. The entire Bible is inspired but not all of it is revealed. Inspiration is the grace to write; revelation, the grace to know, especially truths which could not otherwise be known by our limited human intelligence and above all matters of primary importance in doctrine and morals. As for data about prehistoric events such as the origin of the world, the great St. Augustine wisely remarks in summary that "God does not reveal how the heavens go, but how we go to Heaven!"[13]

All of this may be interesting and helpful, but the inevitable question arises, How is the ordinary layperson expected to gain the knowledge required to understand the meaning intended by the human writers of the Bible? In an earlier age, that query was far more difficult to answer, but in our "age of Scripture," thanks to extraordinary advances in archaeology, history, and geography as well as ethnology, philology, and related sciences, we are fortunately in a much more favorable position for understanding in general the human authorship of the Bible.[14] Wonderful! But is that enough? No, I do not think so!

We human beings want to know, insofar as possible, who the particular human authors were, why they happened to write what we have in the Bible, and how they proceeded to develop their ideas in such a way as to produce the works as they are. When we pick up any book, do we not instinctively check to see who the author is as well as why and how he or she came to write the volume, so that we may know not only whether we will go ahead and read it, but also and above all what we will be looking for in the writing? Now, bearing in mind that all the biblical books were authored by humans writing humanly, although under divine inspiration, is it not natural for us to want to know who those human authors were, what they were like, why they wrote their works, and how they set about organizing their ideas so that we might know what to look for in our reading of their books? *It is precisely to help the reader to answer such questions that I have undertaken to write this book.*

An important endeavor, granted, but how can it possibly succeed? Is it not true that for most of the books of the Bible we do not even know the names of the human authors,[15] let alone why and how they wrote their books? This is true enough for the Old Testament, but in the New, or Christian, Testament we do have a *good idea of who composed* the particular books as well as some indications of why and how they wrote them. I hope to take that information, drawn partly from historical tradition, and partly from well-founded speculation based on documented research and weave it into a readable and credible account which may help the New Testament reader to identify more closely with the human authors of the individual books. Not that the resulting portraits of those authors are guaranteed to be accurate in every detail, for the "stream cannot rise above its source,"[16] but plausible pictures, although subject to controversy, are to my mind better than no pictures at all. As the famous Chinese proverb expresses it, "I go tsin, i wan tzu," that is, "One picture is worth ten thousand words!"[17]

By reason of limitations, both in the length of these volumes and in the availability of sources, I have decided to confine my portraits of the New Testament writers to five, comprising those who are generally regarded as the five main human authors of the New Testament: *Mark, Matthew, Luke, Paul, and John.* Because they and their writings are alive in Christ and in the Holy Spirit, I hope that these studies will help them to come alive anew for the reader. In my treatment of them, I assign each author a descriptive (and alliterative) adjective which may help to fix his individual portrait in the reader's imagination and memory. In singling out these five authors, who are responsible for the vast majority of New Testament books, I do not at all intend to slight such outstanding authors as Peter, James, and the writer of the magnificent Epistle to the Hebrews (who was not St. Paul),[18] but rather to help at least these five to become real and alive to my readers. If I can manage to do that in the case of even one or two of these human authors, I will consider my time and effort well spent indeed, and perhaps my feeble attempt will move others far more knowledgeable than I to succeed where I have fallen short.

The treatment of each of the five New Testament authors will comprise, in general, three parts: (1) a somewhat imaginative *portrait* of the person himself and a dramatic *scenario* of the special circumstances that seem to have occasioned his writing, (2) a brief *analysis* of his work (or works) to discover its principal characteristics and message, and (3) some personal and communal *applications* to our own times and lives. For the sake of personal and group study, each chapter will be followed by questions for reflection and discussion together with suggestions for further reading.

The translation of the Bible that I will normally use in this enterprise is the New American Bible, which seems to be the most familiar to my fellow Catholics, for whom this volume is principally but not exclusively intended, but I shall not hesitate to use whatever translation best captures the meaning of the original Greek, even making my own translation whenever that appears to be necessary. To avoid confusion, I will indicate which translation I am using in each of my quotations or allusions, according to the following designations, listed alphabetically: JB for the *Jerusalem Bible*,[19] NAB for the *New American Bible*,[20] NEB for the *New English Bible*,[21] NIV for the *New International Version*,[22] RSV for the *Revised Standard Version*,[23] and WFD for my own translation. At times, it may be helpful and even necessary to quote directly in transliteration from the original *Koine*, or Common Greek, which became the international language under Alexander the Great and in which the entire New Testament was written, but only in order to clarify a point or disclose the riches of the text.

Before concluding this introduction, I want to express my debt of gratitude to the administration and faculty, students and staff, and especially the kind and helpful librarians of Saint Thomas Seminary in Denver, Colorado, where much of my initial research and writing was done in the summers of 1988–90, as well as to my fellow Vincentians of Timon House in Houston, Texas, where the work was completed, and of course to the editors and staff of The Liturgical Press, without whose patient assistance this modest effort might never have reached publication.

Warren F. Dicharry, C.M.
Vincentian Evangelization
Timon House, Houston, Texas

NOTES

1. Our simple and familiar word "Bible" has had a long and fascinating history. It began as a Greek feminine loanword *býblos* from the Egyptian noun for papyrus and the "paper" made from it, hence the name of ancient Byblos in Lebanon where papyrus was imported from Egypt into Phoenicia. Then the word was modified to *bíblos* and the neuter diminutive *biblíon*, which came in time to be the word of preference for a scroll or book. The plural of this neuter, namely *tà biblía*, meaning "the scrolls or books," was used without any other indication by the Greek-speaking Jews and Christians in reference to the Sacred Scriptures, so great was their reverence for them. But when the neuter plural noun *biblía* for "books" was transliterated into Latin it became a feminine singular *biblia*, meaning "a book or the book." Thus it was that what had originally and correctly been regarded as a collection or library of books, came in time, through Latin and French, to be understood as "a book or the book," namely the Bible *(Theological Dictionary of the New Testament*, 1964, s.v. "bíblos, biblíon").

2. Texts on inspiration: Exod 24:4; Isa 34:16; 1 Macc 12:9; Mark 12:36; John 5:39; 10:35; 2 Tim 3:15-17; 2 Pet 1:19-21.

The belief in inspiration and the endeavors to explain it are two very different matters. I will make no attempt in this brief introduction to solve the mystery of inspiration. Instead I refer the reader to treatments of this thorny issue by acknowledged authorities on the subject, listed in alphabetical order, with the reminder that we are, after all, dealing with a mystery of grace: Luis Alonzo-Schökel, *The Inspired Word* (New York: Herder and Herder, 1965); James Burtchaell, *Catholic Theories of Biblical Inspiration Since 1810* (Cambridge, England: University Press, 1969); Pierre Grelot, *The Bible, Word of God*, trans. Peter Nickells (New York: Desclee, 1968) 35–79; Jean Levie, *The Bible, Word of God in Words of Men*, trans. S. H. Treman (New York: Kenedy, 1961) 203–301; Karl Rahner, *Inspiration in the Bible*, 2nd ed., trans. Charles Henkey, rev. Martin Palmer (London, England: Burns & Oates, 1964); *Theological Dictionary of the New Testament*, s.v. "pneûma"; Bruce Vawter, *Biblical Inspiration* (Philadelphia: Westminster, 1972).

3. *See* Pope Pius XII, "Divino Afflante Spiritu" (1943), *Rome and the Study of Scripture*, 6th ed. (St. Meinrad, Ind.: Grail, 1958) 96–99.

4. *The Jewish Encyclopedia*, 1916, s.v. "Inspiration"; S. David Sperling, "Judaism and Modern Biblical Research," *Biblical Studies: Meeting Ground of Jews and Christians*, ed. Lawrence Boadt, Helga Croner, and Leon Klenicki (New York: Paulist, 1980) 19–44; Martin Cohen, "Record and Revelation: A Jewish Perspective," *Biblical Studies* 147–71; Vatican Council I, "Dei Filius, ch. 2: De Revelatione," *Bible Interpretation*, ed. James McGivern (Wilmington, N.C.: McGrath, 1978) 191–92.

5. What I have said above under n. 2 about the mystery of inspiration pertains also to the related mystery of inerrancy. In addition to the list of books given above one should check the following Church documents: Pope Leo XIII,

"Providentissimus Deus" (1893), *Rome and the Study of Scripture* 23–25; Pope Benedict XV, "Spiritus Paraclitus" (1920), *Rome and the Study of Scripture* 48–51.

6. *See* Raymond Brown, "Hermeneutics," *The Jerome Biblical Commentary,* ed. R. Brown, Joseph Fitzmyer, and Roland Murphy (Englewood Cliffs, N.J.: Prentice-Hall, 1968) 2:606–10 (hereafter cited as *JBC*).

7. *See* Pope Pius XII, "Divino Afflante Spiritu" (1943), *Rome and the Study of Scripture* 92–93; Vatican Council II, "Dogmatic Constitution on Divine Revelation" (1965), *The Documents of Vatican II,* ed. Austin Flannery (Northport, N.Y.: Costello, 1975) 756–58.

8. *Ibid.* 756–58. This comparatively brief section of the Vatican II Constitution on Divine Revelation summarizes almost all the key points in prior Church documentation about the Bible.

9. *See* Pope Pius XII, "Divino Afflante Spiritu" (1943), *Rome and the Study of Scripture* 93–95; Brown, "Hermeneutics," *JBC,* 2:610–19.

10. *See* Raymond Brown, *The Birth of the Messiah* (Garden City, N.Y.: Doubleday, 1977) 143–55.

See also the development of the "Son of Man" idea from a symbol of redeemed Israel in Dan 7:13-14 to a messianic individual in the Apocryphal Book of Henoch to Jesus' use of it to indicate both his humanness and his messiahship. *See* Louis Hartman, "Daniel," *JBC* 1:436; Raymond Brown, "Apocrypha," *JBC* 2:538; David Stanley and Raymond Brown, "Aspects of New Testament Thought," *JBC* 2:773.

Another good example may be Gen 1:26-27, where we humans are described as made "to the image and likeness of God." Even in a literal sense it could have several meanings intended by the human author (or succession of authors), for unlike the Greek philosophical mind so prone to define, divide, and distinguish, the biblical intuitive mind tended to view things in a more holistic, existentialist manner. *See* St. Augustine, *Christian Instruction,* trans. John Gavigan, The Fathers of the Church, ed. Ludwig Schopp (New York: Cima, 1947) 147. Hence, these possible literal meanings: (1) humans have intelligence and free will like God himself; (2) we also have dominion, like God, over creation (Gen 1:28) but a dominion of stewardship; (3) as "male and female" we have the awesome power, like God and with God, to "create" new human life (v. 28). But in addition there may be one or more spiritual meanings, for example: (1) humans were formed "to be imperishable" (Wis 2:23); (2) above all, we were created in God's "image and likeness" in the profound sense of being intended for union with Jesus Christ, "the image of the invisible God" (Col 1:15), "the perfect representation of the Father's being" (Heb 1:3) into whose image we were predestined to be conformed or transformed (see Rom 8:29; 2 Cor 3:18; Col 3:10). More on this matter so crucial for our spiritual life can be found in my book *To Live the Word, Inspired and Incarnate* (Staten Island, N.Y.: Alba House, 1985) 35–39.

11. This is a rather free but very emphatic rendering of Pope Pius XII's encyclical "Divino Afflante Spiritu," *Rome and the Study of Scripture* 98; see also St. John Chrysostom's commentary on Gen 1:4; 2:21; 3:8 in J-P Migne, *Patres Graeci* (Paris: Petit Montrouge, 1862) 53:35, 121, 135.

12. *See* John McKenzie, *The Two-Edged Sword* (Milwaukee, Wis.: Bruce, 1957) 60–71; John McKenzie, "Aspects of Old Testament Thought," *JBC* 2:755.

13. This catchy aphorism seems to be a free but powerful summary of St. Augustine's comment on Gen 2:28 in "De Genesin ad Litteram," J-P Migne, *Patres Latini* (1841) 34:278, cited in Pius XII's "Divino Afflante Spiritu," *Rome and the Study of Scripture* 82.

14. *See* Pope Pius XII, "Divino Afflante Spiritu," *Rome and the Study of Scripture* 97.

15. *See* Burtchaell, *Catholic Theories of Biblical Inspiration* 249–50.

16. William Smith, *Oxford Dictionary of English Proverbs*, 3rd. ed., rev. F. P. Wilson (Oxford: Clarendon, 1974) 779.

17. Anonymous Chinese proverb in John Bartlett, *Familiar Quotations*, 14th ed., rev. and enl., ed. Emily Morison Beck (Boston: Little, Brown, 1968) 149b.

18. Despite the ascription of this Epistle to St. Paul in the Lectionary, it is almost universally agreed among Scripture scholars today, Catholic and otherwise, that Paul was not the author in any commonly accepted sense. Origen (A.D. 185–253), who is generally considered the founder of biblical science, regarded it as Pauline in only the broadest sense. Even earlier Tertullian (A.D. 155–220?) attributed it to Barnabas. The truth of the matter is that this magnificent Epistle is, unlike Paul's Letters, unsigned and listed in the New Testament outside the Pauline corpus. The author is unknown but does give evidence of a Jewish Christian Alexandrian origin as well as great expertise in Greek philosophy and rhetoric. For this reason the opinion of Luther, Zahn, Manson, Spicq, and others that Paul's fellow evangelist Apollos (see Acts 18:24-28; 1 Cor 1-4) is the most likely candidate has much to recommend it. *See* Myles Bourke, "The Epistle to the Hebrews," in *JBC* 2:381–82. Other sources are Alfred Wikenhauser, *New Testament Introduction*, trans. Joseph Cunningham (New York: Herder and Herder, 1958) 453–54; F. F. Bruce, *The Epistle to the Hebrews* (Grand Rapids: Eerdmans, 1977) xxxv–xlii; Philip Hughes, *A Commentary on the Epistle to the Hebrews* (Grand Rapids: Eerdmans, 1977) 19–30; Raymond Brown, *Christ Above All: The Message of Hebrews* (Downers Grove, Ill.: InterVarsity Press, 1982).

19. *The Jerusalem Bible*, ed. Alexander Jones (Garden City, N.Y.: Doubleday, 1966).

20. *The New American Bible*, rev. (Camden, N.J.: Nelson, 1987).

21. *The New English Bible*, ed. Sandmel, Suggs, and Tkacik (New York: Oxford University Press, 1976).

22. *The Holy Bible: New International Version* (Grand Rapids: Zondervan, 1978).

23. *The Holy Bible: Revised Standard Version / Catholic Edition*, ed. Orchard and Fuller (Collegeville: The Liturgical Press, 1966).

NERO'S ROME

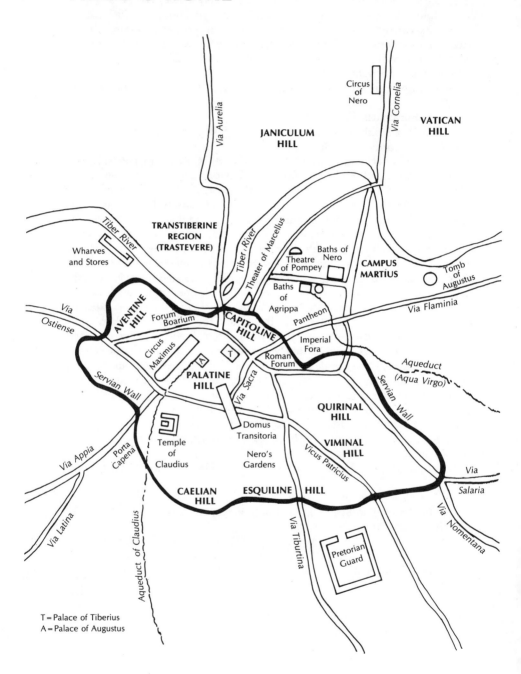

N —→

Via Aurelia

JANICULUM
HILL

Circus
of
Nero

Via Cornelia

VATICAN
HILL

Tiber River

Wharves
and Stores

TRANSTIBERINE
REGION
(TRASTEVERE)

Tiber River

Theater of Marcellus

Baths of
Nero

Theatre
of Pompey

CAMPUS
MARTIUS

Tomb
of
Augustus

Via
Ostiense

AVENTINE
HILL

Forum
Boarium

Circus
Maximus

Baths
of
Agrippa

Pantheon

Via Flaminia

CAPITOLINE
HILL

Imperial
Fora

Roman
Forum

Aqueduct
(Aqua Virgo)

Servian Wall

A

T

PALATINE
HILL

Via Sacra

QUIRINAL
HILL

Servian Wall

Via Appia

Porta
Capena

Temple
of
Claudius

Domus
Transitoria

Nero's
Gardens

Vicus Patricius

VIMINAL
HILL

Via
Salaria

Via Latina

Aqueduct of Claudius

CAELIAN
HILL

ESQUILINE   HILL

Via Tiburtina

Via Nomentana

Pretorian
Guard

T = Palace of Tiberius
A = Palace of Augustus

1
Marvelous Mark and the First Gospel[1]

THE STORY OF MARK

Along with Persecutions[2] (Mark 10:30)

No one in Rome could remember a hotter, drier summer. Most of the elite had already left the Eternal City for cooler climate. One of the first to flee, the emperor Nero,[3] was heard to mutter something about the "Infernal City" as his chariot raced toward the west-coast town of Antium,[4] his birthplace and summer resort. And yet it was still only July! In the past, this kind of oppressive and stifling heat had not succeeded in driving Romans out of their city until the following month. But they were gone, leaving behind those who had nowhere to go: impoverished nobles and knights, patricians and plebeians, who either could not afford or had lost summer homes; some of the officials and politicians whose duties or fears precluded their departure; merchants between trips and soldiers between wars; and above all the poor in their hovels and the slaves guarding their masters' mansions. They could think of no worse fate than having to languish in Rome through such a beastly summer! None, that is, until the historic Great Fire of Rome on the night of July 18–19, A.D. 64.[5]

It began near the vast Circus Maximus[6] on the south side of the ancient city. There, in a hollow of closely packed shanties and shops, a tiny wisp of smoke appeared as if by spontaneous combustion. Unnoticed at first, it quickly exploded into a leaping flame, piercing the darkness like a gleaming sword raised in angry revolt. The scorching sirocco which had tormented the city and its environs for weeks now

17

dealt its coup de grâce, consuming the slums like kindling and driving the flames irresistibly northward toward the very heart of Rome with its grand temples and palaces.

Cries of terror and despair shattered the night. The entire corps of Roman *vigiles*,[7] or firefighters, was dispatched to contain and extinguish the blaze, but to no avail. Their initial fireline, hastily installed in a desperate attempt to save the great city, was no sooner established than it was breached and swallowed up by the conflagration. The emperor Nero, who had been summoned from Antium at the first alarm, arrived at Rome just in time to see first his *Domus Transitoria*[8] then his palace on the Palatine, both of them filled with his cherished ornaments and artistic awards, reduced to smoking rubble.

On and on like an invincible army the holocaust continued to spread, consuming without distinction palaces and temples, spacious homes and simple hovels, theaters and gardens. After five days the onslaught was halted at the Esquiline Hill[9] by a colossal firebreak, only to rekindle and destroy still more of the stricken city until, on the ninth weary day, it was at long last brought under control.

Ten of Rome's fourteen districts[10] lay in smoldering ruins. Countless numbers of people, especially the poorest of the poor, perished in the smoke and flames, their noisome charred and rotting corpses strewn everywhere, while dazed and demented survivors wandered aimlessly about or huddled in surrounding fields in a state of total shock. The once magnificent city now resembled an enormous garbage dump, even vaster and uglier than Jerusalem's infamous Gehenna,[11] the Jewish symbol of hell itself!

Without delay Nero gave the order, first to shelter the homeless, then to bury the dead, and promptly after that to begin rebuilding Rome on a far grander scale with more permanent materials, starting with his own projected *Domus Aurea*.[12] News of this order, along with awareness of the emperor's earlier plans to construct a new and greater capital city and name it after himself,[13] began to generate among the many homeless and bereaved inhabitants the rumor that the erratic ruler himself had ordered the fire started, prevented it from being extinguished, and even used the horrible conflagration as ideal scenery for his sung reenactment of the tragic destruction of Troy.[14]

Ironically, the rumor of Nero's responsibility for the Great Fire quickly became as impossible to control as the blaze itself. The more measures he conceived to halt it, the more it continued to spread. No matter that his *Domus Transitoria* and his Palatine palace with their priceless treasures had been among the first buildings destroyed. The angry populace was determined to vent its collective wrath on whoever was responsible for its misery, and the principal suspect was clearly the emperor Nero himself. The fast-deteriorating situation could very easily result in his assassination, not unlike the fate of his uncle, Gaius Caligula.[15] He must act, and act quickly, to turn aside the relentless wrath of his people. He must find a convenient scapegoat on whom they could exhaust their rage. But who could that be?

"Why not the Greeks or Egyptians or Parthians?" proposed different councilors[16] in quick succession, though without much conviction. "What about those hardheaded Jews?" suggested one of the older councilors. "They've resented Roman rule ever since Pompey captured Jerusalem!"[17] "Yes," replied a contemporary, "but that was over a hundred and twenty years ago, and they've never attempted anything this drastic before. Who's going to believe they'd do it now?" "Look," interrupted Nero sharply, "I myself considered blaming the Jews, if only because their Transtiberim quarter survived the fire, but I just can't do it. As you're all aware, my beloved Poppaea[18] would fly to the defense of her Jewish friends. No, there just doesn't seem to be any workable solution, does there?" And Nero slumped down in his improvised throne, his fear and despair plainly visible on his round, effeminate face.

Then Tigellinus,[19] Nero's sadistic favorite, who was himself a prime suspect as the emperor's henchman during the Great Fire, hit upon an ingenious suggestion. "Why don't we point the finger at the Christians?" he asked almost casually. "The Christians?" repeated Nero, rolling the idea around his cunning mind. "Yes, of course! Why not the Christians? How clever! How diabolically clever you are, Tigellinus, my baseborn buddy! Don't you see, my slow-witted councilors? Many Christians also live in Transtiberim, but unlike the Jews, they're comparatively new in Rome and a puzzle to most Romans. Who knows what they're capable of? Besides, they're a secret society,[20] and for that very reason, they're at the same time a threat to all Romans as well as a target for any and all accusations, no matter how outlandish they may seem!" At the very thought, Nero rubbed his pudgy hands with childish glee and out of his sensual mouth erupted a torrent of triumphant laughter.

A view of the Tiber looking toward St. Peter's Basilica.

"But that's not all, divine Caesar," pursued Tigellinus. "I have learned through my secret agents that they worship as their founder (yes, even as their god!) an uneducated carpenter from a despised village in Galilee who was denounced by the Jewish Sanhedrin as a false messiah, condemned by the Roman governor as a revolutionary, and crucified as a common criminal!"[21] Tigellinus paused to let the emperor savor this damaging description.

Aware of Nero's superstitious fears, he decided to omit any mention of the Christians' reported conviction that this same Jesus, whom they call their Christ, or Anointed One, truly rose from the dead and appeared alive and in person to many of their number.[22] Instead, he chose to arouse the Emperor's contempt to a state of frenzy by calmly adding, "It's even reported to me on good authority that these Christians, in their secret ceremonies, actually eat human flesh and drink human blood!"[23]

"Enough!" bellowed Nero. "These Christians aren't just stupid religious fanatics; they're absolute madmen! Cannibals! They deserve to be destroyed, not just as pyromaniacs, but as enemies of the state

20

The River Jordan at the approximate spot where Jesus was baptized by John.

and of all humanity! Yes, by all means give the order! Arrest the Christians! Let our imperial wrath lend support to our beloved people, and let our new Rome be rid of this inhuman sect once and for all!'' And so the carnage began, as described vividly but with merciful brevity by the Roman historian Tacitus:

> First, then, the confessed members of the sect were arrested; next, on their disclosures, vast numbers were convicted, not so much on the count of arson as for hatred of the human race. And derision accompanied their end: they were covered with wild beasts' skins and torn to death by dogs; or they were fastened on crosses, and, when daylight failed, were burned to serve as lamps at night. Nero had offered his gardens for the spectacle, and gave an exhibition in his Circus, mixing with the crowd in the habit of a charioteer, or mounted on his car. Hence, in spite of a guilt which had earned the most exemplary punishment, there arose a sentiment of pity, due to the impression that they were being sacrificed not for the welfare of the state but to the ferocity of a single man.[24]

If the entire population of Rome had been in a state of shock over the cruel conflagration which had decimated their families and deva-

Sea of Galilee.

stated their property, the whole Christian community was now in such a trauma of fear and grief, panic and despair, that it defied description. Just converted to faith in Jesus Christ and proud of being both Roman and Christian, they suddenly found themselves ostracized by the state and society, despised as enemies of the human race, hunted down as criminals, and condemned to the most barbarous and degrading forms of execution imaginable.

Was this what it meant to be a Christian? No indeed! Many, if not most, had felt that in becoming Christian, they were joining a noble movement which held the promise of stemming the tidal wave of decay in Roman life and morals.[25] Little did they dream that they would be branded as vicious criminals, unfit to live among humans, especially Romans! No wonder they felt that their entire world had collapsed around them[26] and, in many cases, decided to save themselves by renouncing their new faith and denouncing their fellow Christians.

This whole state of affairs was especially heartrending to the Christian leaders who had worked so hard and so long to win these converts, had nurtured them as "newborn babes,"[27] and had tried to teach them the fundamental values of love and fidelity only to see them collapsing under the very first onslaught of persecution. Some were indignant at these turncoats, who were not even as brave as the Stoics.[28] Others were more understanding and compassionate, being fully conscious of their own human weakness. Among these, the most notable were Simon Peter,[29] the Galilean fisherman whom Jesus had chosen as the first leader of his infant Church and his secretary-companion John Mark,[30] the Jerusalem city dweller who had embraced the faith as a mere youth. Both were acutely aware of their own past cowardice in the face of danger: Peter especially in his triple denial[31] of Jesus during the trial before the Sanhedrin and even later in his contradictory conduct at Antioch;[32] Mark particularly in his flight from the Garden of Gethsemane[33] and afterward in his desertion of his cousin Barnabas and their fiery spokesman Paul on their very first missionary journey.[34]

Not only did they refrain from condemning their fellow Christians in their failures, but being "of one heart and one mind,"[35] they shared with each other their mutual concern and their strong conviction that something had to be done, and done quickly for the many Christians who were wavering between suffering for Christ and saving their skins. Yes, something must be done, but what? And by whom?

Peter, as always, was the first to clear the air. Fixing his younger companion with coal black eyes, which contrasted sharply with his leathery face framed by snow-white hair and beard,[36] he came right to the point. "Mark, my son, I know that my days are numbered. As leader of the Church, I am the primary target of the emperor's spies and executioners. Any day now, I will be arrested, just as the Lord predicted.[37] They will put me to death, probably by crucifixion like the Lord himself, although I am the least worthy of such a privilege. I only hope and pray that this time I will be able to trust completely in his strength rather than my own. You and I both know what can happen when we rely on our own human enthusiasm."

Mark, middle aged but feeling like a youth again before his aged friend, winced with the painful reminder of his weakness but said nothing, waiting for Peter to continue.

"Our beloved brother Paul,[38] as you well know, has been away from Italy ever since his release from prison two or three years ago. Wherever he is right now, he may have very little knowledge of our precarious situation. So who does that leave to do something? Only you, my dear friend and faithful secretary! It is time for you to be more than a secretary, to write what the Church, especially our Roman Christians, needs to hear and to read in this dangerous time." And with that Peter's wrinkled old face broke into a radiant smile.

"But . . . but . . . that's impossible!" stammered the younger man. Shorter than Peter and of a slighter build, his neatly trimmed hair and beard a distinguished gray at the edges,[39] John Mark was aghast at the direction of Peter's thought. He counted it a great blessing to be a personal friend and confidant of both Peter and Paul and to be able to help them secretarially with his knowledge of Aramaic and Hebrew, Greek and some Latin. But never had he envisioned being called upon to take more of a leadership role in the Church. Bolstered by these reflections, he continued, "Please reconsider, Peter. I do appreciate your confidence, and you know I'd do anything I can to help you and the Church, especially at this trying time. But I really don't believe I'm qualified to be anything more than a secretary, and I'm quite happy to continue doing just that. Besides, who in the world would listen to me or read anything I'd write on my own? You and Paul can write letters, and because of who you are, they carry an aura of authority. The faithful devour them as if they come from the Lord himself. And, in a very true sense, they do. But if I make a speech or write a letter, it's only an ordinary speech or letter. True, I've had the privilege of being a companion and secretary to both you and Paul, but I don't wear your mantle of authority. So I do believe that someone else, perhaps Linus or Cletus or Clement, or all three together,[40] should write a letter or do whatever needs to be done in our worsening situation. Don't you agree?"

Peter did not hesitate a moment. "No, Mark my son, I don't agree at all. As helpful as letters have been, especially those of our brother Paul,[41] the present crisis demands something more than a letter. Besides, I've already discussed this with my three presbyters, Linus, Cletus, and Clement. They're in full agreement with me and have strongly encouraged me to pursue this with you."

Mark could not hide the confusion on his face as he blurted out, "Pursue what, Peter? I'm sorry, but I just don't follow you. I've the feeling you've got something definite in mind, but I don't have the faintest idea what it is. Please help me understand what you're driving at!"

"Just be patient, my son. I do have something in mind, but just how definitely is another question. It's hard for me to explain what's not quite clear in my own thinking. But let's begin with the present crisis. We Christians are now outlawed by Rome and are being unjustly accused of all kinds of unnatural crimes. As a result, many are bravely accepting torture and death as witnesses to the Lord, but others are weakly renouncing their faith and denouncing their Christian brothers and sisters to save their own lives, and still others are being torn between fidelity and apostasy. Now, if Jesus himself were still here in the flesh, what would he do?"

Mark thought a moment. Slowly, a kind of inner light began to suffuse his entire face. "He would talk, yes, but above all he would lead and strengthen us by his own example. He would go before us like a shepherd leading his flock,[42] or perhaps more like a sacrificial lamb being led to the slaughter."[43] Then a dark cloud passed across his face. "But Peter! The Lord couldn't do that even if he wanted to! He couldn't die again because, as Paul wrote to this very Church of Rome: 'We know that Christ, once raised from the dead, will never die again; death has no more power over him. His death was death to sin, once for all; his life is life for God.'[44] Isn't that true?"

"Of course it is," Peter replied with a grin, "but he won't need to die again. He won't even need to return visibly among us at this time. The point is that he has already shown us how to live and how to die! He has already shown us that if we want to be his disciples, we too must be willing to take up our cross and follow him, even to crucifixion and death![45] That isn't just a figure of speech, as Jesus himself made me realize at Caesarea Philippi.[46] But what we have lacked so far and what we so desperately need in the present crisis is a vivid account of his life and death, an account so real that we can see him, feel him, and follow him just as if he were still living and dying all over again before our very eyes." Peter paused to let his words exert their effect on Mark's mind and heart. As he expected, he could see the fire in his friend's eyes grow steadily brighter.

"What a challenge!" Mark was thinking. "What a challenge for my eager Christian spirit and limited writing skills! To enable Jesus Christ to live again in the minds and hearts, the lives and deaths, of his followers, over thirty years after his saving death and resurrection! But how can I, John Mark, possibly accomplish such a thing? I'm neither a witnessing apostle like Peter and John or even like Paul, nor can I claim the writing skills of Luke[47] or of Silas,[48] Paul's secretary (and Peter's too), or of that famous preacher, Apollos[49] of Alexandria.''

He was about to voice all these objections when Peter anticipated him. ''Yes, Mark, I know what you're thinking, but you're exactly the person our Lord and his Church need at this very time to do what I've outlined. You don't have to be an apostle because you've got the benefit of all the eyewitness accounts you've heard from me over the years, not only in my preaching and teaching but also in our many private conversations, full of so many intimate details,[50] every one of which is engraved on your memory as well as mine. Besides, as my secretary here in Rome, you've been at the heart of the Church's life and teaching. You're thoroughly familiar with her kerygma,[51] her public proclamation about Jesus Christ. You're also fully aware that in all our crises and questions, we implore Jesus, our chief shepherd, to guide us through his Holy Spirit in applying the words and deeds of his life to our own[52] so that we may always be faithful to his example and teaching. From this wealth of material, most of which you've written down, I'm completely confident, my dear Mark, that you'll be able to give our Christians a graphic portrait of Jesus as he truly was and is.[53]

''Nor do you need the writing skills of a Luke or a Silas. They're excellent, even elegant, writers, but elegance is not primarily what we need right now. You're a good writer, Mark, in fact, the very best we have at coming right to the point without any distracting frills. All you'd have to do is portray Jesus just as he was: the powerful Son of God casting out devils,[54] curing all kinds of illness,[55] even raising the dead to life,[56] but still the humble Son of Man and Servant of God[57] devastated by the ominous prospect of death by crucifixion,[58] yet accepting the will of his Father lovingly and courageously. Our people need to see and feel the *real* Jesus, beset by the same human weakness[59] and limitations,[60] the same fears and depressions, the same temptations and trials, as we experience; no, even greater than we can ever have,[61] yet he bore them all and never sinned![62] Besides, don't we owe it to Jesus, who is truth itself, to let all fair-minded people know and love him just as we do? Didn't he himself command us to proclaim the good news about him to all creation?[63]

''And, if you need further convincing, think a few moments about this: If the Church is persecuted so brutally in the city of Rome today, she'll be persecuted in the whole wide world tomorrow,[64] and she'll need the same kind of support everywhere that she needs in Rome today. And in addition, with my passing and that of the other apostles, the Church will need to have Jesus' words and deeds available in a far more permanent form[65] so that she can always nourish and renew herself through contemplation of him as he truly lived and taught and died amongst us. O Mark! The more I think and talk about it, the more convinced I am that Jesus himself is calling you to do him this very special service!''

At last Mark capitulated. Never before had Peter been so urgent and determined in requesting his help. What else could he do but promise the revered apostle to begin without delay the task of trying to organize the available material into a readable work of some kind? Just what kind, he had absolutely no idea! Nor was this the time to try to figure that out, for Peter had made it clear that this was his farewell request, and the very thought of their impending separation after so many years together filled him with such a feeling of profound depression that it quickly drove every other consideration from his mind.

Peter's words were nothing short of prophetic. Within a week he was hunted down, arrested, and summarily condemned to crucifixion in the Circus, or Hippodrome, of Gaius (Caligula) and Nero at the foot of Vatican Hill across the Tiber from devastated Rome.[66] Mark longed to join him in death as they had been so long joined in life, but martyrdom at this time would have prevented him from carrying out Peter's final request. So he had to content himself with watching the ghastly business from the safe distance of the Janiculum Hill.[67] Fortunately, despite his years of secretarial work his eyes were still sharp, and from his vantage point he could clearly observe all the details of Peter's crucifixion. Like his beloved Master and all who were condemned to the cross, Peter had been scourged in the merciless Roman fashion,[68] though not as severely as Jesus because of his age. Nor was he wearing that horrible crown of thorns like Jesus[69] or carrying his cross himself,[70] for he was too feeble for that. Like Jesus, however, his wrists[71] were being nailed to the crossbeam with those unmistakably sickening blows. But wait! What was happening now? How very strange! Peter was being raised feet first and crucified upside down, his great head of shaggy white hair almost touching the ground! Of course! Wasn't that just like Peter? Hadn't he declared less than a week ago that he felt unworthy of suffering death in exactly the same way as his Master? What a noble martyrdom! And what a shining model for the persecuted Church of Rome and soon of the whole world! Now and for all time to come, Mark felt instinctively, the Vatican Hill and the circus of Nero would be identified with Peter, the rock on which Jesus had built his Church.[72]

Peter did not languish long in his unnatural position. Soon it was evident that his battered old body was hanging lifeless from the cross. Waiting until the soldiers and the few remaining spectators had left the scene, Mark and other devoted Christians proceeded to remove the precious burden from the cross, and after washing and wrapping it in the customary shroud, they buried it in a shallow grave within the nearby Vatican Hill cemetery, marking it with a few of the stone slabs that lay about in the area.[73]

Mark yearned to remain throughout the night as a guard of honor at Peter's resting place, but two thoughts in particular forced him to leave: one, that Peter after his heroic martyrdom was already in glory with his Lord and Master; and the other, that the pressing needs of the persecuted Christian community and the urgent plea of their martyred leader compelled him to begin immediately to fulfill the promise which he had made to his dear friend and mentor. Both of these considerations served to assuage his human grief and drive him with a calm but firm determination to work quickly and with a minimum of distractions until his special task was done.

But as Mark hurried to his home his hyperactive mind was full of questions. "What kind of writing am I supposed to do? A history? No, for it has to be the true story of a person, the most extraordinary person who ever lived on this earth, and such an opus is usually called a biography, not a history. But it cannot qualify as a biography either, since it will be concerned with only the three years of Jesus' public life and ministry, crowned by his painful death and glorious resurrection. Nor can it be a mere collection of Jesus' acts and sayings, because Peter insisted on the need of focusing on the example of Jesus in his wondrous deeds, yes, but most of all in his saving death and resurrection." As a matter of fact, Mark could not think of any literary category in which to place his projected work, so he concluded that he would just have to put aside such literary considerations and wait to see what the end result would be. For now it was enough that he had promised to fulfill Peter's final request to present Jesus in action and suffering as honestly as possible. The important thing was to begin!

But how to begin this unusual writing? With a flash of memory, Mark suddenly recalled how Peter had repeated Jesus' command to preach the good news to all creation[74] and how Paul had written so boldly to the Roman community about "the good news being the power of God leading everyone who believes in it to salvation."[75] He recalled further that the expression "good news" had enjoyed a long and happy usage not only in secular life and Jewish Scriptures but also by John the Baptist, Jesus himself, and Paul.[76] And finally, he realized that if any people ever needed good news it was the persecuted Christians of Rome. With all this in mind, Mark decided then and there to title his writing "The good news of Jesus Christ the Son of God!"[77] By this he meant not only the "glad tidings" about the saving life, death, and resurrection of Jesus but also and more importantly that Christ himself is the good news, so eagerly but unknowingly sought by the sad and sinful world and so longed for by the fragile and fearful Church of Rome. Pleased with this happy choice, Mark smiled to himself. Could Peter be helping him already from heaven? How typical of the impetuous apostle, and for that matter, of Mark himself, Peter's true disciple, to jump headlong into the work with a blockbuster title like that! Little did Mark dream, however, that his happy choice of title would also provide the name for an entirely new literary creation know as a "gospel." How providential! What a debt of gratitude we owe Mark as well as Peter and, above all, the Holy Spirit, the Spirit of Jesus, who inspired them both!

It seemed that Mark had no sooner reached his home and begun to search out his collection of papyrus notes than a messenger tapped furtively at his door. Instinctively, Mark froze. Could it be his turn already? What about his solemn promise to Peter? But his fears were allayed when he recognized the messenger and read the message. It was from the Roman presbyters, Linus, Cletus, and Clement,[78] expressing their sympathy with Mark in his temporary separation from his spiritual father and friend but rejoicing with him that Peter had won such a glorious victory. As he read further, Mark glowed with happiness and gratitude at the invitation to join them and other Christians who could safely come in a celebration of the Eucharist honoring the memory of their martyred leader. Finally, Mark instinctively nodded his approval on reading further that at the same time and place, someone would be selected to continue Peter's role as shepherd of the flock, lest the visible body of Christ in Rome and beyond remain any length of time without a visible head and so that the morale of God's people might be bolstered through the example and leadership of a new standard bearer. Meanwhile, Mark was asked to join his prayers to theirs for the guidance of Christ and the Holy Spirit, so that just as Peter himself had successfully conducted the choice of Matthias to take the place of Judas in the role of apostle,[79] the Church might now be able to discern Jesus' choice of a worthy vicar to continue the role of shepherding his flock as Peter had so ably done in life and in death.

Within a week the meeting was held. The Eucharistic celebration, led by the three presbyters, was warm and touching. And the task of choosing Peter's successor was accomplished quickly, smoothly, and without rancor. The logical candidates were of course the presbyters, Linus, Cletus, and Clement; but in a spirit of humility, charity, and unity Cletus and Clement immediately urged the choice of Linus, who had been a presbyter the longest and Peter's "right-hand man," whereupon the whole assembly unanimously and enthusiastically accepted the happy choice as coming from Jesus himself and the Holy Spirit. Finally, right after dismissing the faithful with a special blessing, Linus sought out Mark, and assuring him that he was speaking not only for himself but for Cletus and Clement as well, he begged him to continue as secretary and above all to implement Peter's last request as soon as possible.

Encouraged by this additional entreaty, Mark hastened home and without a moment's delay got to work, determined to lose no time in the fulfillment of his sacred commission and confident that somehow Peter would assist him in its accomplishment. But first, of course, he had to finish collecting all the papyrus notes that he had been gathering for so many years. Some were very brief, some much longer. Most were notes taken of Peter's preaching, teaching, and conversations; but many were from various other sources, and a large number recorded the discussions and decisions of Church leadership in applying words and deeds of Jesus to current problems and questions. All of them, Mark felt, were important and should be kept in mind for inclusion in his "good news" about Jesus Christ.

Once he had rediscovered all his notes, Mark began to read each one in turn, slowly at first, then more and more rapidly as he began to realize what a treasure he had accumulated over the years. Yes, what a treasure, but how could he possibly organize it into the kind of dynamic story about Jesus that Peter had envisioned? How indeed?

"Well, to begin with," he mused to himself, "every story has to have a beginning, a middle or development, and an ending. In the story of Jesus, what would those be? How did Jesus himself begin his public ministry? Let's see. Of course! It was with his baptism in the River Jordan by his forerunner, John the Baptist,[80] accompanied by his messianic anointing with the Holy Spirit symbolized by the descending dove,[81] with the Father's voice proclaiming his sonship and servanthood,[82] followed by his forty days in the desert fasting and conquering the temptations of Satan.

"So much for the beginning. Now what should the middle section contain? Well, what else but his ministry in and around Galilee, followed by his steadfast journey to Jerusalem and all that awaited him there? And was it not in this middle section that Jesus clearly manifested what Peter had emphasized so much, namely that he was the Messiah of Israel and even the Son of God, as he had shown by his miracles and his domination of Satan; and yet he deliberately and courageously journeyed to Jerusalem where he knew exactly what his end would be: total identity as Son of Man and Servant of God in his sufferings and death, crowned by his triumphant resurrection?[83]

"Wait a minute! Isn't that what we call the Church's kerygma?[84] Her public proclamation about Jesus Christ, as we've heard from the beginning, especially in the sermons of Peter and the other apostles? Certainly it is! All right then, I'm on safe ground! But one question keeps nagging me: Where should I draw the dividing line between establishing Jesus as Messiah and Son of God and yet showing him as Son of Man and Servant of God? Where else but at Peter's profession of Jesus' messiahship at Caesarea Philippi? Isn't that really the climax of Jesus' ministry in Galilee and beyond? And didn't Jesus, right after that, begin to head for Jerusalem and even predict all that would befall him there?[85] Yes, of course! All right, now I'm beginning to see the outline of the story!

"But there are still questions that I have to answer; for example, how do I organize this wealth of material that I've collected from Peter and the others—accounts of miracles and expulsions of devils; parables, brief sayings, and declarations made in the context of a setting; the opposition of Jewish religious leaders, lack of faith and acceptance on the part of the people generally; and even failure to understand and appreciate Jesus Christ on the part of his apostles?

"Well, in general, I can see that the miracle stories and exorcisms will fit best in the first part, for they certainly indicate Jesus' power and authority as Messiah and Son of God. By the same token, much of the unbelief of the people and the opposition of their leaders would also arise in the first part, for these attitudes did not happen out of the blue later in Jesus' life but had to be building up all along. And the preaching and teaching of Jesus must have pervaded his entire public ministry—in the beginning as part of his revelation of the kingdom of God which he had come to establish, and in the second part as examples of what he expects of disciples who are willing to follow him to his destiny in Jerusalem.

"But within this outline, how shall I arrange all the things I've just been thinking about? In a time sequence? Impossible, since I don't even know the chronological order for most of the episodes. And certainly Peter in his talks never bothered much with the chronological order. Then what about a geographical order of arrangement? Now, that offers some real possibilities. For example, besides the general areas of Galilee and Judea, notably Jerusalem, there are also a number of other geographical indications such as Capernaum or Nazareth or the area around the Sea of Galilee or across the sea in the Decapolis (the Ten Greek Cities) or in the district of Tyre and Sidon (comprising part of what is now Lebanon). Why don't I just go through the material and group events in geographical cycles[86] with a view to arranging them in some kind of order?

"So far so good, but still there remains the problem of so much material and so little time and space to include it. Time and space, after all, are virtually interchangeable, for the more extensive the writing I end up doing, the more time it will take the Church leaders and members to copy it. This leaves me with a real dilemma! On the one hand I need time and space to compose a really vivid account of Jesus' life, but on the other hand I must do my level best to keep the overall work as brief and compact as possible. How can I manage to reconcile these two opposites? Ah! I think I have the solution: summaries!

"What I can do is narrate some of the more dramatic miracles and exorcisms and highlight some of the more pivotal events and teachings, handling the rest with brief, comprehensive summaries. In fact, those summaries can serve as well to open or close the various units that will make up the book as a whole.[87] I do believe it will work!

"Now, what should I do about such matters as style and structure? Well, in regard to style, I have neither the time nor the skill to compose a truly stylish work. Even my Jewish background tends to militate against my writing anything in stylish Greek without more rhetorical training than I have time for. Nor is that what Peter really asked of me. No, he wanted a straightforward, no-frills story of Jesus, letting his life and sufferings, his death and resurrection, speak for him and his genuine followers without any editorial preaching on my part. So I'll just not concern myself with trying to polish my style.[88] Nor will I try to use any fancy structures, such as chiastic arrangements or concentric circles,[89] other than the purely practical geographic cycles just mentioned. Some familiar structural touches may help, such as the use of parallels, triplets, inclusions, and perhaps word chains, but I'll keep them to a minimum and use them only when they'll help to enhance the richness of meaning in Jesus' story.[90] In general, any outline of development I use will be simply one that will make my story of Jesus clear, forceful, and compelling."

Now, what was the end result of all that had occurred—the Great Fire of Rome, the first persecution of Christians, the final entreaty of Peter before his death, the election of Linus and his seconding of Peter's request of Mark, and finally the latter's preparatory reflections? Our little Gospel According to Mark, which we are now in a position to analyze briefly in order to determine if and how the rather imaginative account I have given of its writing seems to be justified by the Gospel itself. That is the subject of the analysis which follows immediately.

BRIEF ANALYSIS OF MARK'S GOSPEL

In the interest of time and space as well as clarity and learning, this analysis and those of the four other main human authors of the New Testament will be presented in summary outline form, which should be easily understood if the reader has already perused the first, or story, part and, hopefully, also the endnotes[91] thereof. Our analysis is divided into two parts: an overview of the principal considerations which give us a sense of the Gospel, then an outline which provides us with a graphic idea of its total development.

I. Overview

   A. General impression

      1. A brief, fast-moving, action-packed portrait of Jesus of Nazareth, Messiah of Israel and Son of God but also Son of Man and Suffering Servant, best read straight through to feel its urgency

      2. Apparently written for Gentile Christians, since Jewish expressions are always translated, Jewish customs always explained, for example, Boanergés (3:17), *talitha koum* (5:41), customs and Korbân (7:3-4, 11), *ephphatha* (7:34), Bartimaeus (10:46), *Abba (14:36), Golgotha (15:22), Eloi,* etc. (15:34)

      3. Apparently written in a Roman environment, considering the number of Latinisms,[92] for example, *denárion* (denarius, 5:37; 12:15; 14:5), *kênsos* (tax, 12:14), *kodrántes* (quadrans, 12:42), *krábattos* (bed, stretcher, 2:4, 9, 11, 12; 6:55), *legión* (legion, 5:9, 15), *kenturíon* (centurion, 15:39, 44, 45), *xéstes* (jug, pitcher, pot, 7:4), *spekoulátor* (special-duty soldier, executioner, 6:27). Of these, the last three are found only in Mark.

      4. A "no frills" Gospel,[93] featuring

         a) a simple, racy, journalistic style, straightforward and unpolished, featuring present-tense narratives, many summaries, regular use of *kaí* (and) *eúthús* (immediately);

         b) vivid storytelling details, for example, the cure of the paralytic (2:1-12), the expulsion of the legion of devils (5:1-20), the death of John the Baptist (6:1-5), the transfiguration of Jesus (9:2-8), the prayer and agony in the Garden of Gethsemane (14:32-42);

         c) candid portrayals of and references to

            (1) Jesus' "family?"[94] (3:21), doctors (5:26), the crowds[95] generally *(passim),*

(2) Jesus' apostles, for example, Peter (8:33), John (9:38), James and John (10:35-37), all three (14:33, 37, 40-41), all the apostles (4:13, 40; 6:50; 7:18; 8:14-21; 9:32, 34; 10:41; 14:50),

(3) Jesus himself in his

   (a) Human emotions, for example, pity (1:41), anger (3:5), disgust (8:12), impatience (8:17-21, 33), tender love (10:16, 21), fear and depression (14:34-36),[96]

   (b) Human limitations,[97] for example, regarding knowledge (2:26; 5:30; 13:32), power (6:5), goodness (10:18).

5. Mark a "disordered" Gospel?

  a) Yes, according to Papias, bishop of Hierapolis, and according to the chapter divisions.

  b) No, in itself, as will be seen from the outline. The chapter divisions, introduced into the Vulgate Latin translation at the University of Paris in 1228 by Stephen Langton (later cardinal-archbishop of Canterbury), are generally faithful to the thought divisions in the rest of the Bible, but in Mark this is not the case. The reader is advised to ignore the chapter divisions when reading Mark and follow instead the outline which will be provided.

B. Composition

  1. Circumstances

  The two principal theories about the setting of Mark's Gospel place its composition either somewhere in the Middle East[98] shortly before or after the destruction of Jerusalem in A.D. 70 or in Rome during the Neronian persecution around A.D. 65. Of the two, the latter, which I have followed in this study, seems far preferable both from external and internal evidence.[99]

  2. Authorship

  a) This Gospel is universally attributed to Mark, a native of Jerusalem, a youthful convert and son of a prominent Christian widow, a disciple of Paul, and secretary-disciple of Peter (Acts 12:25; 13:5; Col 4:10; 2 Tim 4:11; 1 Pet 5:13).

b) Mark was ideally suited, being bilingual in Aramaic and Greek, the beneficiary of so much detailed knowledge about Jesus from Peter and others, and (like Peter) experienced in the traumatic trials and failures besetting the Roman Church after the Great Fire (8:32-33; 14:51, 66-72; Acts 13:13; Gal 2:11-14).

3. Purpose

   To strengthen the Roman Christians suffering persecution under Nero by portraying Jesus Christ, Son of God yet Suffering Servant, as their model

4. Sources

   a) Peter

   (1) "Memoirs of Peter" according to tradition (for example, Papias, A.D. 130)

   (2) Confirmed in general by internal evidence

   (a) Eyewitness details: Jesus asleep on a cushion (4:38), people reclining like flowerbeds (6:40), process, or sacramental, cures (7:31-37; 8:22-26), the transfiguration (9:2-8), not the time for figs (11:13), location of the discourse on the end of Jerusalem and the world (13:3), Simon, the father of Alexander and Rufus (15:21)

   (b) References and parallels to Peter
   Called "Satan" (Peter's humble report on himself, 8:33), *talitha koum* in parallel with *Tabitha koum* (5:41 and Acts 9:40), clean and unclean food and people (7:19 and Acts 10:15)

   b) The Church, in her

   (1) Kerygma—her basic proclamation about Jesus Christ underlying all the Gospels and the discourses in Acts comprising John's baptism and witness, the Galilean ministry, the journey to Jerusalem, the saving events in Jerusalem

   (2) Reminiscences, preaching, and teaching from A.D. 30 to 65, especially responding to questions and problems, for example, regarding fasting (2:18-20), blood ties (3:31-35), mission work (including anointing with

oil, 6:7-13), persecution (8:34-38; 10:30; 13:9-13), divorce and remarriage (forbidden to women too, reflecting gentile practice, 10:2-12), infant baptism (10:13-16)

(3) These reminiscences are couched in the different forms emphasized by form criticism and enumerated by Vincent Taylor as follows: 19 pronouncement stories, 17 miracle stories, 29 stories about Jesus, 22 parables and groups of sayings, to which he adds 18 Markan constructions and some 15 summaries.

c) Mark's own experiences, observations, and reflections about Christ and Christianity and especially about the nature of Christian "followship," or discipleship, as required by Jesus.

C. The end result
The good news, or Gospel, of Jesus Christ, the Son of God, our earliest and in so many ways our most attractive Gospel because in it Mark "tells it like it is" about Jesus Christ, both in himself and in his followers. An outline of Mark's Gospel follows immediately, after which we will reflect on some applications of this remarkable Gospel to our personal and communal life in today's world.

II. Outline of Mark's Gospel

A. Prologue or overture (1:1-13)

1. Title
The good news of Jesus Christ, Son of God (1:1)

2. Introduction
O.T. witness of John the Baptist (1:2-9)

3. Commission
Jesus anointed with the Spirit as Messiah, Son and Servant of God (1:10-11)

4. Testing
Jesus driven by the Spirit to combat with Satan in the desert (1:12-13)

B. Part 1: Mystery of Jesus the Messiah and Son of God (1:14–8:30)

1. Jesus and the crowds (1:14–3:12)

a) Introduction: summary of Jesus' preaching and call of the first disciples (1:14-20)

b) Jesus' power: teaching, exorcising, healing, confounding (Capernaum Cycle, 1:21–3:6)

c) Conclusion: summary of Jesus' popularity and witness of demons (3:7-12)

2. Jesus and his own people (3:13–6:6)

    a) Introduction: summary of Jesus' call of the twelve apostles (3:13-19)

    b) Jesus' power: (Lake Cycle, 3:20–5:43)

        (1) Misunderstood by relatives and religious leaders (3:20-35)

        (2) In parabolic preaching, explained only to disciples (4:1-34)

        (3) Over nature, devils, sickness, even death ([Markan sandwich, 5:21-43] 4:35–5:43)

    c) Conclusion: summary of Jesus' popularity at home but rejection by his own (6:3-6)

3. Jesus and his apostles (6:7–8:30)

    a) Introduction: summary of the apostles' mission and return (Markan sandwich, 6:7-32)

    b) Jesus' power: (Foreign Cycle, 6:33–8:26)

        (1) In first feeding and sequels: walk on water, sea calmed, other miracles, Jewish teachers confounded, gentile miracles (6:33–7:37)

        (2) In second feeding and sequels: Pharisees rejected, disciples rebuked, cure of the blind man at Bethsaida (8:1-26)

    c) Conclusion (climax of Part 1): Peter's confession of Jesus' messiahship (8:27-30)

C. Part 2: Mystery of Jesus, Messiah, Son of Man and Servant of God (8:31–16:20)

    1. Way of the Son of Man, Suffering Servant of God (Journey Cycle, 8:31–10:52)

        a) First prediction of suffering and sequels (8:31–9:29)

(1) Prediction, Peter's misunderstanding, instructions on discipleship (8:31–9:1)

(2) Sequels: transfiguration, teaching on Elijah, special exorcism (9:2-29)

b) Second prediction of suffering and sequels (9:30–10:31)

(1) Prediction, disciples' misunderstanding, instructions on discipleship (9:30-50)

(2) Sequels: teaching on marriage, children, riches, rewards (10:1-31)

c) Third prediction of suffering and sequels (10:32-52)

(1) Prediction, James and John's misunderstanding, instructions on discipleship (10:32-45)

(2) Sequels: cure of the blind man at Jericho and his discipleship (10:46-52)

2. Judgment of the Son of Man on Israel and world (Jerusalem Cycle I, 11:1–13:37)

a) Triumphal entry: judgment on Israel (fig tree, Temple cleansing, evil tenants, 11:1–12:12 [Markan sandwich, 11:12-25])

b) Triumphal debate: judgment on Israel and the world (12:1–13:37)

3. Victory of the Son of Man: death and resurrection (Jerusalem Cycle II, 14:1–16:20)

a) Prelude: anointing; betrayal; Passover and Eucharist; prayer and agony; arrest (14:1-52)

b) Climax: trials and denials; passion, death, and burial; centurion's confession (14:53–15:47)

c) Postlude: empty tomb (16:1-8); endings[100] (16:9-20)

MARK'S GOSPEL AND OUR LIFE

This final section of chapter 1 is designed to help the reader derive the choice spiritual fruit contained in the Gospel of Mark. It is not enough to read or hear, to study and understand, the Word of God. No, we must above all put it into practice in our personal and communal life,[101] as Jesus so often reminds us (see Matt 7:24-26; Luke

6:46-49; John 13:17; etc.). For us Christians, to "profess [and practice] the truth in love" (Eph 4:15, NAB) is more than to believe the truths of our faith, to keep the commandments, and to worship the Lord on Sundays and holy days. It is to live in relationship with our loving God by a covenant of love[102] (see Exod 19:3-6), of which the Ten Commandments (see Exod 20:1-17), later reduced to the two great commandments (see Deut 6:4-5; Lev 19:18; Mark 12:29-31 and parallels), specify the basic conditions. More than that, it is to live in close relationship with Jesus Christ, with the three Persons of the Holy Trinity, and with one another by baptism into the new covenant[103] (see Mark 14:22-24 and parallels), whose conditions are spelled out in the two great commandments of love mentioned above, in the challenging Beatitudes (see Matt 5:3-12), and in the new commandment of love (see John 13: 34; 15:12, 17). To be fully Christian is nothing less than to be transformed into Jesus Christ himself (see Gen 1:26-27; Rom 8:29; 2 Cor 3:18), to so surrender ourselves to him and let him so take possession of us that today, in our own time and circumstances, he can continue his life and ministry, seeing through our eyes, listening with our ears, speaking with our tongue, thinking with our mind, loving with our heart, and suffering with our body[104] (see Col 1:24). With all this in mind let us now delve into the first of our crucial subjects in Mark, namely, How human was Jesus?

The Sacred Humanity of Jesus

One of the most burning questions today not only for Scripture scholars and theologians but also for spiritual persons striving to live their call to union with and transformation into Christ is this: How human was Jesus Christ[105] during his life here on earth? As a divine person who assumed a human nature, was his human mind endowed with the beatific vision and all infused knowledge throughout his life? Was his human nature gifted with unlimited power and his human will naturally beyond even the possibility of sinning?

There was a time, particularly before Vatican II with its return of emphasis on scripture as the "soul of sacred theology,"[106] when theology manuals[107] would have answered these questions with a resounding "Yes, of course!" After all, it was argued, Jesus' human nature was intimately united with his divine person by the hypostatic union and therefore must have possessed every privilege that was not metaphysically impossible. That is certainly a distinct possibility, but actually it does not coincide with the the evidence of Scripture, especially the Gospel of Mark, nor even with the dogma of the Council of Chalcedon, held in A.D. 451, that there is no mixture of the divine and human natures in Jesus.[108] For these reasons, contemporary Scripture scholars and theologians[109] tend rather to speculate on how great was Jesus' loving self-emptying (see Phil 2:5-8) in regard to his human knowledge, power, and impeccability. Let us now examine these three important considerations as they are reflected in the Gospel according to St. Mark.

Among most scholars the question is usually formulated in this way: Was the human Jesus conscious of being the Messiah of Israel and the unique Son of God? Perhaps the question is asked in this way on the assumption that if indeed Jesus was so aware, then in his human nature he must have enjoyed the beatific vision, been endowed with all infused knowledge, possessed divine power, and been totally beyond the possibility of sin. However, this conclusion does not necessarily follow. There is another way in which the human mind and heart of Jesus could have been aware of his messiahship and unique sonship, namely, through faith and intuitive knowledge, derived from the attainment of the heights of mystical union. This would explain why he needed that long period of seemingly ordinary life at Nazareth (see Mark 6:1-3), during which he "was advancing [literally cutting forward, as in rowing, plowing, or carpentry?] in wisdom, age [or height, maturity], and grace [or goodwill, graciousnesss] before God and men" (Luke 2:52, WFD). This would also explain the need of divine confirmation of his mystical faith-conviction at his baptism: "You are my son,[110] my beloved! In you I am well pleased [or take delight]" (Mark 1:11, WFD), and at his transfiguration: "This is my son, my beloved! Hear him [above Moses and Elijah]!" (9:7, WFD).

Having to live by faith and mystical union would also explain Jesus' desperate need of prayer, even all-night contemplation (see Mark 1:35; Luke 6:12), as well as his devastating agony, desperate plea, and filial surrender to the will of his "Daddy" (the approximate meaning of Aramaic *Abba*[111] (see Mark 14:32-36) in the Garden of Gethsemane. Finally, this would also explain the ambivalent portrait of Jesus in Mark's Gospel, where there are passages which seem to deny and an equal

number of texts which seem to affirm or at least imply a consciousness of his messiahship and divine sonship.

Taking the negative first, we see Jesus being baptized by John the
Baptist (see 1:9), driven by the Spirit into the desert (see 1:12), and
being thoroughly tempted there by Satan (see 1:13). We see him possibly regarded as mad by "those with him [his relatives?]" (3:21) and
certainly accused by the Jerusalem scribes of being possessed by Satan[112] (see 3:22). We also see Jesus apparently not knowing who had
touched him (see 5:30) or who the high priest was[113] that enabled David
to escape from Saul (see 1 Sam 21-22; Mark 2:26) or when the end-
time would occur (see 13:32). We also behold Jesus exhibiting every
kind of human emotion, as already indicated,[114] and various kinds of
human limitation. For example, Jesus, according to Mark, is unable[115]
to work miracles at Nazareth (save for a few cures) because of the Nazarenes' unbelief (see 6:5-6). To the rich young man he asks the enigmatic question, "Why do you call me good? No one is good but God
alone" (10:18, NAB). He disclaims the right to seat[116] anyone at his
right or left in glory (see 10:40). And finally he is absolutely devastated
in the Garden of Gethsemane (see 14:34), mocked as a false messiah
(see 15:18, 32), and on the cross he feels totally abandoned by God
himself[118] (see 15:34).

To these many instances which seem to suggest that Jesus was un-
aware of being the Messiah of Israel and the unique Son of God, Mark's
Gospel, when read with an open mind, adds at least as many indications that he was truly conscious of his messiahship and divine sonship. For instance, at his baptism by John, Jesus comes immediately
out of the water without any confession of sins as was done by others
(see 1:5, 10); then he sees the heavens split open[119] and the Spirit
descending into him while he is addressed by the voice (of God) from
heaven: "You are my beloved Son. On you my favor rests" (1:10-11,
NAB). In the case of the paralytic (see 2:1-12) Jesus forgives his sins
(see 2:5), reads minds (see 2:8), and with the staggering statement
"That you may know that the Son of Man has authority on earth to
forgive sin"[120] (2:10) he effortlessly heals the man (see 2:11-12). In 2:28
Jesus makes the surprising declaration that "the Son of Man is lord
even of the sabbath!"[121] In his exorcisms he is identified by the evil
spirits as "the Holy One of God" (1:24), "the Son of God" (3:11), and
"Son of God Most High" (5:7) while he manifests absolute power[122]

over them all by silencing and expelling them (see 1:25-26; 3:12; 5:8-13). Even while denying any (human) knowledge of the date of the end-time, he declares his divine sonship: "But concerning that day or hour, no one knows, neither the angels in heaven nor the Son, [no one] except the Father" (Mark 13:32, WFD).

And the same can be said of Jesus' frequent use of that enigmatic self-description, "the Son of Man." On the one hand it simply means "man," thus identifying Jesus as human (see Ps 8:5; Ezek throughout); on the other hand it also calls to mind the figure of "one like a son of man coming on the clouds of heaven" (Dan 7:13-14, NAB), which clearly referred in Daniel to the Israelite "empire" but came in time to refer to the Messiah, as we see in Jewish intertestamental literature.[123] Thus, as embodied in Jesus' own self-designation, especially when on trial for his life (see Mark 14:61-62), he is both thoroughly human and at the same time the heavenly Messiah. Even the dehumanizing sufferings which he underwent, he himself had predicted no less than three times and well in advance[124] (see 8:31; 9:31; 10:33; and parallels in Matthew and Luke), to which we should also add the powerful parable of the tenants in Mark 12:1-12, where he predicts his death as "the son whom he [God] loved"[125] (Mark 12:6, NAB).

It seems, then, especially from the Gospel According to Mark and the Council of Chalcedon that (1) Jesus, in his human nature, possessed neither the beatific vision nor all infused knowledge during his earthly life; (2) he was conscious of being the expected Messiah and even the unique Son of God, a conviction derived from faith, mystical experience, and God's personal revelation; and (3) that as human he was limited not only in knowledge but also in power, although in both he far exceeded other humans because of his lifelong growth in "wisdom, age, and grace" (Luke 2:52).

The question remains, however, whether Jesus, as human, limited, and able to be tempted was capable of sin but actually never sinned. In this question we are faced with a dilemma. If Jesus could not sin, how could he be tempted? If he could sin, how could this be compatible with his being the very Son of God? Is it possible that he was impeccable, not metaphysically but morally, that is, so confirmed in grace, so united with his Father's will, so filled with the Holy Spirit, that while theoretically or metaphysically he was able to sin and therefore truly able to be tempted, in fact he lived his entire life without the slightest trace of sin? This is what the Bible itself seems to imply, for it never says that Jesus could not sin but only that he *did not sin,* for example in John 8:46; 2 Cor 5:21; Heb 4:15.

However, there is still a theological problem here. The infinite value of Jesus' life, death, and resurrection, which sufficed to satisfy his Father's justice and to save the human race from its sinfulness, derived from the fact that while his actions and sufferings were human, they were also divine. Expressed in Thomistic terms, *actiones et passiones sunt suppositorum,*[126] which means, freely translated, ''Actions and sufferings are attributed to persons.'' If, then, Jesus had been able to sin, that sin would have been attributable to his divine person, the Second Person of the Holy Trinity, which is impossible. But if he could not sin, how could he really be tempted?

Is there a way around this impasse? I suggest that for a possible solution we need to return to Jesus' limited knowledge as human. As a divine person he was absolutely impeccable, but in his human mind he was aware of this only by faith (Jesus was not a philosopher!), and therefore he could still be tempted. In any case let us remember that we are dealing with the profound mystery of the incarnation and hypostatic union, and all we can do with our own human limitations is try to understand Jesus' humanity as fully as possible and thereby be able not only to know and love him but also to identify with him, imitate him as fully as possible, and above all be transformed into him. What a privilege is ours: to be in love with both the divine person and the human personality[127] of Jesus, Son of God and Son of Man!

The Nature of Christian Discipleship

Next let us turn to the nature of Christian discipleship, which is another major emphasis in the fascinating Gospel of Mark. Bear in mind that in our account of the writing of Mark's Gospel, we speculated that in the persecution under Nero there were many apostates[128] (as well as many martyrs), probably because the Roman Christians generally may have tended to embrace Christianity as offering a higher set of moral standards than the perverted paganism that was destroying Roman life,[129] not fully realizing that to be a Christian meant to follow Jesus Christ even to the cross. That is why they needed Mark's simple, unvarnished story of Jesus, powerful Son of God yet humble Son of Man and Suffering Servant of God. Following Jesus to the cross is what

Christian discipleship meant then, and this is what it still means today. In the words of a well-known poster depicting a lion in the arena, "Christianity didn't use to be a spectator sport; it still isn't!"[130]

A key question is this: Almost two millennia have passed, but are we any clearer about the nature of Christian discipleship than were the first-century Roman Christians? Do we yet realize that being a Christian does not simply mean living a good moral life, as necessary as that is, but living in intimate union with Jesus, continuing his life and ministry in the world today, and if necessary remaining united with him even through painful sufferings and death? How seriously do we identify with Jesus' self-description, "The Son of Man has not come to be served but to serve—to give his life in ransom for the many" (Mark 10:45, NAB)? For that matter, how many of us truly take to heart that categorical imperative with which Jesus challenges us, "If anyone would come after me, he must deny himself and take up his cross and follow me" (Mark 8:34, NIV)?

Just as the first-century Roman Christians desperately needed Mark's first painful but salutary portrait of Jesus, the Son of God but Suffering Servant of Yahweh, along with his pressing invitation to follow him to the cross, so do we need it today. Probably much more so![131] Not only is our basic instinct for self-preservation constantly "looking out for number one,"[132] not only are we totally surrounded with "necessities" which people of former times and even in many areas today would not even dream of as luxuries, but today we are literally bombarded by the secular media, especially television, both in stories and commercials, with the deceptive untruths: (1) that this life is all there is or at least the only one worth living for; (2) that peace, joy, and happiness can only be achieved by the avoidance of pain and suffering of any kind and the fulfillment of our desires for wealth, fame, and pleasure, the so-called "lifestyle of the rich and famous";[133] and (3) that suffering and death are the ultimate evils, to be avoided at all costs.[134]

As if this triple threat were not enough to shake our Christian faith-convictions, there are Christian preachers and writers today who, like the false prophets of old, do not hesitate to present these same secular untruths in the guise of Christian principles based on the Bible. For example, some have reverted to the "Deuteronomic theology"[135] of totally temporal rewards and punishments characteristic of early Israelite thought and living before any awareness of an afterlife; before the "questioning books" of Job, Qoheleth or Ecclesiastes, and Wisdom led to a truer theological picture; and above all before the suffering servant of Yahweh in Second Isaiah[136] and Jesus, the Son of God become the the the Suffering Servant, exemplified the redemptive value of suffering. (After all, Jesus did not save the world by his preaching, teaching, and miracles but by his suffering, death, and resurrection!) Sometimes the same preachers, sometimes others in virtually every branch of Christianity, insist that according to the Bible, God hates suffering and always removes it from us if we but pray with enough faith. What a travesty, perhaps even a prostitution, of biblical teaching! Did Jesus not pray with enough faith in the Garden of Gethsemane? Did Paul not pray with enough faith for the removal of his "thorn in the flesh" (2 Cor 12:7-10)? What is really needed is an open-minded, open-hearted reading and hearing of the Bible in its divine and human authorship as it was written and intended to be understood. Then we would be able to counter today's secular untruths with the true teaching of Jesus Christ, mainly in these particulars:

1. This earthly life, precious as it is, constitutes only a shadowy preparation for that true life of the Spirit which begins even here with our baptism and is to reach perfection with our death, or rather birth, into eternal life. The Greek New Testament even uses distinct words for these two kinds of life: *psyché* for earthly life and *zoé* for spiritual or eternal life. Indeed, compared with our eternal life, our earthly life, no matter how long or how full, is less than the nine months in the womb as compared to the longest and fullest human life. Why then are we so desperately determined to remain in the womb forever, as if that were even possible?[137]

2. True joy, peace, and happiness come only when we truly seek union with God in love and service of him and of our fellow human beings, for in the words of St. Augustine, reflecting the biblical, three-dimensional anthropology of flesh-person-spirit, "You have made us for yourself, O Lord, and our hearts are restless until they rest in you."[138]

   The so-called joy, peace, and happiness that are sought through wealth, pleasure, and fame are not real but counterfeit, and the pages of human history are littered with the emptiness and despair of the "rich and famous."[139] In the cryptic words of Jesus reported in Mark 8:36, NIV, and repeated in Matt 16:26 and Luke 9:25, "What good is it for a man to gain the whole world, yet forfeit his soul?"[140]

3. The greatest evil is not suffering but sin, yet we humans seem more intent on avoiding suffering than on avoiding sin. In itself suffering is neither good nor evil. Those who enjoy suffering *in itself* are not saints but masochists. It is how we handle suffering that makes all the difference. First of all, suffering is unavoidable, for it is part of our earthly life. Either we try to avoid it at all cost and when despite all our efforts and remedies we still encounter suffering, we end up discouraged, depressed, and despairing; or we realistically accept the inevitability of suffering, find a meaning in it, embrace it for our own good and that of others, and, miraculously, suffering becomes sacrifice, pain is transformed into the most profound joy and peace and happiness.

And if it be objected by some that they neither crave great wealth, fame, and pleasure nor do they encounter extraordinary sufferings, so what is said here does not apply to them. They need to realize that it is a question not so much of what they are attached to but of how deeply and addictively they are attached. Jesus was speaking to all, rich and poor, in his Sermon on the Mount.[141] And as for the amount of suffering that may come our way, again it is not a question of how much we endure but of the love and patience with which we do so. If, for example, we cannot bear ordinary discomforts and inconveniences, it is idle for us to claim that we would endure great sufferings cheerfully. If chronic illnesses throw us into deep depression, how will we ever bear acutely painful and life-threatening afflictions? But let us return to Mark.

It is an intriguing thought that *Mark*, who is mentioned affectionately in both Peter's General Epistle (see 1 Pet 5:13) and Paul's Letter to the Colossians (see Col 4:10), may have learned from both of them the precious value of suffering in union with Christ for his own sanctification and for the spiritual benefit of others. Peter states in 1 Pet 4:13, NAB: "Rejoice in the measure that you share Christ's sufferings. When his glory is revealed, you will rejoice exultantly." And Paul, in Col 1:24, NAB, delineates the redemptive value of suffering: "Even now I find my joy in the suffering I endure for you. In my own flesh I fill up what is lacking in the sufferings of Christ for the sake of his body, the Church." As a true follower of Jesus, Paul fully realizes that by accepting his sufferings with joy and with a redemptive purpose, he is actually allowing Christ to continue his suffering in and through him for the continuing salvation of the world and, above all, for the ongoing redemption and reformation of his body, the Church.

The Church in Mark's Gospel

The mention of the Church in Paul's powerful statement provides the cue to give at least a brief consideration to Mark's treatment of the Church in his Gospel. Unlike the Gospel according to "Matthew," which we will consider next, Mark certainly does not give major emphasis to the Church, perhaps because he is primarily concerned with Jesus not as teacher and founder of the Church but as the model for the suffering Christians of Nero's Rome. Mark does not deliberately underplay the importance and role of the Church; rather he seems to take it for granted as an unmentioned part of the scene. In countless ways, if we are perceptive in reading between the lines, we can detect the Church as alive, present, and operative, at least in its incipient stages.

For example, the principal sources of Mark's Gospel, as we have already seen, are (1) the eyewitness accounts about Jesus by Peter, the leader and spokesman for all the apostles (see Mark 1:36; 3:17; 8:29, 32; 9:5; 10:28; 11:21; 14:29, 37, 54; 16:7) and the one chosen by Jesus to lead his followers after his departure, as is clearer in Matt 16:13-19; Luke 22:31-32; John 21:15-19; (2) the kerygma,[142] or proclamation of the Church about Jesus Christ, based on the eyewitnessing of the apostles and comprising the baptism and witness by John the Baptist, the ministry in Galilee, the journey to Jerusalem, and the saving events in Jerusalem and underlying all four Gospels as well as the principal discourses in the Acts of Apostles; and (3) the insights and decisions of the Church in recalling Jesus' words and deeds and applying them to questions and problems that arose in the Church's life.[143] In other words, it is largely the Church which forms the source of what we read in the Gospel According to Mark.

Further, in Mark's Gospel we see Jesus inviting the first disciples to follow him (see 1:16-20; 2:14); then choosing from among all his followers the twelve apostles, beginning with Peter, to be his community of twelve after the twelve tribes of Israel, forming the nucleus of his Church (see 3:13-19); and as "apostles" (ones sent), to be the vanguard of his worldwide missionary endeavor[144] (see 16:9-20). Not only do we then observe the Twelve with him in his various preaching opportunities, healing occasions, and confrontations with Jewish leaders (see 3:20-7:23), but we also see them receiving special instructions not granted to the others (see 4:1-41; 7:23), being sent out by Jesus on the home missions in a special trial run not unlike the practice of field education in modern seminaries (see 6:7-7:1), and being further trained for their future role as foreign missionaries in a kind of peripatetic[145] or walking seminary (see 7:24-8:10) culminating in a "final examination" (comprising two principal questions) in the district of Caesarea Philippi (see 8:27-29).

Then, in the great journey to Jerusalem, the Twelve are further instructed on a deeper level in the meaning of the Christian *hodós*,[146] or journey to the spiritual or heavenly Jerusalem (see 8:31-10:52), a journey which Luke will later expand into ten chapters of spiritual instruction not only for the apostles but for all Christians (see 9:23-19:27), all "followers of the way" (see Acts 9:2; 16:17; 18:25-26; 19:9, 23; 22:4; 24:14, 22). Even or especially in Jerusalem the Twelve constitute the early Church observing and preparing to witness not merely to Jesus' victorious debates with his various adversaries[147] but above all to the saving events of the triumphal entry; the institution of the Eucharist and inauguration of the new covenant; the agony and prayer in the garden; and the trials, death, and resurrection of Jesus (see Mark 11-16).

In all of this there are even hints of the Church's effective combination of word and sacraments, the former in the many examples of Jesus' preaching and teaching as well as in the apostles' "practice run" in preaching; the latter in the story of Jesus' own baptism by John the Baptist (see Mark 1:4-11), his forgiveness of the paralytic's sins (see 2:1-12), his use of material substances in his process cures (see 7:31-37; 8:22-26), the apostles' use of oil[148] to anoint the sick and cure them (see 6:13), and of course in Jesus' institution of the Eucharist as the Christian covenant and Passover sacrifice (see 14:22-25). Please notice that in this collection of word and sacraments we have not used the so-called longer ending of Mark 16:9-20, which has a number of references to preaching and sacraments but is generally regarded as largely borrowed from other Gospels by another writer.[149]

In conclusion then, while Mark's main emphasis is on personal commitment to Jesus Christ, Son of God and Son of Man, particularly when faced with violent persecution, his entire picture of Christ and his followers would be incomplete and, as it were, hanging in midair without the consciousness of the Church as part of the picture. Mark is primarily concerned with the "followship" of Christ, yes, but that followship of Christ is lived out, as we see in the case of the apostles, in fellowship with all others who are also following Christ.[150] I emphasize "all" here because, amazingly, Mark alone includes a statement of Jesus which is the epitome of ecumenism, namely, "Anyone who is not against us is with us!"[151] (Mark 9:40). How sad that it has taken us all these centuries to recognize and embrace the ecumenical attitude which our Savior clearly taught the apostles and, through them, all of us. All we can say, in all humility, is "Better late than never!"[152]

* * * * *

It is difficult to leave Mark because he exhibits so much that we twentieth-century Christians can identify with: his candor and realism, his fresh, unsophisticated presentation, his insightful portrait of Jesus, his uncompromising description of discipleship. Not only can we recognize them but we desperately need to make them our own if we are to be faithful followers of him who showed us how to live and how to die. It is with regret, then, but also with renewed admiration and dedication that we bid farewell to the first evangelist, St. Mark.

NOTES

1. I refer to Mark as marvelous not only because, according to the vast majority of Scripture scholars, he wrote the first Gospel and initiated Gospel literature but also because he emphasized the marvels of Jesus as Son of God and Messiah, clearly showing his power over sin and Satan, sickness and death, as well as over the things of nature such as food and storms; yet in spite of that he meekly died a cruel and degrading death for our sakes like the suffering servant of Isa 53.

The ascriptions of the Gospels to Matthew, Mark, Luke, and John are not part of the original text and are not accepted by all, but in the case of Mark, Scripture scholars are in general agreement that the ascription is correct, for why otherwise would Mark, who was not an apostle or well-known Church leader, be thus singled out? They also tend to agree that this Mark was most probably the same as the Mark, or John Mark, mentioned in Acts 12:12, 25; 13:5, 13; 15:37-39 as well as in Col 4:10; Phlm 24; 2 Tim 4:11; 1 Pet 5:13. He was a wealthy and well-educated Jew from Jerusalem, and like many Jews of the time, he was at ease in Greek and probably some Latin as well as his native Aramaic and some Hebrew. Also like Paul and many others he had two names: the Hebrew/Aramaic "John," meaning "Yahweh is Gracious," and a very common Greek/Latin name "Marcos/Marcus," signifying "Hammer." Sometimes he is referred to as a Hellenistic Jew, but that description would fit only in a wide sense, for true Hellenistic Jews not only knew Greek but used it as their primary language, whereas Mark's primary language seems to have been Aramaic, as indicated by the thought patterns in his Gospel.

The common opinion among Scripture scholars that Mark wrote the first Gospel is based largely on its comparative simplicity as well as the apparent dependence on Mark of the other two synoptic Gospels, "Matthew" and Luke.

2. This verse, my own translation of *metà diogmôn*, is found only in Mark among Jesus' promises to those who have left all things to follow him, and appearing surprisingly in that context, it forms an ideal scriptural capsule of the historical setting of Mark's Gospel.

3. The infamous emperor known by the short, almost laconic, name of Nero was born on December 15 in A.D. 37 and named Lucius Domitius Ahenobarbus (Bronze Beard) after his grandfather, who had married Antonia, the daughter of Augustus' sister, Octavia, and Marc Antony. Nero's parents were Cnaeus Domitius Ahenobarbus and Agrippina the Younger, great-granddaughter of Augustus and his first wife, Scribonia, through the marriages of their daughter Julia to Agrippa and of their granddaughter Agrippina the Elder to the noble Germanicus, brother of Claudius and father of Agrippina the Younger and Gaius Caligula. Thus Nero was able to trace his ancestry back to both Augustus and his sister, Octavia, but he became emperor only through the sinister machinations of his unscrupulous mother, Agrippina the Younger, who contrived to marry her uncle, the emperor Claudius, then prevailed on him to adopt her son (bestowing on him one of his own names, Nero, and also his own daughter, Octavia, in marriage), after which Agrippina apparently had Claudius poisoned and her son, Nero, declared emperor on October 12, A.D. 54.

Once enthroned, Nero showed himself a worthy heir of murderous forebears by eliminating all possible rivals for power or restraints on his lust, including his stepbrother Britannicus, his wife Octavia, and even his own mother, Agrippina. For much more on the first Roman emperor to persecute the Christians *see* Michael Grant, *Nero:Emperor in Revolt* (New York: American Heritage, 1970).

4. Ancient Antium, Nero's birthplace and summer residence on the Tyrrhenian Sea, is now the resort town and port of Anzio, south-southeast of Rome, with a population around twenty-three thousand, made famous in World War II as the site of one of America's most costly beachheads.

5. The date was significant, particularly to the superstitious like Nero himself. On this same date, July 19, 390 B.C., Rome was sacked and burned by the Gauls, a humiliation which she never forgave or forgot. To add to the superstition, Tacitus states that "others have pushed their researches so far as to resolve the interval between the two fires into equal numbers of years, of months, and of days," finally explained by Grotefend in 1843 as based on the number 418 which, in years, months, and days, adds up roughly to 454, the number of years between 390 B.C. and A.D. 64. Tacitus, *Annals XV:XLI*, trans. John Jackson, The Loeb Classical Library, ed. T. E. Page (Cambridge: Harvard University Press, 1951) 279.

In this work, I am using the designations "B.C." and "A.D." (before Christ and anno Domini, in the year of the Lord) for the times before and after Christ because they are more familiar to my readers, but one must remember that this rearrangement was not done until about A.D. 525 by Dionysius Exiguus, a Scythian monk and abbot of a Roman monastery who unfortunately erred by at least four years. The Roman reckoning was according to years since the supposed founding of Rome (A.U.C., or *ab urbe condita*, meaning "from the city founded"). *See* Addison Wright, R. Murphy, and J. Fitzmyer, "A History of Israel," *The Jerome Biblical Commentary*, ed. Raymond Brown, Joseph Fitzmyer, and Roland Murphy (Englewood Cliffs, N.J.: Prentice-Hall, 1968) 2:696 (hereafter cited as *JBC*). In recent years, B.C. has often been replaced by B.C.E. (before the common era) and A.D. by C.E. (the common era, i.e., the era common to Jews and Christians).

6. The word *circus* in ancient times meant a hippodrome or chariot race course. The two that functioned at Rome in Nero's time were the circus of (Caligula and) Nero where St. Peter was martyred and later buried and where the great Vatican basilica bearing his name now stands, and the Circus Maximus, or Great Hippodrome, whose extensive ruins are still quite visible in modern Rome. Later the Emperor Domitian, dubbed "Nero Redivivus" (Nero Reborn) on account of his cruelty, built another hippodrome (or more accurately, a stadium for athletic games) whose clear outlines are still visible in the delightful Piazza Navona. *See* Alberto Carpiceci, *Rome 2000 Years Ago* (Florence: Bonechi, 1981) 98, 121–24, 148–52.

7. The *vigiles*, thought to number about seven thousand, were "members of a force organized at Rome by Augustus as a fire brigade, originally of slaves (23 B.C.), later (A.D. 6) of freedmen, each cohort having charge of two city regions; some police and, exceptionally, military duties were added." *Oxford Latin Dictionary*, ed. P. G. W. Glare (Oxford: Clarendon, 1984) 2051.

8. Nero's *Domus Transitoria* (Transitory House) was so called not because it was only temporary (which it was not meant to be) but because it formed a passageway, or transition, from his magnificent mansion on the Palatine Hill to the west and his estates on the Esquiline Hill to the east. It was intended as an entranceway to his projected mammoth *Domus Aurea*, or Golden House. Its ruins now rest beneath the partially restored Temple of Venus and Rome constructed a century later by Hadrian at the south end of the Roman forum. *See* Grant, *Nero*, especially the map, p. 153 and explanations, p. 164.

9. The Esquiline Hill, one of the famous seven hills of Rome, rises to the east of the Roman forum, the center of the city, opposite the Palatine Hill to the west and between the Viminal and Caelian Hills to the north and the south respectively. On it stretched the beautiful Gardens of Maecenas, a famous Roman statesman and literary patron (70–8 B.C.), until Nero included it in the extensive area of his Golden House and Gardens after the Great Fire.

10. In regard to this statement in Tacitus, *Annals* XV:XL, 277, n. 3, John Jackson remarks, "Both the archaeological and the literary evidence show this assertion to be too sweeping," yet he fails to offer a more accurate figure. At any rate, even half of the fourteen districts would still represent enormous destruction.

11. "On the west of Jerusalem is the Valley of Hinnom (Josh 15:8; 18:16), swinging around the southern end of the mount to meet the Kidron (Valley) in the southeast at Haceldama (Acts 1:19). This valley (Ge-Hinnom or Gehenna) acquired an unpleasant reputation because it was used for the burning of garbage and the worship of pagan gods (especially through the human sacrifice of infants to Moloch by burning). 1 Kgs 11:7; 2 Kgs 16:3; 23:10), whence the derived meaning of Gehenna as 'Hell.' " Robert North and Raymond Brown, "Biblical Geography," *JBC* 2:648. *See also* Jer 2:23; 7:32; 19:6ff.; Isa 66:24; Mark 9:43-48; Matt 5:29-30; 10:28; 18:9; 23:15; Luke 12:5.

12. According to Michael Grant and others, Nero's Golden House and Gardens comprised at least 125 acres (more than half again as large as Vatican City) but probably covered more like 370 acres. "Never before or since, in the whole course of European history, has a monarch carved out for his own residence such an enormous area in the very heart of the capital" (Grant, *Nero* 169). However, Nero's Domus Aurea was very short lived, being demolished by the Emperor Vespasian (A.D. 69–79), whose Flavian amphitheater (popularly called the Colosseum on account of the adjacent colossal statue of Nero, changed to represent the sun god) covers no more than one-tenth of the area occupied by the Golden House and Gardens. *See* Tacitus, *Annals* XV:XLII, 278, n. 2.

13. *See* Tacitus, *Annals* XV:XL, 277, and n. 2.

14. "The report had spread that, at the very moment when Rome was aflame, he (Nero) had mounted his private stage, and typifying the ills of the present by the calamities of the past, had sung the destruction of Troy" (Tacitus, *Annals* XV:XXXIX, 275). "While the city was burning, it was rumored that Nero had been so moved by the sight that he took his lyre, put on his singer's robes and sang through the whole of a tragic song of his own composition called the 'Fall of Troy,' which was perhaps based on his epic 'The Trojan War.' Such, then, is the famous story that Nero fiddled while Rome burned; though if he played any instrument it was a lyre and not a fiddle" (Grant, *Nero* 152).

15. Gaius Caesar, nicknamed "Caligula" (Little Boot) by the troops of his most noble and universally loved father, Germanicus, the nephew of Tiberius and brother of Claudius, became emperor at the death of Tiberius, possibly by Gaius' own hand, in A.D. 37, the year of Nero's birth. He ruled a mere four years, during which he changed from a popular monarch to a feared and

despised monster characterized by every excess of lust and cruelty, until he was stabbed to death by members of his Praetorian Guard on January 24, A.D. 41. *See* Suetonius, *The Twelve Caesars,* trans. Robert Graves (Baltimore: Penguin, 1957) 149–79.

16. For Nero's councilors, *see* Grant, *Nero* 137–40.

17. 63 B.C. *See* Wright, Murphy, and Fitzmyer, "The Hasmonean [Maccabean] Rulers," par. 114, in "A History of Israel," *JBC* 2:671.

18. *See* Grant, *Nero* 140–48, especially 148.

19. *Ibid.* 137–38.

20. The reputation of a secret society may have stemmed from the custom in the early Church of not divulging information to others about Christian rites and truths, reflecting Jesus' own caution: "Do not give what is holy to the dogs or throw your pearls in front of the pigs, lest they trample them under their feet, and then turn and tear you to pieces" (Matt 7:6, WFD). However, this did not justify the opinion that they were like the mystery religions of Eleusis, Greece, and elsewhere, whose rites and secrets could be shared only with the initiated. In fact, other than a prudential circumspection no secrecy was imposed, and the so-called *disciplina arcani* (discipline of the secret) did not become strictly observed until the formal organization of the catechumenate in the third century and remained in force only until the fifth century. Even then, however, there was no oath or promise of secrecy asked of the catechumens. (*New Catholic Encyclopedia,* s.v. "Secret, Discipline of the," 1967, [hereafter cited as *NCE*]).

21. *See* Matt 26:47-27:50; Mark 14:43-15:41; Luke 22:47-23:49; 18:1-19:30; Acts 2:14-36; 3:11-26; 10:34-43; 13:16-43.

22. *See* Matt 28:1-20; Mark 16:1-20; Luke 24:1-53; John 20:1-21, 25; Acts 1:11; 9:1-19; 22:1-21; 26:1-23; 1 Cor 15:1-11.

23. This is, of course, a reference to the Holy Eucharist in very crude and cannibalistic language which distorts Jesus' promise and institution of the Eucharist in John 6:1-69; 1 Cor 11:23-34; Matt 26:26-30; Mark 14:22-26; Luke 22:14-20.

24. Tacitus, *Annals* XV:XLIV, 283–85.

25. For the sad state of morals in Rome, we need only turn to Tacitus, *Annals* XV:XLIV, 283, ". . . the capital itself, where all things horrible or shameful in the world collect and find a vogue." And this is more than confirmed in Paul's Letter to the Romans, written six years earlier, in which he blames the pagans' rejection of the true God for the pervasiveness of unbridled immorality, especially homosexuality among both sexes, together with "every kind of wickedness, evil, greed, and depravity. They are full of envy, murder, strife, deceit and malice . . . senseless, faithless, heartless, ruthless . . ." (Rom 1:18-32, NIV).

26. The shock experienced by the Roman Christians over the outbreak of persecution may seem surprising in view of the warnings of both Paul in Rom 8:17-18 and Peter in 1 Pet 4:12-19, but it must be remembered that (1) Paul wrote in general terms; (2) Peter addressed himself to the Christians of "Pon-

tus, Galatia, Cappadocia, Asia, and Bithynia,'' all in Asia Minor; and (3) there is a vast difference between a general, theoretical prospect of suffering and a real, personal threat of death, as any of us who have lived in a time and place of persecution know from experience.

27. 1 Pet 2:2, NAB.

28. Stoicism was ''a philosophical school named after the *stoa*, i.e., the porch or painted colonnade where Zeno (366–264 B.C.) of Citium (an ancient Phoenician town near the present-day city of Larnaca in Cyprus), its first exponent, used to teach in Athens. Stoicism stresses the seriousness of life. It emphasizes the individual and the concrete in opposition to Platonic ideas or Aristotelian universals. Among its characteristics . . . are the primacy of the practical, the ideal of mental tranquillity, a pervading materialism, and generally a marked affinity for Oriental values and attitudes'' (*NCE*, s.v. ''Stoicism'').

Of the three stages of Stoicism, the third, which was almost entirely concerned with ethics, was the dominant moral philosophy in the Roman Empire, e.g., at Tarsus and especially at Rome itself, during the last century B.C. and the first century A.D. As lived and taught by such famous men as Cicero (106–43 B.C.), Seneca (A.D. 4–65), incredibly the tutor and early councilor of Nero, and Epictetus of Hierapolis in Asia Minor (A.D. 50–138), it stressed self-control and self-sufficiency, honor and patriotism, courage and serenity under trials. In some ways it prepared the way for Christianity, especially through its emphasis on self-control, but in its self-assured humanism it also presented an obstacle to the humility, selfless love, and self-surrender so basic to Christianity. In our own time there seems to be a resurgence of Stoicism in the current emphasis on self-sufficiency and self-help.

29. Simon, or Simeon bar Jonah (Simon, son of John: ''Simon'' possibly meaning ''Yahweh has heard,'' and ''John'' meaning ''Yahweh is gracious''), a native of Bethsaida in Galilee (see John 1:44) but living in Capernaum (see Mark 1:29; Matt 8:14; Luke 4:38), was chosen by Jesus in spite of his weaknesses to be the leader of his Church (see Matt 16:13-20; Luke 22:31-32; John 1:42; 21:15-17; Acts 1:15-26; 2:14-41; 3:1-26; 4:1-22; 5:1-32; 9:32–11:18; 12:1-17; 15:1-12; 1–2 Pet) and given the significant name ''Cephas'' (from *kepha*, the Aramaic for ''rock'') or *pétros* (Greek for ''rock''). Any attempt to deny the primacy of Peter (and his successors) on the basis of translating *Pétros* as ''little rock'' in contrast with Jesus as ''bedrock'' violates both the text and context and, above all, ignores the fact that Jesus would have been speaking not in Greek but in Aramaic, where there is no ambiguity. For more on this see my book *To Live the Word, Inspired and Incarnate* (Staten Island, N.Y.: Alba House, 1985) 452. Second Peter is considered by most Scripture scholars not to be genuinely Petrine, largely because it seems to depend on the Epistle of Jude, but the pseudonymous use of Peter's name does indicate something of his position and authority in the Church. While Mark contains the least about Peter's primacy (probably due to its general acceptance in Rome), his entire Gospel evidences a dependence on the testimony of Cephas and a reflection of his character.

30. *See* Acts 12:12, 25; 13:5, 13. *See also* n. 1 above on Mark.

31. *See* Matt 26:69-75; Mark 14:66-72; Luke 22:54-62; John 18:15-37.

32. *See* Gal 2:11-14. Far from being a denial of the primacy of Peter in the Church, this passage rather confirms it, for it was precisely because of Peter's exalted position that Paul's bold action derived its force. Nor was Paul accusing Cephas of teaching error. After all, was it not Peter who had received the first gentile converts into the Church (see Acts 10) and had led (or would lead) the Council Of Jerusalem in its landmark dogma (decision) about gentile converts (see Acts 15)? Rather, Paul was confronting Peter about his failure to live up to his own convictions by practicing a kind of "de facto" segregation regarding the gentile Christians, thereby causing them to feel like second-class members of the Church.

33. *See* Mark 14:51-52. It is thought by many Scripture scholars that the young man referred to in this passage, who is mentioned only in Mark's Gospel, must be Mark himself. In fact, it is the opinion of some, myself included, that the Last Supper may have been held in Mark's own home because, again only in Mark's Gospel, Jesus gives his disciples this sign for locating the prearranged site of his Last Passover Supper: "Go into the city, and a man will meet you carrying a jar of water" (Mark 14:13, NEB). What a perfect signal! Men did not normally carry water jars, women did! But if Mark had no sisters and his mother was busy preparing for the Passover, Mark himself may very well have been the man carrying the jar of water. If so, then this would explain his presence at Gethsemane in his night clothes. As a young man, he was supposed to be in bed, but out of curiosity he may have witnessed the main events of the Last Supper and then out of continuing curiosity followed Jesus and the Eleven to the Garden of Gethsemane, where he had the dubious honor of being the first "streaker."

Nor does the mention of an *oikodespótes* or "master of the house," in Mark 14:14 and Luke 22:11 rule out this possibility. The Greek word may indeed refer to a householder or owner, but it may also mean a housekeeper or butler, a major-domo or maitre d'hotel, in charge of the household for Mary, Mark's widowed mother, whose home was evidently large enough to require a maid or portress named Rhoda (Rose) and to accomodate "many others gathered in prayer." This seems clear from the account of Peter's miraculous release from prison in Acts 12:1-17, NAB. And the fact that Peter after his release instinctively went "to the house of Mary the mother of John (also known as Mark)" argues strongly for the identification of this home with the "upstairs room, spacious, furnished, and all in order" for the Last Supper (Mark 14:15; Luke 22:12, NAB) as well as the site of some of the appearances of the risen Christ (see Luke 24:36-48; John 20:19-29) and the location of events in the early chapters of Acts, e.g. Acts 1:12-2:4; 4:31. On *oikodespótes, see* Maximilian Zerwick and Mary Grosvenor, *A Grammatical Analysis of the Greek New Testament*, rev. ed. (Rome: Biblical Institute Press, 1981) 155, 270; and on this opinion generally *see* William Barclay, *The Men, the Meaning, the Message of the New Testament Books* (Philadelphia: Westminster, 1976) 15.

34. *See* Acts 13:13. It is not clear why Mark left Paul and Barnabas at this point in the first missionary journey, but Barclay offers some possible reasons: "He may have gone home because he was scared to face the dangers of what was notoriously one of the most difficult and dangerous roads in the world, a road hard to travel and haunted by bandits. He may have gone home because it was increasingly clear that the leadership of the expedition was being assumed by Paul, and Mark may have felt with disapproval that his uncle was being pushed into the background. He may have gone home because he did not approve of the work which Paul was doing. Chrysostom—perhaps with a flash of imaginative insight—says that Mark went home because he wanted his mother!" *The Gospel of Mark*, The Daily Study Bible Series, rev. ed. [Philadelphia: Westminster, 1975] 3). Mark's desertion of Paul and Barnabas obviously occasioned the subsequent alienation of those two great missionaries (see Acts 15:36-41), but Paul and Mark must have been reconciled later, according to some of Paul's letters from prison (see Col 4:10; Phlm 24; 2 Tim 4:11).

35. Acts 4:32, NAB. If it was true of all the Christians in this passage, how much more true must it have been of Peter and Mark, whom the former refers to as his son (see 1 Pet 5:13).

36. My description of Peter is of course only approximate but is based in general on drawings, paintings, mosaics, and statues, which exhibit a remarkable degree of uniformity and can be found in an abundance surpassed only by those of Jesus and Mary in catacombs, basilicas, early churches, crypts, and the recent excavations under St. Peter's Basilica at Vatican City. One of the best collections of representations of St. Peter is gathered in James Lees-Milne, *Saint Peter's: The Story of Saint Peter's Basilica in Rome* (London: Hamish Hamilton, 1967) 12–40. *Consult also* John Beckwith, *Early Christian and Byzantine Art* (London: Penguin, 1970).

37. *See* John 21:18-19.

38. As we shall see, Luke's Acts of Apostles ends with Paul under house arrest in Rome, thus fulfilling the theme stated in Acts 1:8 that the apostles were to be Christ's "witnesses in Jerusalem, and all Judea and Samaria, and to the end of the earth" (WFD). However, Paul was not put to death at that time. Rather, after two years of minimum security under house arrest during which his accusers did not arrive from Jerusalem, he was legally released around A.D. 62–63. Then, perhaps after a visit to Spain (see Rom 15:28), he returned to Greece (see Titus 3:12) where he may have been at the time of the Great Fire and persecution of Christians. However, he apparently returned to Rome before the persecution ceased with the suicide of Nero in A.D. 68 and, as a Roman citizen, was beheaded on the Ostian Way in A.D. 67 or 68.

39. It is difficult to present a clear picture of St. Mark, since it seems that few portraits of him exist other than under the symbolism of a lion, accomodated by the Fathers from the four living creatures in Ezek 1:10; 10:14; Rev 4:7, which seem to represent all of creation. When Mark is depicted, as in Beckwith, *Early Christian and Byzantine Art*, pl. 100, he appears as a young man

with a full head of black hair and a black beard, penning his Gospel with grim determination, or as in Lees-Milne, *Saint Peter's*, 36, as an elderly man largely bald and looking older than Peter himself. But according to my calculations he would have been middle-aged when he wrote his Gospel, as he is portrayed in *NCE*, s.v. "Mark, Gospel according to," and that is the way I have tried to portray him. (As to the portrait of an elderly Mark in Lees-Milne, I wonder if that is not actually a picture of Peter and Paul rather than Peter and Mark.)

40. Linus, Cletus, and Clement were leading figures in the Italian Church of the first century and succeeded Peter as bishop of Rome and therefore vicar of Christ, or pope, in the order mentioned: Linus (64–79), Cletus (79–92), and Clement (92–101). All three were martyred and are so honored in the Roman canon or first Eucharistic Prayer of the Mass. Two may possibly be mentioned scripturally as companions of Paul in his Roman imprisonments: Clement in Phil 4:3 and Linus in 2 Tim 4:21. One, namely Clement, is listed among the apostolic Fathers by virtue of his beautiful Letter to the Corinthians urging loving unity in the spirit of Paul, their founder. (*NCE*, s.v. "Anacletus [Cletus], Pope, St.," and "Clement I"; "Letter of St. Clement of Rome to the Corinthians," trans. Francis Glimm, *The Apostolic Fathers*, The Fathers of the Church [New York: Cima, 1947] 3–58).

41. *See* 2 Pet 3:15-16. While this Epistle is generally considered by Scripture scholars today as pseudonymous, it certainly reflects the sentiments of Peter, whose esteem and affection for Paul, in spite of the confrontation of Gal 2:14, is depicted in numerous representations dating back to the early Church. *See* Lees-Milne, *Saint Peter's*, e.g., pp. 30 and 54. They are honored together in the liturgy of June 29 as princes of the apostles and as founders of the Church at Rome, even before they arrived there personally, because of Peter's Pentecostal Sermon which converted three thousand Jews, some of whom were from Rome (see Acts 2:10), and because Paul helped to shape them into a viable Church through his powerful Letter to the Romans.

42. *See* Isa 40:10-11; Ezek 34:11-16, 22-24; John 10:11-16.

43. *See* Isa 52:13–53:12, notably 53:7b; Jer 11:19; Acts 8:32.

44. Rom 6:9-10.

45. *See* Matt 16:24-28; Mark 8:34-38; Luke 9:23-27; John 12:24-28.

46. *See* Matt 16:13-23; Mark 8:27-33.

47. Mark would undoubtedly have met Luke, probably not in Jerusalem or any other city but in Rome itself where Mark was already with Peter when Luke arrived with Paul around A.D. 60, as he relates in Acts 28:11-16. "For two full years Paul stayed on in his rented lodgings, welcoming all who came to him" (Acts 28:30, NAB). It must have been during those two priceless years that Paul and Mark, perhaps through the gentle persuasion of Luke himself, succeeded in putting the past behind them and were thoroughly reconciled with each other, as we see reflected in Col 4:10 and particularly in Phlm 24, where Mark and Luke are mentioned in the same sentence. It must also have been during this time, before Paul sent Luke away to assume charge of one of his Churches, probably Philippi, that Mark came to know Luke, even be-

fore the latter's Gospel and Acts, as a gentile Christian of exceptional talents combined with total dedication and, above all, as a compassionate and cherished friend in Christ.

48. Silas, whose name is a shortened, more familiar Aramaic or Greek form of the Latin *Silvanus* or *Silvester*, meaning "Woodsman" or "Man of the Forest," is encountered in Acts 15:22-41, first as a representative of the Council of Jerusalem to Antioch, then as Paul's choice to replace Barnabas and Mark on his second missionary journey, the first into Europe. Just when Silas reached Rome is not clear, but he did assist Peter in writing his "encyclical," known as First Peter (see 1 Pet 5:12), even though Mark was present and mentioned in the work (see 1 Pet 5:13). My own opinion is that Peter normally used Mark as his secretary when writing in Aramaic or sending ordinary letters in Greek but that for his first (and perhaps only) circular letter, addressed to the Churches in Asia Minor, he borrowed the well-educated Silas, who had the talents and training to put his ideas into more elegant Greek. The result? A masterpiece! But Peter himself does not shine through the elegant Greek. No wonder, then, that he insisted on having Mark rather than Silas tell the story of Jesus just the way it happened. How much alike were Peter and his "son," Mark!

49. Did Mark ever meet Apollos, the great Alexandrian philosopher and orator, who was perhaps a disciple of the famous Jewish and Greek philosopher, Philo, then was converted from Judaism to Christianity, preached at Ephesus (see Acts 18:24-26), Corinth (see Acts 18:27–19:1; 1 Cor 1-4), and later at Crete (see Titus 3:13) and according to a growing number of Scripture scholars, was the most likely author of the eloquent Epistle to the Hebrews? We have no record indicating that the Jerusalem disciple was ever in Ephesus or Corinth, let alone when Apollos was in those cities.

Mark, then, may have known Apollos only by reputation, which of course would be enough to justify his feelings of inferiority. There is an ancient tradition that sometime in his life Mark was involved with the Church at Alexandria, but it would most probably have been after Apollos had left there for Ephesus and then Corinth, so it is not likely that he encountered Apollos there or still less that he himself converted Apollos, even though that would not be the first or last time that a comparatively simple but saintly person has been the instrument of God in leading a great intellectual to Christ (see Matt 11:25; Acts 18:26; 1 Cor 1:27-31).

50. A few examples of such eyewitness details found only in Mark's Gospel are Jesus asleep on a cushion during the storm at sea (see Mark 4:38); the people reclining on the grass "like flowerbeds" (Mark 6:40); the process cures, perhaps in preparation for the sacrament of the sick (see Mark 7:31-37; 8:22-26); the fruitless fig tree outside the time for figs (see Mark 11:13); the location of the eschatological discourse (see Mark 13:3); plus scenes like the transfiguration (see Mark 9:2-8) and agony in the garden (see Mark 14:32-47).

51. The early Church's kerygma, or public proclamation in regard to Jesus, is generally considered to contain these four main points: (1) the baptism of Jesus by John the Baptist and his messianic approval from heaven (see Mark

1:2-13), (2) the ministry of Jesus in Galilee and beyond (see Mark 1:14–8:30), (3) the journey in fact and faith to Jerusalem (see Mark 8:31–10:52), and (4) the saving events in Jerusalem (see Mark 11:1–16:20). In general these underlie not only the four Gospels but also the main discourses in Acts, e.g., 2:14-39; 10:34-43; 13:16-41.

52. What is referred to here is what form critics call *sitz im leben kirche* (the Church's life situation) in which the Church, faced with questions and problems, reminisced on what Jesus had done and said in his own life situation (*sitz im leben Jesu*), e.g., regarding fasting (see Mark 2:18-20), divorce (see Mark 10:2-12), infant baptism (see Mark 10:13-16), etc., these responses taking various forms such as *lógia* (short sayings), pronouncement stories (statements in story settings), parables, miracle stories, etc. and being finally incorporated into the Gospels by the evangelists in what is called *sitz im leben evangelisten* (the evangelists' life situation).

This is a valid kind of criticism known to Scripture scholars as *Formgeschichte* (form history or form criticism), developed by Rudolf Bultmann and Martin Dibelius after World War I and popularized in English after World War II by such British scholars as C. H. Dodd and Vincent Taylor. Out of form criticism, which regarded the evangelists largely as collectors of the aforementioned forms, came redaction criticism, developed largely by such post-Bultmannians as Gunther Bornkamm, Hans Conzelmann, and Willi Marxsen, which emphasized the role of the evangelists as redactors or revisors, and finally the new literary criticism or composition criticism, developed by a host of modern interpreters, which stresses the role of the evangelists as true authors albeit incorporating the findings of both form criticism and redaction criticism.

Where I would differ with the form critics, besides the rejection of their philosophical bias, e.g., against the possibility of miracles (a possibility which Catholics and most Protestants accept), is in the interpretation of the word "Church." When the form critics speak of the Church as remembering Jesus' deeds and words in order to answer questions and solve problems in her life situation they speak in generalities, whereas I see the Church as led by particular individuals such as Peter, its principal human leader and Paul, its greatest missionary; and I envision them, especially Peter, gathering with their presbyters to solve problems in the light of Jesus' words and deeds with Mark and perhaps other secretaries recording these. Thus, Peter, Paul, and Mark themselves would be deeply involved in the content of the forms emphasized in form criticism.

For more information on this important subject please see Rudolf Bultmann, "The Study of the Synoptic Gospels," in R. Bultmann and Karl Kundsin, *Form Criticism*, trans. Frederick Grant (New York: Harper & Row, 1962); Martin Dibelius, *From Tradition to Gospel* (New York: Scribner, n.d.); Edgar McKnight, *What Is Form Criticism?* (Philadelphia: Fortress, 1969); John Kselman, "Modern New Testament Criticism," *JBC* 2:13-20.

53. Mark "tells it like it is" with vivid details, especially in the miracle stories; racy journalistic style, characterized by the use of "and" or "immedi-

ately'' as connectives and extensive use of the narrative present; plus candid accounts of Jesus himself (see Mark 14:34-36), his family (see Mark 3:21), his apostles (see Mark 8:33; 9:38; 10:35-37, etc.).

54. In Mark's Gospel Jesus' very first work of power is an exorcism (see Mark 1:23-27), followed by many others (see Mark 1:34, 39; 3:11-12; 5:1-20; 7:24-30; 9:14-29).

55. In Mark Jesus is indeed the wonder healer, his cures like his exorcisms being told to exemplify his power as Messiah and Son of God (see Mark 1:29-34, 40-42; 2:1-12; 3:1-10; 5:25-34; 6:53-56; 7:31-37; 8:22-26; 10:46-52). By way of contrast, please note the other evangelists' use of Jesus' miracles as we study those authors.

56. The daughter of Jairus (see Mark 5:21-24, 35-43).

57. A dominant theme in the second half of Mark (see 8:31-33; 9:12, 30-31; 10:45; 14:32–15:47).

58. In Greek, Jesus' trauma in the Garden of Gethsemane is far more devastating (see Mark 14:32-42) than it seems in translation.

59. *See* Mark 4:38.

60. *See* Mark 6:5-6.

61. *See* Mark 1:12-13; 14:32-42.

62. Jesus forgave sin (see Mark 2:5) and died to save us from sin (see 15:35-39) but was totally free from sin (see Mark 1:11; 9:7; 2 Cor 5:21; Heb 4:15).

63. This statement reflects Mark 16:15, NAB, which is generally thought by Scripture scholars not to be part of the original Gospel of Mark but is accepted by the Catholic Church as inspired and serves to summarize the commission to the apostles in Matt 28:16-20. It could well have been familiar to Peter, somewhat like the saying attributed to Jesus by Paul in Acts 20:35 which is found nowhere in the four Gospels.

64. This is indeed promised by Jesus in his eschatological discourse (see Mark 13:5-31; Matt 24:1-35; Luke 21:5-28) as well as in his last discourse in John 15:18–16:4.

65. This is a common and plausible motive suggested by Scripture scholars for the writing of the Gospels, but it is purely conjectural and I personally tend to look for more personal and situational reasons, as given in this volume.

66. This section of Rome was not destroyed by the fire because it was across the Tiber from Rome proper. This also explains why there was a cemetery at Vatican Hill, since no one was allowed to be buried inside Rome, the only exceptions being Romulus and Remus, the legendary founders of Rome, and Julius Caesar, whose tombs are honored in the Roman forum, and Augustus Caesar, whose huge circular tomb is clearly visible near the Stadium of Domitian or Piazza Navona.

67. Like the Vatican Hill, the imposing Janiculum Hill was not one of the original seven hills of Rome, for it was across the Tiber from Rome proper, but today it is a favorite spot because of its panoramic view of Rome and its fame as the final battle site in the war for the unification of Italy in 1870.

68. Unlike the Jewish scourging which was limited to forty blows (actu-

ally thirty-nine for fear of exceeding the number, see 2 Cor 11:24), the Roman scourging was unlimited and sometimes resulted in the death of those condemned to scourging alone or scourging and crucifixion. The marks of the scourging on the shroud of Turin provide a graphic picture of Roman scourging whether or not the figure thereon is that of Jesus Christ.

69. There seems to be no other known instance of anyone other than Jesus Christ being mocked with such a crown, which apparently was not a circlet of rose thorns as so often depicted but an entire cap of acacia thorns, often three or four inches long like those of a honey locust tree.

70. While the synoptic Gospels (Mark, Matthew, Luke) seem to indicate that Simon of Cyrene carried the crossbeam the whole way for Jesus (see Mark 15:21; Matt 27:32; Luke 23:26), John, whose description indicates more of an eyewitness report, insists that "Jesus was led away, and carrying the cross by himself, went out to what is called the Place of the Skull (in Hebrew, *Golgotha*)" (John 19:16b-17, NAB). Tradition tends to combine the two accounts in such a way that Jesus began to carry his own cross, but when he could no longer do so Simon was conscripted.

71. As demonstrated by Dr. Pierre Barbet in connection with the shroud of Turin, nails through the hands would not have held the body of Jesus, hence they had to be driven through the wrists as indicated in the shroud. *See* Pierre Barbet, *A Doctor at Calvary* (Garden City, N.Y.: Doubleday, 1963) 103-20. However, if Peter was crucified upside down as tradition indicates, then it is possible that nails through his feet could have held his body even if his hands were nailed through the palms.

72. There is good cumulative evidence for the sojourn, episcopacy, crucifixion, death, and burial of St. Peter at Rome, e.g., in John 21:18-19; 1 Pet 5:13; 2 Pet 1:14 (even if not Petrine, it reflects an ancient tradition). *See* Clement I, "First Epistle to the Corinthians," 5 ff. *Patrologia Graeca* I, cols. 217 A-221A; St. Ignatius of Antioch, "Epistle to the Romans," 4, *Patrologia Graeca* V, col. 689 A-B; *Ascension of Isaias* IV, 2 ff., ed. E. Tisserant (Paris, 1909) 116 ff.; "Apocalypse of Peter" in C. Wessely, *Patrologia Orientalis* XVIII 3 (Paris, 1924) 482 ff. This and more is from Margherita Guarducci, *The Tomb of Peter*, trans. Joseph McLellan (New York: Hawthorn, 1960) 25 ff., 184-85nn.

73. On the question of St. Peter's original grave and the apparent discovery of his bones in a separate repository nearby, see the careful study by John Walsh, *The Bones of St. Peter* (Garden City, N.Y.: Doubleday, 1982).

74. *See* Mark 16:15. *See also* n. 63 above.

75. Rom. 1:16, WFD.

76. "Good News," in Greek, *euangélion* from *eu* (well, good) and *angelía* (message, news) from *ángelos* (messenger, angel). For examples of secular usage mostly in royal announcements; of Old Testament usage particularly regarding divine interventions, e.g., in messianic contexts; and of New Testament usage by John the Baptist, Jesus, and above all Paul (some sixty instances!), see *Theological Dictionary of the New Testament*, 1964, s.v. "euangélion" (also abridged in one volume).

77. Literally, "Beginning of the good news of Jesus Christ, Son of God" (Mark 1:1, WFD).

78. On Linus, Cletus, and Clement, see n. 40 above. It is thought by some that after Peter's martyrdom these three early leaders may have governed the Church together. *See* Michael Walsh, *An Illustrated History of the Popes* (New York: St. Martin's, 1980) 23. However, there is no more evidence for such a possibility than there is for the scenario that I have indicated.

79. *See* Acts 1:15-26.

80. *See* Mark 1:2-9.

81. *See* Mark 1:10. Unlike the other three evangelists Mark describes the dove symbolic of the Holy Spirit as descending not just upon him but actually into him (*eis autón*). Strangely, none of the English translations reflects this, yet it is important, for it emphasizes the fact that Jesus, in his humanity (characteristically stressed in Mark), is not only anointed by the Spirit as Messiah (Anointed One, see Isa 61:1-3; Luke 4:14-21) but is even filled with and driven by the Spirit throughout his life. Thus in Mark alone "the Spirit drives him out into the desert" (Mark 1:12, WFD) where he begins his conquest of the evil spirit which perdures all through his public life, starting with the opening exorcism (see Mark 1:23-28), continuing with the condemnation of the "unforgivable sin" against the Holy Spirit (see Mark 3:20-30), expulsion of the legion of evil spirits at Gerasa (see Mark 5:1-20), rebuke of Peter's human attitude toward Jesus' predicted suffering and death (the attitude of many Roman Christians facing persecution) as aligning him with Satan (see Mark 8:33), and concluding with his ultimate triumph over the evil spirit by his death and resurrection.

82. Mark and Luke, unlike Matthew, report the heavenly voice of the Father as directly addressing Jesus when proclaiming him Son and Servant, reflecting Ps 2:7 and Isa 42:1. Many regard this as implying the celebrated messianic secret theory of W. Wrede, *The Messianic Secret in the Gospels*, published in 1901 and summarized in Kselman, "Modern New Testament Criticism," *JBC* 2:12: "The historical Jesus never made any claim to be the Messiah. Only after the resurrection did the disciples realize that Jesus was the Christ. They then read back Messiahship into the earthly life of Jesus and created the 'Messianic Secret' (Jesus' concealment of his Messiahship) to account for the fact that his Messiahship was unknown to them and to the Jews at large before his death. The Messianic secret was therefore a tradition created by the early Christian community and taken over by Mk, who wrote not as an objective historian but from the viewpoint of Christian faith."

Granted that Mark and the other evangelists wrote from the viewpoint of Christian faith, this theory hardly deserves the attention given it over the years. Evidence abounds that Jesus was well aware of his messiahship but silenced public acknowledgement because of false ideas of the time, and that Peter and the other apostles clearly professed his messiahship (see Mark 8:27-30; Matt 16:13-16; Luke 9:18-21; John 6:66-69) but did not fully understand it (or realize his divinity) until after the resurrection (see Mark 8:31-33; 9:32, and parallels).

The voice from the heavens seems to have been addressed only to Jesus and to John the Baptist, with emphasis on the former in Mark and Luke, on the latter in "Matthew" and John. The purpose? For the *human Jesus* to confirm his messiahship and unique divine sonship, both of which he had learned by faith and mystical prayer during the many years of growth at Nazareth "in wisdom, age and stature, grace and favor, before God and people" (Luke 2:52, WFD. Note how I have tried to probe the fullness of meaning). For John the Baptist to identify Jesus especially as the Messiah and Suffering Servant, "the one who is to come" and "baptize in the Holy Spirit and fire" (Mark 1:7-8; Matt 3:11; Luke 3:16), "the Lamb of God who takes away the sin of the world" (John 1:29, 36), even "the Son of God" (John 1:34, WFD, throughout) so that John might be able to herald his coming with understanding and zeal.

83. In Mark's Gospel, followed by "Matthew" and Luke, the first part concludes with Peter's (and the apostles') profession of Jesus' messiahship in response to Jesus' "two-part final examination" (see Mark 8:27-30; Matt 16:13-16; Luke 9:18-21) after their peripatetic training inside and outside Galilee. Then, satisfied that his apostles have at least completed their basic training, Jesus begins immediately to journey toward Jerusalem while predicting (not just once but three times) his imminent death and resurrection and inviting their "followership."

84. The word *kérygma* (proclamation) is based on *kêryx* (herald), which of course fits in nicely with the idea of *euangélion* (good news). *See* n. 76 above.

85. Already treated in n. 83 above.

86. For geographical cycles please see the outline of Mark under the analysis of his Gospel.

87. For the strategic use of summaries see the outline of Mark's Gospel. And for further study of Mark's summaries *see* Vincent Taylor, *The Gospel According to St. Mark* (London: Macmillan, 1959) 85-86. Not that summaries are unique to Mark, since they are found also in Matthew, Luke, and Acts, but it seems probable that Mark led the way in their use.

88. Mark's simplicity of style, sometimes even awkwardness, coincides perfectly with his Jewish background as well as with the needs of the Roman Christians and the desire of Peter. Many of his sentences begin with *kaí* (and) or *euthús* (immediately), and his clauses tend to be more coordinate than subordinate as is characteristic not only of someone writing simply, hurriedly, and in a second language but also of someone versed in a Semitic manner of expression.

89. These "fancy structures" will be fully explained and exemplified when we examine "Matthew," Luke, and John.

90. Examples of simpler structures found in Mark are (1) the parallel theophanies at Jesus' baptism (see 1:10-11) and at his transfiguration (see 9:7-8) and the parallel multiplications of the loaves and fishes for Jews and Gentiles respectively (see Mark 6:34-44; 8:1-9); (2) the triple predictions of Jesus' suffering, death, and resurrection in Jerusalem (see Mark 8:31; 9:31; 10:33-34), his threefold prayer in the garden (see Mark 14:32-42), and Peter's triple denial

(see Mark 14:66-72); (3) the possible inclusion at the beginning and end of the Gospel of the epithet "Son of God" (Mark 1:1; 15:39) and the emptiness of the desert and the tomb (see Mark 1:12; 16:1-8); and (4) the word chains in the parables of the seed (see Mark 4:1-34) and in Jesus' teaching on the kingdom of God, fire, and salt (see Mark 9:43-49).

Another structure that is particularly identified with Mark, a kind of combination of parallelism and inclusion, is popularly called a "Markan sandwich." In this structure, between the beginning and end of the main story another story is interjected which has an important connection with the main story. Some notable examples of Markan sandwiches are these: the raising of Jairus' twelve-year-old daughter to life sandwiching the cure of the woman with the twelve-year-old hemorrhage (see Mark 5:21-43), the mission and return of the apostles sandwiching the arrest, imprisonment, and beheading of John the Baptist as a model of what apostles (and Christians generally) should expect (see Mark 6:7-33); and the cursing and withering of the fig tree, the symbol of fruitless Israel, sandwiching the cleansing of the Temple, symbol of Israel's covenant relationship with Yahweh (see Mark 11:12-25).

While structures may not be as important in Mark as in the other Gospels, attention to the foregoing ones will help in understanding and appreciating some of the subtle nuances of the first Gospel.

91. In a work like this which is intended to appeal to a general readership, it is tempting to omit endnotes altogether, thus making the work so much easier to write as well as to read. However, I have chosen to resist the temptation for these reasons: (1) because I do want these portraits of the five main human authors of the New Testament to be truly documented stories, (2) because I want to give scholars the opportunity to check on the reliability of sources and logic of reasoning used to support my contentions, and (3) even for those who do not consider themselves scholars but who have a hunger for knowledge of Holy Scripture, I want to offer as much information as possible. In practice the general reader may want to read the portraits straight through without reference to the endnotes in order to savor the overall impressions involved, then in a second reading check the endnotes for documentation and further information.

92. *See* Taylor, *Gospel According to St. Mark* 45.

93. The "no frills" tenor of Mark's Gospel is probably due to several factors, e.g., the need of haste in producing the work for the persecuted Roman Christians, Mark's (and Peter's) own temperament, and the importance of presenting a portrait of Jesus that is as human and straightforward as possible. Later we will see that the Gospels of "Matthew" and Luke carefully modify some of Mark's language in order to avoid misunderstandings, especially in regard to Jesus and the apostles.

94. The passage in Mark 3:21 is not quite clear. First of all, the expression usually translated as "his family" (NAB, NEB, NIV), "his relatives" (JB), "his friends" (RSV) is the enigmatic *hoi par' autou* (those with him). Then the rest of the sentence, which is usually translated as "they went to take charge of

him, for they said, 'He is out of his mind' " (NIV), can as easily be understood as, "they went to take charge of it (the crowd, *óchlos*, a masculine noun), for they said, 'It is out of its mind' (or "beside itself"). However, the very next statement reads, "And the teachers of the law who came down from Jerusalem said, 'He is possessed by Beelzebub! By the prince of demons he is driving out demons' " (Mark 3:22, NIV). This seems to favor the reference to Jesus rather than the crowd as being considered "out of his mind," but both translations are possible and compatible with Markan thought.

95. In correlation with Mark's portrait of Jesus' powerful teaching and miracles as Messiah and Son of God is his unique portrait of the amazement, the utter stupefaction, on the part of the witnesses. No fewer than four different Greek verbs are used, namely *ekpléssomai* (1:22; 6:2; 7:37; 10:26), *exístemi* (2:12; 5:42; 6:51), *thaumázo* (5:20; 12:17), and *thambeomai* (1:27) in addition to the Greek verb for fear or terror, *phobéomai* (4:41; 5:15, 33). Whether or not these reactions manifest a lack of faith, as maintained with some reason (see William Lynch, *Jesus in the Synoptic Gospels* [Milwaukee: Bruce] 21), it seems clear to this writer that the main purpose is to impress the reader with the extraordinary power of Jesus as Messiah and Son of God, in spite of which he freely accepts the cruelest of deaths.

96. The examples used are, as indicated, only a sample of Jesus' emotions in Mark's Gospel. For a more complete picture, it will be helpful not only to cite additional instances but also to provide both the Greek words used and the immediate contexts of their usage. Interestingly, while the witnesses' emotional reactions referred to in n. 95 above are somewhat repetitious (thirteen reactions being expressed by only five different Greek verbs), such is certainly not the case regarding Mark's descriptions of Jesus' emotions. Here he never seems to repeat himself, using eleven distinct and powerful Greek expressions in addition to three episodes where the context itself tends to imply Jesus' emotional state. Here is the list, comprising the reference in Mark, Greek expression, its basic form in parentheses, the translation in quotation marks, and the context in which it is used:

1. 1:41—*splanchnistheìs (splanchnízomai)*, "moved with pity or compassion" for the leper who hopes for healing.

2. 1:43—*embrimesámenos (embrimáomai)*, "speaking harshly or peremptorily" in dismissing the leper and forbidding him to tell anyone except the priest "as a witness to them."

3. 3:5—*periblepsámenos autoùs met'orgês (orgé)*, "surveying them with anger" before healing the withered hand.

4. 3:5—*syllypoúmenos (syllypéomai)*, "deeply grieved" at the hardness of their (the Pharisees') heart.

5. 6:6—*ethaúmazen (thaumázo)*, "he wondered or was surprised" at their (the Nazarenes') lack of faith.

6. 8:12—*anastenáxas (anastenázo)*, "groaning deeply in spirit" over the Pharisees' demand for a sign or miracle.

7. 8:17-21—The whole episode implies Jesus' impatience with his apostles in the boat over their obtuseness in regard to the "leaven of the Pharisees."

8. 9:19-29—The whole episode implies Jesus' impatience with his apostles (and others) regarding the possessed boy.

9. 10:14—*ēganáktesen (aganaktéo)*, "he was indignant or upset" over his apostles' shortness with the children.

10. 10:16—*enankalisámenos (enankalízomai)*, "hugging or embracing" the children, showing tender love in action.

11. 10:21—*ēgápesen (agapáo)*, "he loved" the rich young man (with a spiritual love).

12. 11:15-18—The whole context implies Jesus' anger and indignation over the desecration of the Temple.

13. 14:33—*ērxato ekthambeîsthai (ekthambéomai)*, "he began to be greatly anguished" in his agony in the garden.

14. 14:33—*ademoneîn (ademonéo)*, "to be dispirited."

15. 14:34—*perílypós estin hē psychē mou héōs thanátou*, "my soul is very sad or deeply distressed, even to death."

97. In Mark's Gospel more than anywhere else in Scripture we can see Jesus in all his humanness, including his human limitations in knowledge, power, and goodness, but rather than examine such an important subject at this time and place I will wait until I can treat it more fully in the final part of our study of Mark, which looks into the personal and communal applications of Mark's Gospel.

98. Among the minority who favor a near-Eastern origin around A.D. 70 are Paul Feine, Johannes Behm, and Werner Kummel, *Introduction to the New Testament*, trans. A. J. Mattill, Jr. (Nashville: Abingdon, 1966) 70–71; Howard Kee, Franklin Young, and Karlfried Froehlich, *Understanding the New Testament*, 3rd ed. (Englewood Cliffs, N.J.: Prentice-Hall, 1973) 114–16; and Wilfrid Harrington, *Mark* (Wilmington, Del.: Michael Glazier, 1979) xii, in which he seems to have departed from his more traditional opinion in an earlier work, *Explaining the Gospels* (Glen Rock, N.J.: Paulist, 1963) 69–70.

99. The external evidence in the early Church, featuring Papias of Hierapolis, the anti-Marcionite prologue, Justin Martyr, Irenaeus, the Muratorian canon, Clement of Alexandria, Origen, and Jerome, is carefully detailed in Taylor, *Gospel According to St. Mark* 1–7.

The internal evidence, scattered throughout this study of Mark, can be summarized under these headings: evidence of Petrine testimony; translation of Semitic expressions and Jewish customs; presence of many Latinisms; and clear references to persecution throughout the Gospel, especially the Markan sandwich account of John the Baptist's martyrdom (see 6:14-29), Jesus' predictions of his own sufferings and those of his followers (see 8:31-38; 9:30-32; 10:32-34), Jesus' promise of persecutions along with other rewards (see 10:29-30), his apocalyptic prediction of suffering and rejection by those in authority (see 13:9-13), and above all the obvious emphasis on Jesus' own sufferings and death as the model and example for his followers (see 14:27–15:47).

To the above evidence may be added the confirmation of so many modern authors, e.g., Barclay, *The Gospel of Mark* 65; Raymond Brown in R. Brown and John Meier, *Antioch & Rome* (New York: Paulist, 1983) 196–97; W. D. Davies, *Invitation to the New Testament* (Garden City, N.Y.: Doubleday, 1966) 198, 208; C. H. Dodd, *About the Gospels* (Cambridge, England: University Press, 1958) 1–2; Archibald Hunter, *Introducing the New Testament*, 2nd ed. (Philadelphia: Westminster, 1957) 40; John McKenzie, *Dictionary of the Bible* (Milwaukee: Bruce, 1965) 543; George Montague, *Mark: Good News for Hard Times* (Ann Arbor, Mich: Servant Books, 1981) 8–9; D. E. Nineham, *Saint Mark* (London: Penguin, 1974) 65–75; Francis Rhein, *An Analytical Approach to the New Testament* (Woodbury, N.Y.: Barron's, 1966) 92–93; Donald Selby and James Wast, "Introduction to the New Testament," *Introduction to the Bible* (New York: Macmillan, 1971) 74; Robert Spivey, D. Moody Smith, *Anatomy of the New Testament*, 2nd ed. (New York: Macmillan, 1974) 83–84; and Taylor, *Gospel According to St. Mark* 7–8, 32.

In addition there are a number of authors, including such scholars as Paul Achtemeier, Werner Kelber, Willi Marxsen, Pheme Perkins, and Norman Perrin, who feel that the evidence, both external and internal, is inconclusive and therefore they prescind from any particular location for Mark's Gospel. To them, this is the more scientific approach. However, to my mind, not only is the evidence sufficient, but as I indicated in the introduction, I believe that a dubious setting is better than none at all in enabling the reader to understand, appreciate, and live the Scriptures, especially the New Testament.

100. A word should be said about the famous ending(s) to the Gospel of Mark. Both the internal evidence of the Gospel itself and the manuscript evidence seem to agree that Mark concluded his Gospel at the end of what is now Mark 16:8. In typical Markan fashion the work begins and ends abruptly. Unlike the other three Gospels which open with Infancy Gospels or a prologue and close with appearances of the risen Christ to his followers, Mark commences with the blockbuster declaration, "The beginning of the good news of Jesus Christ, the Son of God!" (WFD), followed by the surprise appearance of John the Baptist in the emptiness of the Judean desert; and he concludes with the emptiness of the tomb and the blockbuster declaration of the "young man clothed in white" who tells the three women, "Don't be alarmed! You are searching for Jesus the Nazarene who was crucified. He has risen. He is not here. Look at the place where they laid him. But go and tell his apostles and Peter that he is going ahead of you to Galilee. There you will see him just as he told you" (WFD).

Just as Luke concludes his Acts of Apostles abruptly with the first imprisonment of Paul at Rome for the simple reason that he has fulfilled his aim, expressed by Jesus in his injunction of Acts 1:8, so also Mark ends his Gospel abruptly because he too has fulfilled his purpose, namely to portray Jesus as Messiah and Son of God yet also Son of Man and Servant of Yahweh who freely accepts suffering and death. This is confirmed by the absence of any further ending in two of the most important manuscripts, namely the Codex Vaticanus and Codex Sinaiticus.

To others, however, Mark's ending seemed incomplete, hence three further additions have been made in various manuscripts. The longer ending

(Mark 9–20), an obvious synthesis of Jesus' appearances in the other three Gospels, is printed in brackets in the Greek New Testament of the United Bible Societies and included in all modern English translations. Though not originally Markan it is accepted as inspired by Catholics and many Protestants. The other two endings, designated as the shorter ending and the Freer logion and both included, unnumbered, in the New American Bible but not in other versions, are generally not considered as inspired.

101. This emphasis on living the Word of God is featured in my volume on biblical spirituality, *To Live The Word*, 437 pp., with a beautiful preface by Carroll Stuhlmueller, C.P. Subtitled *An Integral Biblical Spirituality*, this is one of the only works available that uses the entire Bible to construct a comprehensive biblical spirituality which is both understandable and livable and which, therefore, is recommended to all who are seriously striving to live a deep spiritual life.

102. Exod 19:3-6 is a very important text, containing as it does God's invitation to Israel to live in a covenant relationship with him. It reads as follows: "Moses went up the mountain to God. Then the Lord called to him and said, 'Thus shall you say to the house of Jacob; tell the Israelites; you have seen for yourselves how I treated the Egyptians and how I bore you up on eagle wings and brought you here to myself. Therefore, if you hearken to my voice and keep my covenant, you shall be my special possession, dearer to me than all other people, though all the earth is mine. You shall be to me a kingdom of priests, a holy nation. That is what you must tell the Israelites' " (Exod 19:3-6, NAB). Notice that there is not a word in this invitation about commandments or laws. A covenant is an agreement establishing a bond of lasting relationship, and it is relationship that is at the heart of religion, whereas truths, laws, and worship are either means of relationship or flow from it.

For the covenant of Sinai, the conditions or specifications are expressed in the Ten Commandments, which are given in the following chapter (see Exod 20:1-17); and all the other written laws (over six hundred, found mostly in Exodus, Leviticus, and Deuteronomy) were drawn up in the course of Israelite history to ensure the keeping of the commandments, to which they are reducible, and in turn the preservation of the covenant relationship.

Our human nature is such, however, that in time the legalism of the commandments and laws usurped the primacy of attention intended for the relationship of the covenant. This is painfully clear from the attitude of the "experts in the Law," the scribes and Pharisees, toward Jesus, who had come to reconcile Israel and indeed all humankind into relationship with his Father. Notice how often Jesus deliberately does "work" on the Sabbath, the keeping of which was reverenced by the legalists as the most important commandment (see Mark 2:23-28; 3:1-6 and much more in Matthew and John) and how in Mark especially he tries to raise the legalists' minds beyond ritualistic laws to the more important requirements of justice and love and purity (see Mark 7:1-23). And when challenged to name the greatest commandment, Jesus without hesitation lists in Mark 12:29-31 the two great relational commandments into which the ten commandments are reducible, namely the love of God in Deut 6:4-5 and the love of neighbor in Lev 19:18.

103. When Jesus instituted the Holy Eucharist at the Last Supper he simultaneously inaugurated the new covenant, a covenant which had been foretold by Jeremiah (see Jer 31:31-34), a covenant whose initiates by baptism (*eis Christòn*, "into Christ" according to Paul's usage in Rom 6:3; Gal 3:27, etc.) enter into personal and communal relationship with the very risen body-person of Jesus Christ as well as with the mystical body of Christ, the Church. And significantly, Peter in his First Epistle, which is really a baptismal homily, applies to the baptized the same terminology used in the covenant of Sinai: "You, however, are 'a chosen race, a royal priesthood, a holy nation, a people he claims as his own to proclaim the glorious works' of the One who called you out of darkness into his marvelous light" (1 Pet 2:9, NAB). Being human, however, we Christians have also tended to trade relationship for legalism, and must always strive to "be reconciled to God" (2 Cor 5:20, NAB) in the "new covenant, a covenant not of a written law but of spirit" (2 Cor 3:6, NAB).

104. For a fuller treatment of this and the foregoing truths please see *To Live the Word*, 3–53.

105. For a fuller treatment of this fascinating but thorny question, see *To Live the Word*, app. B, 415–24, taking into account the further development of thought contained in this work. It is also important to remember that this is not simply a mental exercise of theologians and Scripture scholars but a question of developing an accurate portrait of Jesus, human as well as divine, so that we may truly know him, fully appreciate his love for us, love him totally in return, grow in union with him, and continue his life, ministry, and sufferings in ourselves.

106. *Vatican Council II: The Conciliar and Post Conciliar Documents*, ed. Austin Flannery (Collegeville: The Liturgical Press, 1975) 764.

107. E.g., Ludwig Ott, *Fundamentals of Catholic Dogma*, bk. 3, sec. 1, ed. J. Canon Bastible and trans. P. Lynch (St. Louis: B. Herder, 1957) 162–72.

108. See Henry Denzinger, *The Sources of Catholic Dogma*, par. 148, trans. Roy Deferrari (St. Louis: B. Herder, 1955) 60–61.

109. E.g., in alphabetical order: Raymond Brown, *Jesus God and Man: Modern Biblical Reflections* (New York: Macmillan, 1967) 79–102; Jean Galot, *Who Is Christ?: A Theology of the Incarnation* pt. 5 (Chicago: Franciscan Herald, 1981) 319–404; Dermot Lane, *The Reality of Jesus: An Essay in Christology*, (New York: Paulist, 1975) 109–29; James Mackey, *Jesus the Man and the Myth: A Contemporary Christology* (New York: Paulist, 1979) 159, 240–47; Karl Rahner, *Theological Investigations*, trans. Karl Kruger (New York: Seabury, 1966) 5:193–215; Karl Rahner and Wilhelm Thuesing, *A New Christology* (New York: Seabury, 1980) 143–59; Leopold Sabourin, *Christology: Basic Texts in Focus* (New York: Alba House, 1984) 56, 59, 101f.; Edward Schillebeeckx, *Jesus: An Experiment in Christology* (New York: Seabury, 1979) 652–69; Piet Schoonenburg, *The Christ: A Study of the God-Man Relationship in the Whole of Creation and in Jesus Christ* (New York: Herder and Herder, 1971) 71–78, 127–35, 140–52; Bruce Vawter,

This Man Jesus: An Essay Toward a New Testament Christology (Garden City, N.Y.: Doubleday, 1973), 133–51.

110. Note that in Mark's Gospel, according to the Greek, not only does the voice address Jesus directly but the Holy Spirit under the symbol of a dove enters into Jesus. This is significant because immediately the Spirit drives Jesus into the desert for his testing, and indeed, throughout his life Jesus is constantly driven by the Spirit.

111. This interpretation of the Aramaic *Abba* as "Daddy" is given special attention in Joachim Jeremias, *New Testament Theology* (New York: Scribner, 1971) 61–68.

112. With all the confusion about the meaning of "the unforgivable sin" it seems clear in Mark's Gospel that Jesus himself labeled as the unforgivable sin that of blasphemy against the Holy Spirit, especially in attributing to the evil spirit the works of the Holy Spirit (see Mark 3:28-30).

113. In 1 Sam 21-22 the high priest involved in helping David was named "Ahimelech," whereas Jesus in Mark 2:26 gives him the name "Abiathar," the only survivor of Saul's massacre of Ahimelech and his whole priestly family who later became the high priest during David's reign. Various explanations are given, such as that Jesus chose to use the name of the priest who would be more important in the reign of his ancestor, David, but if the human mind of Jesus did not enjoy the beatific vision and all infused knowledge there is no contradiction in attributing to him a lack of knowledge about things that he did not need to know in order to fulfill his mission as Messiah and Savior.

114. Jesus' wide-ranging emotions have been listed in the second part of this treatment on Mark, namely the analysis of his Gospel.

115. Mark in his candid fashion relates that Jesus could not work miracles at his hometown because of their lack of faith, while "Matthew," who regularly refines Mark's narrative, changes the wording to "he did not work many miracles there" (Matt 13:58, NAB).

116. Here again we have an interesting example of Markan candor and Matthaean refinement. In Mark the "sons of thunder," James and John (see Mark 3:17), boldly ask for the first places in Jesus' glory, while "Matthew," desiring as usual to show the Twelve in the best light, depicts the mother of James and John as doing the asking. Any good Jewish mother can readily be excused for being ambitious for her sons!

117. See n. 96 above, nos. 13, 14, and 15 on the meaning of the Greek expressions describing Jesus' agony.

118. Some have downplayed Jesus' feeling of abandonment on the cross, pointing out that he is quoting the first line of Ps 22, many verses of which contain elements of his passion. However, this is to apply a Greek-style either-or interpretation, whereas the Semitic mind, both Jesus' and Mark's, is more likely to intend both the reference to the psalm and the traumatic feeling of abandonment.

119. In addition to the content of n. 110 above, it may be helpful to point out a good example of Mark's graphic language, describing the heavens as

"split open" or "torn apart" (*schizoménous*, see Mark 1:10), while both "Matthew" and Luke simply refer to the heavens as "opened."

120. In this episode the Pharisees themselves add weight to the idea of Jesus' divine sonship with their question 'Who can forgive sins except God alone?'' (Mark 2:7, NAB).

121. In Mark 2:27-28, Jesus actually teaches two truths, (1) that the Sabbath rest (the subject of the most important commandment according to the Pharisees) was made for humans in order to enable them to grow in their relationship with God and their families and not vice versa, and (2) that the Son of Man, the heavenly Messiah, is actually Lord of the Sabbath, for he is the very Son of God.

122. Here there is involved the notion of the importance of names and naming. In Gen 2:19-20 Adam's ability to name the animals did not indicate remarkable infused knowledge but rather dominion over the animals as promised in Gen 1:28. So also by naming Jesus the devils tried to establish dominion over him, but Jesus was able to reject their attempt and cast them out. In contrast, in Mark 5:9 Jesus is able to demand and receive the name of the possessing demons, "Legion," then he proceeds to exorcise them, permitting them to enter and destroy the swine to indicate that this was a true exorcism of real devils and not just the cure of a mental illness, which in those days was often misunderstood as diabolical possession.

123. The principal intertestamental works that mention the "Son of Man" are the Book of Henoch and 2 Esdras. *See* Raymond Brown, "Apocrypha; Dead Sea Scrolls; Other Jewish Literature," *JBC* 2:537–38, 540. *See also* David Stanley and Raymond Brown, "Aspects of New Testament Thought," *JBC* 2:773.

124. When the biblical writers wish to give something an extraordinary amount of emphasis they tell it three times, for example in the "Holy, holy, holy" of Isa 6:3, or in the New Testament the stories of Peter's vision and his reception of the first Gentiles into the Church (see Acts 10; 11:1-18; 15:6-11) and Paul's conversion (see Acts 9:1-19; 22:1-21; 26:1-23). So it is with Jesus' predictions of his own approaching sufferings, death, and resurrection, which are recounted three times in Mark, "Matthew," and Luke. Whether the repetition was spoken by Jesus or only written by Mark, "Matthew," and Luke is not clear, but since the wording is different in each prediction and the apostles' reaction is likewise different, it seems more likely that Jesus himself made his predictions three times. This in itself, of course, does not necessarily indicate awareness of divine sonship or even messiahship but only prophetic gifts; yet the solemnity of the predictions, their details, the use of the title Son of Man, all add to the cumulative evidence of Jesus' awareness of his messiahship and divine sonship.

125. The parable of the wicked tenants or husbandmen in the context of the cursing of the fig tree and the cleansing of the Temple, clearly reminiscent of Isa 5:1-7, left little doubt that the wicked tenants represented the religious leaders of Israel, that the prior servants were the prophets, and that the beloved son was Jesus himself.

126. This expression or its equivalent occurs in several articles of St. Thomas Aquinas' masterwork, the voluminous *Summa Theologica,* e.g., in Sancti Thomae Aquinatis Opera Omnia, Editio Parmae, 1852–73 (New York: Musurgia, 1948) vol. III, 2-2, q. 58, a. 2,c, p. 214; vol. IV, 3a, q. 46, a. 12,d, p. 208; 3a, q. 48, a. 6,c, p. 216. The meaning as indicated is that in Jesus as in anyone actions and sufferings are attributed to the person rather than the nature. The word "person" answers the question who? while the word "nature" answers the question what? Who is Jesus Christ? The Son of God, the Word made flesh (see John 1:14). What is Jesus? God and man, divine and human. Thus, while on the one hand the Son of God became as human as possible ('he emptied himself taking the form or nature of a slave, becoming in the likeness of humans," Phil 2:7, WFD) and therefore bore all the limitations characteristic of humans including temptations but not sin, on the other hand, as a divine person all his actions and sufferings were attributed to his divine person and therefore infinitely meritorious.

127. While in Jesus there was and is only one person, the Son of God, the Second Person of the Trinity, it is nevertheless possible and helpful to speak of Jesus' human personality. In doing so we are simply distinguishing between his philosophical personhood, which is divine, and his psychological personality, which is human. In fact, we could speak of his divine personality as well, but in his earthly life, which is the subject of the Gospels, it is above all his human personality which shines forth and with which we can humanly identify.

128. *See* n. 24 above from Tacitus, *Annals* XV:XLIV, 283–85.

129. *See* n. 25 above from Tacitus, *ibid.* and Rom 1:18-32. The novel and television series *I Claudius* by Robert Graves (New York: Random House, 1977) also provide a graphic picture of degenerate Roman morals, beginning with the imperial family which set the tone of Roman life.

130. Author and publisher not indicated on the poster.

131. In what follows some may feel that I am drawing too bleak a picture of our modern world. Perhaps I am, for it is not my purpose at this point to extol all the good and even saintly people whom I myself know personally and to extrapolate that picture generously. My purpose here is to show how there are clear similarities between our world and that of first-century Roman Christianity and therefore how we can benefit greatly by applying to ourselves the salutary lessons inherent in the Gospel according to Mark.

132. The reference here is to the best-selling book by Robert Ringer, *Looking Out for #1* (Los Angeles: L.A. Publishing, 1977) which, like his *Winning Through Intimidation* (Los Angeles: L.A. Publishing, 1974), boldly teaches nothing less than material self-interest, which is poles apart from Christian love. True, Jesus did commend the unjust steward in Luke 18:1-8. However, the commendation was not for being crooked or even greedy but for showing the initiative in material things that he wanted his followers to have in spiritual matters.

133. The reference here is to a recent television program which portrayed

the homes, villas, yachts, etc. of the rich and famous, arousing greed and envy in countless viewers.

134. Today there is growing interest in the science and technology of cryogenics, according to which a deceased person can be frozen and preserved in liquid nitrogen until some future time when the technology will be advanced to the point where it can restore the body to life and heal whatever caused its death or at least where it can "create" clones from the body's, especially the brain's, cells. How pitiable a project, obviously stemming from a total lack of belief in another life, our real life, after death.

135. The term "Deuteronomic theology" is normally applied to a belief and system of rewards and punishments in this life. It was most appropriate and useful during most of Israelite history when there was no knowledge of an afterlife. And why did God not reveal an afterlife to Israel, for example at the time of the Sinaitic covenant? Perhaps for two reasons: (1) because Israel was called not as individuals but as a people and (2) because Israel was called out of Egypt where much of their polytheistic idolatry was centered on the gods of the afterlife. However appropriate Deuteronomic theology was in its time, it certainly is not now, when we not only know about the afterlife but also have the incredible example of Jesus Christ exhibiting the precious meaning and value of suffering.

136. The enigmatic Songs of the Servant of Yahweh occur in what is commonly known as Second Isaiah because it was obviously written during the Babylonian Exile, perhaps a century and a half after the prophet Isaiah. The four songs are found in Isa 42:1-7; 49:1-7; 50:4-9, and 52:13–53:12, the last-mentioned being particularly concerned with the vicarious sufferings of the servant of Yahweh, the perfect type of Jesus, Son of Man and Servant of Yahweh.

137. See n. 134 above.

138. St. Augustine, *The Confessions*, bk. 1, ch. 1, trans. F. J. Sheed (New York: Sheed and Ward, 1943) 3.

139. See n. 133 above.

140. It was allegedly because of the repetition of this verse by Ignatius of Loyola to Francis Xavier that the latter finally shed worldly ambitions, became a Jesuit priest, and went on to develop into the greatest missionary since St. Paul. (But see James Broderick, *Saint Francis Xavier* (New York: Wicklow, 1952) 41, nn. 2 and 3.

141. It was not until I went to China as a missionary that I came to realize how attached the poor can be to their few worldly possessions.

142. See n. 51 above on the meaning and content of the kerygma. The noun *kérygma* is derived from *kêryx* meaning "a herald," the verb of which is *kerýsso* meaning "to herald or proclaim."

143. See n. 52 above on form criticism.

144. There is a sharp contrast between Judaism and Christianity. Yahweh never directed the Jews to go out to the whole world and make disciples; rather by their lives they were to be witnesses to Yahweh and thus attract the Gentiles to the knowledge and love of Yahweh. The apostles, however, were ex-

plicitly directed to evangelize the world, as is crystal clear especially in Matt 28:16-20; Mark 16:15-20; Luke 24:45-48; Acts 1:8.

145. The term "peripatetic" recalls the practice of the great philosopher, Aristotle, who liked to teach his disciples while they were walking around (Webster's Ninth New Collegiate Dictionary, s.v. peripatetic").

146. The Greek *hodós* and the Hebrew *derek*, both meaning "way, path, journey" are frequently used in the Bible, probably because of the great difficulty of finding one's way in the ancient world where, in the absence of highway systems (except the rare Roman roads) and road signs, one was forced to follow the natural paths of the terrain, often marked by human and animal paths. This was always a risky endeavor at best, for it was easy either to get lost or to be attacked by marauders or both. Hence the wider meaning of *hodós* and *derek* as signifying a "way of life.' With the preposition *metá* prefixed to *hodós*, the combination becoming *methodós*, we have the meaning of "method," or a way of doing things. It is significant that before (and even after) Jesus' followers came to be called Christians at Antioch (see Acts 11:26) they were generally known as followers of "the way" or "the new way."

147 . As is clear in Mark (generally paralleled in "Matthew" and Luke), Jesus' adversaries, especially in Jerusalem during the final days of his life, were "the chief priests, the scribes, and the elders," basically the Sanhedrin, or assembly of Jewish religious leaders (11:27), then a coalition of Pharisees and Herodians (see 12:13), then a group of Sadducees, the priestly party (see 12:18), then the scribes or experts in the Law (see 12:28, 35, 38), and finally the chief priests and scribes (and elders), basically the Sanhedrin (see 14:1, 10, 43, 53).

148. The use of olive oil with its soothing properties was a natural choice in the ancient world for healing. Recall that in the parable of the good Samaritan he uses oil and wine (see Luke 10:34), the former probably for its healing properties and the latter as an antiseptic. Oil is used in the sacrament of the sick to signify and effect through Jesus' power the healing of the soul and sometimes also of the body.

149. See n. 100 above.

150. Since there is only "one Lord, one faith, one baptism" (Eph 4:5), all who are validly baptized are basically members of the true Church founded by Jesus Christ.

151. This saying is not to be confused with another which sounds like it, namely, "He who is not with me is against me, and he who does not gather with me scatters" (Matt 12:30; Luke 11:23). In the Markan saying Jesus is speaking of those outside the Church who because of their sincerity and goodwill are really with us. In the Matthean and Lukan saying Jesus is referring to members of the Church who instead of assisting in the work of Christ and the Church actually hinder it by their attitude of laziness, contrariness, and criticism.

152. This familiar saying has been used by many authors throughout the ages. *See* Burton Stevenson, *The Home Book of Quotations*, 10th ed. (New York: Dodd, Mead, 1967) 1073.

RECOMMENDED READING LIST

Best, Ernest. *Following Jesus: Discipleship in the Gospel of Mark.* Sheffield, England: JSOT, 1981.

Lane, Dermot. *The Reality of Jesus: An Essay in Christology.* New York: Paulist, 1975.

Lane, William. *The Gospel According to Mark: The English Text with Introduction, Exposition and Notes.* Grand Rapids: Eerdmans, 1975.

Martin, Ralph. *Mark, Evangelist and Theologian.* Grand Rapids: Zondervan, 1976.

Montague, George. *Mark: Good News for Hard Times.* Ann Arbor, Mich: Servant Books, 1981.

QUESTIONS FOR REFLECTION AND DISCUSSION

1. Why is it important to keep in mind the human as well as the divine authorship of the biblical books?

2. Who was John Mark and what seem to have been the circumstances which caused him to write the first Gospel?

3. What seem to be the main purposes and characteristics of Mark's Gospel?

4. From Mark's Gospel, what is your mental and spiritual picture of Jesus Christ during his earthly life?

5. What are the principal lessons of Mark's Gospel and how can we apply them to our lives today?

ANTIOCH IN SYRIA

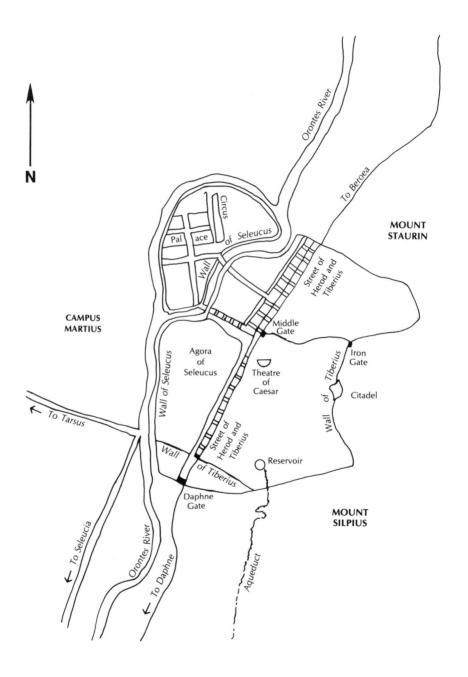

N

Orontes River

To Beroea

MOUNT
STAURIN

Circus

Palace

Wall of Seleucus

Street of
Herod and
Tiberius

CAMPUS
MARTIUS

Middle
Gate

Iron
Gate

Wall of Seleucus

Agora
of
Seleucus

Theatre
of
Caesar

Wall of Tiberius

Citadel

To Tarsus

Wall

Street of
Herod and
Tiberius

of Tiberius

Reservoir

Daphne
Gate

MOUNT
SILPIUS

To Seleucia

Orontes River

To Daphne

Aqueduct

2
Masterful "Matthew" and the Ecclesial Gospel[1]

THE STORY OF "MATTHEW"

New things and old![2] (Matt 13:52)

The huge golden sun hovered over the Great Sea[3] in the west as if unwilling to "finish his course"[4] and retire for the night. As Mattathias[5] hurried from his saddle shop[6] in the Seleucid Agora,[7] along the colonnaded Avenue of Herod and Tiberius,[8] to the southwestern quarter of Antioch-on-the-Orontes,[9] where his modest home near the Daphne[10] Gate awaited him, his mind was filled with many thoughts.

As always, his first thought was of his cherished wife, Esther, so lovely and clever, so affectionate and faithful; then of his three sons, springing up like mustard plants.[11] His second thought was of the beauty all around him: The tired Orontes which, having flowed north all the way from the great Bekaa Valley,[12] now seemed exhausted and content to slide southwestward into the Great Sea at Seleucia;[13] the shining splendor of Antioch the Beautiful, now over three centuries old but ever young in its many cool gardens and colonnaded avenues, its gleaming palaces, theaters, circus,[14] and aqueduct, not to mention its formidable and apparently endless walls.[15] Then, towering over all, the majestic Amanus Range[16] to the north and to the south the Lebanon Range,[17] including terraced Mount Silpius and fortified Mount Staurin, crowned with its impressive acropolis.[18]

Out of the blue it suddenly dawned on Mattathias as he hastened on his way home that the very geographical location of Antioch symbolized those nagging anxieties which hurried his steps faster than usual today. Just as his beloved city appeared to be squeezed between two mountain ranges, so his beloved Jewish Christian community seemed more and more to be menaced by two distinct forces that threatened to snuff out its young life. What these forces were, Mattathias refused to dwell on right now, for he was almost home and did not want to greet his family with a furrowed brow and a face like a great amen. Later, when his friends and fellow leaders[19] of their community had gathered after supper, there would be time enough to wrestle with the entire situation in all its complexity. But for now—ah! there was the welcome sight of his beloved wife and children.

Supper passed quickly with the usual chatter about the day's events. Did Matt meet any interesting people at the shop? Was the business going well? Any humorous situations to relate? And how about Esther's day? Anything unusual? Did she get together with any of their relatives or neighbors or any other Christians, Jewish or gentile? And what about the boys: Jacob, David, and Michael? How was their day at school? What did they learn today? Did they make any new friends? Before he could even remind his family about the scheduled meeting, which the lively conversation had driven from his mind, the first of his guests suddenly arrived. Somewhat embarrassed at forgetting the time, Mattathias quickly recovered and proudly introduced his family to his friend Isaac,[20] who lived up to his name and greeted all of them with a hearty, laughing *Shalom!*[21] That put everyone at ease and made greeting the other arriving guests all the more pleasant. Before long everyone had arrived, so Esther and the boys excused themselves, and the group of seven leaders settled themselves for their discussion.

About what? Why had their good friend and worthy presbyter summoned them together? Each turned to Mattathias with a mixture of curiosity and anxiety. For his part, Mattathias hoped and prayed that he could find the words to express his concerns and that together they would be able to devise some kind of solution. Suddenly realizing the extent of the task, he quickly called upon Isaac to lead them in a prayer for guidance. As if inspired, the latter voiced a petition which was such a beautiful blend of Jewish and Christian prayers that it gave the whole group confidence that the Lord Jesus was in their midst just as he had promised.[22]

"Now, Matt, why are we here?" Leave it to Jonathan to come right to the point! His directness brought a grin to Matt's face and a determination to waste no time in presenting his thoughts. While he was clearing his throat and wondering just how to start, he suddenly recalled his inspiration on the way home and decided to use it in his presentation of the situation as he saw it. But first, in true Semitic fashion, he felt that he needed to set the stage. So, while they listened attentively and supportively, Mattathias began.

"My friends, first let's count our blessings. We're fortunate to dwell in this great city which even rivals Rome and Alexandria,[23] and perhaps surpasses both of them in the freedom and harmony with which we live. Whatever our background, whatever our religion, culture, language, or status, we're all equal citizens[24] of this fabulous city. That's what I call community![25] And for us Jews, isn't it a kind of vindication that we enjoy such freedom in the capital city of the very kingdom[26] which tried its best (and worst) to stamp out the religion of our ancestors in the time of my namesake, Mattathias, the father of our famous Maccabees? But most wonderful, Jewish and gentile Christians here in Antioch live in such harmony that it can truly be said of us, 'See how these Christians love one another!' "[27]

"Yes, yes, Matt," interrupted Nathan, "but you haven't brought us together just to remind us of how fortunate we are, have you? Tell us what's really on your mind!"

"I'm sorry, Nathan. Of course you're right. To be honest, I'm just finding it difficult to get around to our problems as I discern them. However, a thought I had just this afternoon as I was returning home from work may enable me to illustrate what's bothering me. It suddenly occurred to me that just as our great city of Antioch is nudged, even squeezed, between mountain ranges to the north and south, so also our Jewish Christian community in Antioch is being threatened from both sides by forces that can be described as coming from the north and south.

"Let's look at the southern threat first. Twelve years[28] ago we, like the whole world, were shocked at the utter destruction that befell the sacred city of Jerusalem. As Jewish Christians, however, our dismay was tempered by the realization that our blessed Messiah and Savior had very carefully predicted what would happen and prepared us for the sad event.[29] Besides, we also fully realized that the stupid Zealots[30] and their sympathizers brought this devastation on themselves by their constant rebellions against the power of Rome. But the Zealots were

A view of Antioch-on-the-Orontes, where the Gospel of ''Matthew'' may well have been written.
A view of the Mount of the Beatitudes, traditional site of the Sermon on the Mount in ''Matthew.''

A view of Jerusalem, where the saving passion, death, and resurrection of Jesus took place.

not alone to blame; surely the greed of the Sadducees[31] and hypocrisy of so many Pharisees[32] also contributed greatly. However, that's history. What concerns me now is the present situation.

"As we all know, the Zealots ended their lives at Masada; the Sadducees lost their livelihood and function with the destruction of the Temple; and the Essenes disappeared from their monastery at the Dead Sea, which leaves only one sect, the Pharisees. With great tenacity they've somehow managed in the twelve years since then to regroup at Jabneh[33] and concentrate all their efforts on reviving Judaism."

"Ah!" interjected Malachy, "I think I begin to see what you're leading up to. An important part of the Pharisees' rebuilding project is to win back to Judaism as many of our Jewish Christians as they can. They despise all of us as *minim*, or heretics, and feel that it's their sacred duty to correct our thinking and win us back to their teaching, or else bar us from their synagogues and pray for our destruction. It means a parting of the ways. To me, that's really a blessing in disguise, for we need to live what we are, Jewish Christians and not Pharisaic Jews, but I'm concerned about our ultraconservative members, who tend to be more Jewish than Christian, more of the past than the future.''

"Precisely my point, Malachy!" replied Mattathias, "and all I can add is that just this morning I've learned that we Jewish Christians are no longer welcome at the synagogues. If we do show up, we'll be cast out! We who are the true Jews! How will our people be able to handle this? I fear that many may revert to Judaism! When you think that our gracious Lord chose our people as his own centuries ago and that we all grew up with traditional Jewish practices—synagogue services on Sabbaths and feasts, Jewish prayers, the use of mezuzahs,[34] and so on, it's easy to see how traumatic this can be for our people. And when you see zealous Pharisees proselytizing[35] day and night, well, I'm worried. Israel was never sent out to convert the world as we were, yet the Pharisees are trying to do just that, and having some success. The question is, What can we do to protect and strengthen our people in this crisis?''

"Now I understand your concern, Matt," added Jonah. "In fact, there's also a threat from the Judaizers,[36] with their insistence that genuine Christians have to keep the whole Jewish Law. Even after the decision went against them at the Council of Jerusalem,[37] they still cling to their position, which in effect denies the value of Jesus' saving death and resurrection. They move heaven and earth to win others over, both Jewish Christians and gentile converts.''

"I certainly agree," Nathan chimed in, "that we have to do whatever we can to devise an effective defense against this spreading plague from the Pharisees and Judaizers, but didn't you say, Matt, that there's also a threat from the north? I just can't imagine what that could be, but I'm anxious to find out. Would you mind telling us about that even before we try to counter the threat from the south? Perhaps we can find a single formula that will be able to solve both problems at the same time.''

"Good thinking, Nathan! I knew that, as always, I could count on all of you to be open-minded in grasping problems and creative in finding solutions to them. The threat from the north, as I like to call it, stems from the fact that Christianity, which was founded by Jesus, a Jew among the Jews, is fast becoming Graeco-Roman. I don't mean that this is all bad. After all, just as we owe so much to the Roman roads and the Pax Romana in our efforts to 'go and make disciples of

all the nations,'[38] as Jesus commanded us to do, so also we owe much
to the Greek language, thought, and culture in bringing the message
of salvation to the whole Greek-speaking world. We citizens of Antioch should be aware of this more than any others. After all, this is
where the 'followers of the way'[39] (as we used to be known) first made
large numbers of converts among the Gentiles.[40] This is where we first
came to be called Christians, or partisans of Christ,[41] to distinguish
us from the followers of Judaism. This is where blessed Peter came
and served after his imprisonment and miraculous release in Jerusalem.[42] Finally, this is where we commissioned the first missionaries
to the gentile world at large in the persons of blessed Paul and Barnabas.[43] So in a very true sense, we can take pride in calling the Church
of Antioch the mother Church of the Gentile world and the missionary center of the Church at large. All this is true and we rejoice therein,
but there's also a negative side. The more Gentile, the more Greek and
Roman the Church becomes, the more it distances itself from its Jewish roots. Those roots, of course, are not perfect but they do have something special to offer and the Church will be the poorer if she loses
them.''

"Hold on, Matt!" It was Henoch's turn to be heard. "I'm afraid
I just don't follow you. Isn't it an advantage to use the Greek language
and culture in approaching the Greek-speaking world? How else can
we hope to win it for Christ? And aren't the Greek language and
thought far more precise[44] than our Hebrew or Aramaic language and
thought, and for that reason more useful in explaining our beliefs to
others?''

Mattathias sighed. How could he ever explain what he felt in his
heart, what he intuitively knew to be true? Perhaps an example would
serve best in this situation. "Henoch, my friend, do you recall the
powerful letters of our brother Paul? He wrote in beautiful Greek, that
is certainly true. He also used frequent references to Greek athletics
and even theater.[45] But his mentality remained Semitic. For example,
in his allusions to our human nature he spoke of flesh and spirit[46] rather
than of body and soul. His whole thought process remained simple,
direct, intuitive, holistic[47] (if I may use such a term) rather than the
abstract, analytical, and philosophical approach so characteristic of the
Greek mind. Didn't he himself experience the failure of his philosophical address at the Areopagus in Athens[48] and determine afterwards

to 'know nothing but Jesus Christ, and him crucified?'[49] Yes, I repeat, the Church will be much poorer if she abandons the Semitic, Eastern culture out of which she was born and becomes totally identified with the philosophizing of Athens and politicizing of Rome.''

"I couldn't agree with you more, Matt," assured his cheerful friend Isaac. "But I feel I must add a word of my own. What I mean is this: We've been talking about doing something to counter the threats to our dear Jewish Christian community, threats which you've explained very clearly, but don't we have positive reasons for getting something done? For example, shouldn't we be trying to devise or discover something that will help us in our preaching and teaching about the Lord Jesus, especially to our fellow Jews? Don't we owe them that much? Don't we owe our Master that much? Oh! Another thought that strikes me is this: As you've pointed out, it's been some twelve years since Jerusalem was destroyed. We know now that Jesus' return in glory was not intended to happen at that time. In fact, it may not happen for a long time. Meanwhile, we have the Church which he founded and through which he continues to teach and guide us. Shouldn't we help our Jewish Christians to understand that they're still God's chosen people; as Jews, yes, but above all as Christians, chosen to continue the life and ministry of Jesus in his Church?"[50]

Mattathias' smile stretched across his face. "My dear, dear Isaac, I might have known that the Holy Spirit would inspire you with such basic but beautiful thoughts, which simply had not occurred to me. Thank you, my friend!" Then, after a thoughtful and prayerful pause Mattathias went on. "Tell me, Isaac, has the Spirit also suggested to you what the Lord may be asking of us in order to respond to these needs which we have delineated? If so, please share with us whatever you may have in mind."

Sheepishly Isaac responded in a voice that was barely audible. "Well," he began, "I don't know whether this is from the Holy Spirit or not, but I can't help thinking that what we need, what we've been talking about without identifying it, is another gospel, a Jewish gospel!"

"Of course!" exclaimed Mattathias. "That is exactly what we've been talking about! Thank you so much, Isaac, for being perceptive enough to point that out. The more I think about it, the more sense it makes. We're all familiar with the well-known Gospel that Mark wrote to answer the needs of the persecuted Christians in Rome, and

I guess we quite naturally thought that was the only gospel that could and should be written. But why should it be the only gospel? Why not another gospel, one that is written in different circumstances for different readers, with different purposes, emphases, and characteristics? Why not, above all, a thoroughly Jewish gospel?''

As if struck by lightning or by a new Pentecost, the seven were electrified. Suddenly they were all talking at once, so great and childlike was their enthusiasm. Another gospel, a Jewish gospel! Surely this was what the Lord Jesus, through his Holy Spirit, was asking of them! The very thought had them wild-eyed with excitement! Then, little by little, more sobering thoughts began to intrude, such as What would a Jewish gospel look like? How would it be like Mark's Gospel and how would it differ? What sources were available for the writing of this gospel? Above all, who would write it?

That final question was the one that riveted everyone: Who indeed should write this Jewish gospel? Instinctively they realized that they could not do the actual writing as a group. No group or community ever writes anything.[51] It takes a particular individual to do the composition, with the rest of the group offering suggestions and corrections. But who would be the actual author? To a man they all began to disclaim any writing ability, then little by little all eyes turned toward Mattathias.

"Matt, do you trust us?" they asked. "Of course I do!" he declared. "Then we choose you and urge you to write this Jewish gospel which we believe the Lord himself is asking for. We'll help in any way we can, but somebody has to do the actual writing, and we honestly think that you're the one best qualified to do it, the one the Lord himself is asking to do it. After all, as a Hellenist,[52] a Greek-speaking Jew, even a former Pharisaic scribe,[53] as our scholar-in-residence with an extensive personal library of scrolls, and finally as our *presbýteros*, our elder, our priest, you're certainly the one among us who's best qualified to understand the needs (as you've already shown) and to write a gospel that will fill those needs."

"All right," Mattathias finally agreed, "I bow to the will of the Lord speaking through you.[54] I'll certainly do my best, but I'm fully aware of my deficiencies, so I'm counting on you, all of you, to assist me with your suggestions, your corrections, and above all your continuing prayers and encouragement. Now here's what I suggest. Let me do some thinking, praying, and planning in the hope of arriving at an idea of what this gospel should look like, what sources I can employ, how I can best address the needs that surfaced this evening, and above all how I should portray our blessed Lord Jesus and how I need to delineate his Church, even what structures will best fulfill our purposes. These are questions that need to be answered in my own mind before I can even begin. Questions which we cannot answer this evening, both because of their nature and because of the lateness of the hour. When the answers to these questions become clearer in my own mind, then I'll get back to you for your evaluation of the direction I'm taking. Also, just as quickly as is feasible, I'll share our ideas with Bishop Ignatius.[55] Not that I anticipate any problems there, since he's always supportive of our Jewish Christian community, but he deserves our deepest reverence and respect. Besides, he may have some additional suggestions to make.

"Agreed? Well then, let's sing a *hallel*[56] and call it a night. I hope you forgive me for this rather long and involved meeting, but I know you appreciate its importance and the fact that there was simply no point at which we could have adjourned until now. It's quite dark outside so do be careful on your way home. Thank God that Antioch has street lamps[57] to light your way, the only city in the world, to my knowledge, that is so equipped. So, *Shalom!* my dear friends. Walk home in safety and tranquillity, and may the Lord be with you always!"

"And also with you, Matt!" chorused his friends.

After saying goodnight to his friends, Mattathias fully expected to slide into bed beside Esther with great care not to wake her. What was his surprise to find her in bed but fully awake and eagerly waiting to talk with him! "Esther my love, why are you still awake?" he asked with a worried look. "Is something wrong? Has any of the boys taken ill tonight?"

"Not at all, my dear," Esther quickly assured him. "I just couldn't sleep. I know your meeting was about something very important, and I'm dying to learn what it is. Can you talk about it, or is it a confidential matter?"

Mattathias paused a moment reflecting, then eagerly blurted out, "Of course I can talk about it with you, my love, for you're always so understanding and prudent. In fact, it will do us both good to discuss it, first simply because I know I can't sleep without sharing everything with you, and secondly because I'm confident that you can be a great help to me and my friends in this whole matter.''

Then Matt quickly dressed for bed and reported to his wide-eyed partner all that had transpired at the meeting: the concerns voiced about the pressing negative and positive needs of the Jewish Christian community, the solution pinpointed by Isaac and agreed upon by all, namely a Jewish gospel, and the unanimous choice of himself to write it.

Esther listened in rapt silence, her ears perfectly attuned to Matt's careful account, her expressive eyes, heightened color, and quickened pulse betraying her enthusiasm over the gospel project as well as her pride in the choice of her husband to do the actual writing. ''Oh, my dear! What a privilege you have! I know you can do it because I know you. I'll do my very best to keep our boys, and anyone or anything else, from interrupting you. And if I can also do anything positive to help you, dearest, please do me the honor of asking for my assistance.''

''Thank you, thank you, my love!'' Matt's face glowed. 'I value your assistance very highly, and this is such an important and blessed task that I'm sure I'll be needing your help at every turn. But let's not forget that particularly in a work like this, there's only so much that we humans can do. It's the Lord himself,[58] through his Holy Spirit, who will see to it that this gospel will be written, even through such lowly instruments as ourselves.''

''What do you plan to use as your sources, dear? And do you have them in your fine library, or will you have to borrow them, perhaps even travel great distances to obtain them?''

''Not an easy question to answer, love! As you're well aware, not only did I not know the Master[59] personally, I've never even lived in the land of Israel.[60] So I can't provide a direct, eyewitness account of his words and deeds. However, I'm not without some extremely valuable helps. Thanks to my lifelong habit of collecting scrolls, I have in my own library the Gospel According to Mark,[61] which details in such a direct and simple way the life, death, and resurrection of Jesus. This can certainly serve as my foundation, though I may change some of the wording because Mark had to write in such a hurry. Then another source, unused by Mark, is the little copy of Jesus' Sayings,[62] which some of our people believe was written by the Apostle Matthew himself. That's also in my own personal library. For the rest I'll just have to see what else I need and try to find proper sources for the necessary material."

"You mentioned the Gospel of Mark, my dear. How will this Jewish gospel be different from that one?"

"Well, in many ways, as I see it. Remember that Mark wrote in Rome for the gentile Roman Christians suffering persecution under the emperor Nero. He wrote briefly and hurriedly, picturing Jesus as the Son of God, yet by his choice also the Son of Man and Suffering Servant. A very powerful Gospel, but greatly different from the Jewish gospel that we need. For example, we're Jewish not Gentile Christians, so I don't need to translate Jewish expressions or explain Jewish customs. Also, I can freely employ typical Jewish usages, such as symbolic numbers and favorite Jewish literary structures. We're not suffering persecution from the Romans, but we *are* being bothered by those proselytizing Pharisees and Judaizers, so we'll definitely want to portray Jesus as the promised Messiah, the master or teacher of incomparable wisdom, and the founder (like Moses but much greater) of the new and true Israel, the kingdom of heaven, the Church, with new leadership, new sacraments, and a whole new understanding of salvation. Do you begin to see the picture, my love?"

"Oh yes, my extraordinary husband! And I thank God for bringing us to Jesus, for giving us to each other in Christ, for blessing us with our three boys, and for calling you to lead the Jewish Christian community. I also thank you, dear, for sharing with me this exciting news. Now I think we can both go to sleep in the love and peace of Jesus. Good night, my dear!"

"And good night to you, my wonderful wife!" responded Mattathias as, with a tender kiss, they slipped into a deep and restful sleep in each other's arms.

The very next day Mattathias took time off from his saddle shop to pay his respects to Bishop Ignatius and share with him the outcome of the previous night's meeting. Ignatius welcomed him warmly. "My dear Mattathias, come in, come in! It's so good to see you! I do admire your insistence on following the rabbinical tradition of working for your living, but I regret that it leaves so little time for us to get together and discuss the needs of the Church, especially the mutual needs of Jewish and Gentile Christians here at Antioch and its environs."

"I know, Ignatius," replied Mattathias apologetically, "and I really must give further consideration to the question of my continuing to work at my saddle shop, particularly in view of what I've come to talk about."

At that, Ignatius' curiosity rose dramatically and his kindly, luminous eyes fixed themselves on Mattathias with eager expectation. When the latter had finished his summary account of the meeting, Ignatius leaned back with a broad smile suffusing his face. 'My dear Mattathias, I'm so very pleased with you and your chosen leaders of the Jewish Christian community. To be honest, I've been wondering for some time if we shouldn't have another gospel besides Mark's. His is a masterwork, of course, and deserving of all reverence, especially because it owes so much to the recollections of blessed Peter. But I feel the need of another account which will provide much more of what our dear Master said, not just in *lógia* (small sayings) but, above all, in longer discourses.

"Hopefully, your Jewish gospel will supply that need, showing Jesus especially as the peerless teacher as well as the founder of the Church to continue his teaching, serving, and saving mission in the world today. I can't help feeling that you're being called to provide not just the Jewish Christian community but the entire Church, indeed the entire world, with this new portrait of Jesus Christ, and I can assure you of my ongoing prayers for your success in this work of God, this labor of love. In fact, if there are other ways in which I can help you, please do not hesitate to ask. If, for example, you would like to browse through my own library to see if there are any scrolls you can use which may not be in your fine library, believe me, you're to feel perfectly free to do so. By the way, will this gospel be written in Greek, Aramaic, or Hebrew? I must confess my own hope that the language will be Greek so that it may be available to the widest possible readership."

Mattathias was obviously pleased with the reaction of Bishop Ignatius. He could not have asked for a more understanding, loving, and enthusiastic response. But on the final point concerning the gospel's language, he had to admit that the question had not come up for discussion. Perhaps this meant that his fellow leaders of the Jewish Christian community were taking for granted that "their" gospel would be couched in Aramaic; still all of them were more fluent in *koiné,*[63] or Common Greek, and in view of the bishop's express desire for something aimed at a wider readership, the language should certainly be Greek. He hastened to assure Ignatius on that score.

No sooner had he done so, however, than Ignatius added another thought which had not occurred to Mattathias or to his fellow Jewish Christian leaders. "There's yet another reason why I'm looking forward to this gospel, a reason I think you'll agree with. It needs to be a Jewish Christian gospel, yes, but it needs to include our Gentile Christians as well because of two important considerations: first of all, to show clearly that both Jews and Gentiles[64] are called to form one Church in love, peace, and harmony such as we enjoy here at Antioch; and secondly, to make the point that Gentile Christians need to be careful not to make the same mistakes[65] that so many Jews have made and thereby render themselves unfit for the kingdom of God." Mattathias was truly astonished at the bishop's insights and with eager enthusiasm promised that he would certainly include the Gentile Christians, mainly for the reasons Ignatius had just given.

With buoyant step Mattathias "floated" from the residence of Bishop Ignatius. How could anyone ask for more indications of the will of God? How could anyone hope for greater support and more efficacious prayers than he had just been promised by the saintly bishop of Antioch? With deep gratitude and humble trust Mattathias hastened home, eager to begin the work of reviewing his sources and organizing his material in the way that would best fulfill the needs and purposes of the proposed gospel.

For the next several days Mattathias pored over the Gospel of Mark, the Sayings of Jesus, and various other, briefer documents in the hope that something would emerge which would indicate how to organize the material. At last it did. To portray Jesus the Messiah or Christ of Israel, the teacher or rabbi of wisdom, the prophet or interpreter of God's will, the mediator of a new covenant and law, and the founder of a new Israel, a new chosen people of God, the kingdom of heaven on earth, the Church, why not feature five great discourses of Jesus about the new Israel which would clearly show that Jesus is the one to be followed, not the Pharisees, and that the Church, not Pharisaic Judaism, is now the new Israel, the new people of God?

Why five discourses? To parallel the Torah, or Pentateuch, the first five books of the Bible: the story of Israel's call, salvation, covenant,

Law, and community. In fact, it would also recall the five books of Psalms, that unique collection of Israel's prayers and songs.

But which five discourses of Jesus should he use, wondered Mattathias, as the pegs on which to hang all the rest? "Let's see what the Gospel of Mark and the Sayings of Jesus have to offer," was his first reaction.

First, from the Sayings,[66] a great sermon in which Jesus teaches with supreme authority his higher and more demanding law of love, in a sense the "constitution" of the kingdom of heaven, the Church. And to emphasize the parallel with Moses' reception of the covenant and Law on Mount Sinai, why not locate this discourse of Jesus on a mountain?

Secondly, from Mark and the Sayings,[67] a great missionary discourse in which Jesus temporarily shares his authority with the leadership of the Church, namely the apostles, directing them on a kind of "trial run" to evangelize the "lost sheep of the house of Israel." At the same time, this serves as "marching orders" for the whole Church, notably in showing how to evangelize the entire world (beginning with the Jews) and how to cope with the opposition they will encounter.

Thirdly, also from Mark and the Sayings,[68] a collection of Jesus' parables on the nature of his Church, the earthly kingdom of heaven, describing its outer and inner growth and its inclusion of sinners as well as saints (for it is a means, not an end in itself) and distinguishing between his challenging teaching in parables to others and his careful explanations to his apostles.

Fourthly, from Mark, *Q*, and other sources,[69] straight talk about the Church and the quality of leadership that Jesus desires, one that is above scandalous behavior and is characterized by love, concern, and forgiveness; in a word, shepherding rather than ambitiously lording it over the people of God.

Fifthly, from Mark, the Sayings, and other sources,[70] an eschatological discourse, providing a forecast of the future of the Church and all humankind together with dire predictions of the punishment to come on Israel, largely because of the deplorable attitude and conduct of the proud, oppressive, and hypocritical scribes and Pharisees.

"However," thought Mattathias, "I can't just string these discourses together, otherwise the result won't be a gospel but a collection of sayings and parables. I need to intersperse the discourses with narratives, especially of Jesus' miracles. Mark used the miracles to establish Jesus' power as Messiah and Son of God. I think I'll use them simply as preparations for the discourses, showing first of all Jesus' authority in deed and then his authority in word. In this way, I won't need to provide the graphically detailed narratives of Jesus' miracles so characteristic of Mark, which I must confess I've neither the interest nor the ability to match, still less to surpass.

"But wait a minute! It certainly won't be a gospel if I don't include the most important series of events, the sufferings, death, and resurrection of Jesus, 'Yahweh is salvation.' After all, Jesus saved us from our sins not by his preaching, teaching, or miracles but by his passion, death, and resurrection. That's the very heart of the matter. All right then, for this as for the narrative of his public life and ministry in general, I'll lean to a great extent on Mark but with a fuller account of Jesus' resurrection appearances and particularly with emphasis on his final commission to his apostles and, through them, to all of us to 'make disciples of all the nations.'[71]

"So far so good!" mused Mattathias, "but what about structures? To us Jews, they're a crucial part of writing. As Jews in a Hellenized world we're bicultural, and we're fully aware of the difference between the ways in which the Greeks and Jews develop and express their thoughts. For a Jewish gospel, we should certainly use typical Semitic structures such as parallelism, inclusion-conclusion, concentric circles, and chiasmus.

"Beginning with the simpler structures, I can already see that there will be a parallel[72] between the authority of Jesus and that of his apostles. And an inclusive-conclusive[73] structure should be easy enough to devise. As for concentric circles,[74] that structure is already built in as we progress from Jesus' authority in his Sermon on the Mount to the sharing of his authority with the apostles, mainly in his final commission.

"But what about the structure that we call 'chiasmus'?[75] Ah! That may well be the most significant of all. And I do believe that it's already included in the arrangement of discourses as I've lined them up. Surely there's a clear parallel between the Sermon on the Mount and the eschatological discourse on the Mount of Olives as well as between the missionary and ecclesial discourses, leaving as the high point of the entire gospel the parabolic discourse on the nature of the kingdom of heaven, the Church.

"If there's a chiastic arrangement among the discourses, there's also one among the narrative portions which intersperse them, except for one notable instance. I have no major narrative at the beginning to parallel the salvation events of Jesus' death and resurrection at the end. What can I do, if anything? I have it! I can preface the gospel with an account of the birth and infancy of Jesus. That will not only parallel his death and resurrection but also provide at the same time a bridge from the Hebrew Testament (showing the fulfillment of messianic prophecies) and a preview of the rest of the gospel. Great! Thank you, Lord, for giving me that inspiration and, in fact, for seeing to it that this Jewish gospel is practically writing itself! Now I must run this past my friends and fellow leaders as soon as possible. I can't help believing that they'll be pleased, but I'm also anxious to incorporate in the gospel their valuable corrections and suggestions."

Within a week Mattathias had gathered his friends together again and, to their amazement, was able not only to report on the approval, encouragement, and suggestions from the bishop (which pleased everyone but surprised no one, for all revered Ignatius) but also to present a rough outline of how the proposed gospel seemed to be developing. He could feel the joy and support from his friends as he carefully explained the process of his thinking step by step. They fully realized that the major part of the task still remained to be done, for all they were seeing was the skeleton, but the prospect looked good for having their own (yet more than their own) gospel within a matter of months or at most, years, depending on Matt's freedom to carry on the slow and often painful task of writing, first on wax tablets and then on papyrus or perhaps parchment.

"Are there any corrections, suggestions, or questions?" Mattathias, in his humility, was not only open and willing to receive corrections and suggestions but even eager to do so for the sake of the gospel. The others, however, had only some questions about comparatively minor matters. For example, Nathan wanted to know what kinds of typical Jewish characteristics, besides the structures, would be included in the gospel. To that question Mattathias had to admit that he had not yet worked out all the details, but he was able to give some indications of what these Jewish features might be. For instance, the symbolism of numbers might well show up in a genealogy[76] which he was thinking of including in the birth and infancy account. Also, whether because of Jewish or ecclesial emphasis, it would probably happen that wherever Mark had spoken of one person, for example, one blind man, one demoniac, and the like, the Jewish gospel because of its emphasis on community[77] would very likely speak of two or more.

Isaac, in his gentle concern, wanted to know if and how Mattathias would be able to modify some of Mark's statements which seem to put the apostles and even Jesus himself in a less than favorable light.[78] Mattathias quickly assured him that such a concern would be at the forefront of his mind in working out the details of the gospel, because he himself was very anxious to portray Jesus and the apostles in a favorable light. One thought along these lines that had suggested itself to him was to change the episode in which James and John asked for the first places in the kingdom.[79] He saw no harm in having their mother do the asking, for any good Jewish mother could be excused for being ambitious for her sons. At that they all had a hearty laugh, which helped to relax the whole group, particularly Mattathias.

At the conclusion of the meeting, each one made a point of expressing his personal appreciation to Mattathias for the extraordinary amount of work that he had accomplished in such a short time. Matt was most grateful for their expressions of appreciation and their eager anticipation of the finished work, but he was touched most of all by the extraordinary remark of his ingenuous but profound friend Isaac: "Matt, I rejoice with you, for it's clear that you were called and prepared to be the scribe of the Lord, learned in the kingdom and able to bring forth from your treasures both new things and old!"[80]

ANALYSIS OF "MATTHEW'S" GOSPEL

As with Mark, so also with this Gospel, our brief analysis will be made even briefer and hopefully clearer by being presented in outline form and in two parts: first, an overview of the principal considerations which will give us a sense of the Gospel, and secondly, some outlines which will help the reader to appreciate the masterful and even meticulous human authorship involved in this Gospel. Insofar as is feasible, we shall follow the same order of points in our examination as we did with Mark's Gospel so that the reader may more easily see the comparisons and contrasts existing between the Gospels of Mark and "Matthew."

I. Overview

A. General impression

1. A longer and more serene portrait of Jesus Christ, Messiah of Israel, authoritative teacher of truth and wisdom and martyred founder of a new Israel, a new people of God, the earthly kingdom of heaven,[81] the Church, with new and authoritative leadership

2. Written primarily for Jewish Christians as is evident from the many Old Testament quotations;[82] typical Jewish concerns (messiah, true Israel, etc.); rabbinical argumentation (Scripture sometimes used out of context, see Hos 11:1;[83] Matt 2:15), Jewish emphasis (e.g., on numbers: two, three, seven); Jewish structures (parallels, inclusion-conclusion, concentric circles, chiasmus); use of Jewish expressions and practices without the need of translation or explanation, for example, in the Infancy Gospel (1–2), the Sermon on the Mount (5–7), the woes against the Pharisees (23), and the eschatological or endtime discourse (24–25)

3. A Jewish but also anti-Jewish Gospel[84] in the sense of being a polemic against Pharisaic Judaism, as is clear especially in the Sermon on the Mount (5–7), the condemnation of hypocrisy (15:1-20), and the multiple woes (23:1-39)

4. A gospel of discourses, particularly five great sermons: montane (5–7), missionary (10), parabolic (13), ecclesial (18), eschatological (23–25), and also two lesser ones, that of the Baptist (3:1-12) and of Jesus' final commission (28:16-20). For these the narrative, particularly the miracles, are used as preparations. In contrast with Mark where the "marvels of Jesus" are vividly described as proofs of Jesus' divine/messianic power, the same miracles in "Matthew" are recounted in summary, stereotypical fashion, simply as previews of the discourses.

5. An ecclesial or Church Gospel, alone among the four gospels using the word *ekklesía* (church:[85] a people called not just out of Egypt like Israel but out of all the nations to be God's new chosen people, the true Israel, comprising Jews and Gentiles in equality and harmony with new and authoritative

leadership, new and true teaching, sacraments, and morality based on love)

6. A refined Gospel in the sense that "Matthew," unlike Mark, portrays Jesus and the apostles in the most favorable light, systematically changing or omitting Mark's candid language when it seems too open to misinterpretation: the "mad scene" of Mark 3:21 (omitted), the reason for preaching in parables of Mark 4:10-12 (*hína,* "so that," converts to *hóti,* "because," in Matt 13:13-15), Jesus' failure to work miracles at Nazareth in Mark 6:5-6 because of unbelief ("could not" becomes "did not" in Matt 13:58), the ambition of James and John in 10:37 (changed to their mother's ambition for them in Matt 20:21)

B. Composition

1. Circumstances

From among the various theories of the location and time of composition of the Gospel according to "Matthew," I have chosen to place it at Antioch in Syria, the third-greatest city of the ancient world (after Rome and Alexandria), where Jesus' followers were first called Christian (and later Catholic) and where Gentile and Jewish Christians (majority and minority) lived in harmony but were threatened by resurgent militant Pharisaic Judaism around A.D. 82–85[86]

2. Authorship

a) From an early period in Church history this Gospel has been traditionally attributed to the Apostle Matthew. Today, however, this attribution is almost universally discounted for four principal reasons.

(1) The testimony of Papias of Hieropolis,[87] who is quoted by Eusebius as first making the attribution, is only heresay and not altogether reliable.

(2) Even he seems not to have been speaking of a gospel but of a collection of sayings of Jesus in the Hebrew (Aramaic?) language, which would not fit our Gospel.

(3) The author obviously depends on the Gospel of Mark even for the call of Levi, or Matthew the Apostle.

(4) The author exhibits a vague knowledge of Israel and

its geography,[88] which would be characteristic of a non-native.

b) So far as we know, then, the authorship of this Gospel is anonymous.[89] However, in my dramatized reconstruction of its conception and writing I have chosen the name Mattathias (Gift of Yahweh), which is another form of the name Matthew, and I have tried to endow him with all the traits indicated by a reading of this Gospel. Hence I have described him as a Jewish Christian and former rabbi,[90] married with children, supporting himself and his family through manual labor as a saddlemaker, well educated both in Judaism and Christianity, fluent in both Greek and Aramaic with a substantial personal library of scrolls, and sensitive to events and conditions both inside and outside the Church of Antioch.

3. Purposes

a) Proposed by the author and his co-leaders

(1) To counter the inroads of resurgent Pharisaic Judaism at Jabneh under Gamaliel II by showing Jesus Christ to be the Messiah of Israel teaching us how to live and founding the Church, which is the new and true Israel, while Pharisaic Judaism is a false or pseudo-Israel

(2) To provide Jewish Christians with the means of knowing and growing in their Christian faith and sharing it with others, mainly Jews, far and wide

(3) To ensure that Jewish Christianity would not be totally absorbed and snuffed out by Graeco-Roman or Gentile Christianity

b) Proposed by St. Ignatius of Antioch and perhaps other Gentile (Greek) Christians

(1) To provide all Christians, Gentile as well as Jewish, with a more complete gospel, notably of Jesus the teacher and founder, than was already available in the Gospel of Mark

(2) To remind Gentile Christians that as humans they are in danger of making the same mistakes as the Jews

had and therefore of incurring the same punishment, "the weeping and gnashing of teeth in the outer darkness" (Matt 22:1-14; 25:31-46, etc.)

4. Sources

a) The Gospel According to Mark generally for the narrative portion, the order of events, and the miracles

b) The Sayings of Jesus, or *Q*, for much of the discourse material, especially what "Matthew" has in common with Luke and Mark omits

c) The kerygma, or public proclamation of the Church, which underlies all the Gospels and the main discourses in Acts

d) Reminiscences of the deeds and words of Jesus, particularly as they address various problems and questions in the Church. These were available to "Matthew" in various forms, for example: miracle stories (need-deed-result, 8:14-15); *lógia*, or sayings (Sermon on the Mount, 5–7); parables (parabolic discourse, 13); pronouncement stories[91] (on divorce and remarriage, 19:3-9; compare with the *lógion* on divorce in 5:31-32); and liturgical formulae (compare the multiplication of loaves and fishes with the institution of the Eucharist, 14:19; 15:36; 26:26-28).

e) An unknown source or sources available to "Matthew" for those portions unique to his Gospel, for example, the Infancy Gospel, which is written even less for historical purposes than the rest of the Gospel. Like the first eleven chapters of Genesis, the Infancy Gospel of "Matthew," as of Luke, is a kind of prehistory overture setting the stage and providing a preview of the Gospel proper, which begins with the baptism by John the Baptist as indicated in the kerygma. Nor are the Infancy Gospels of "Matthew" and Luke from the same source.[92] Only the little that is common to both of them can be counted on as historically true, namely, that Jesus Christ the Son of God was born at Bethlehem of a virgin called Mary who was married to a descendant of David named Joseph and that he grew up as an obscure carpenter at Nazareth in Galilee.

C. The end result

A second Gospel, a Jewish Gospel, presenting the exemplary life and ministry, the saving death and resurrection of Jesus Christ, the Son of God and Messiah of Israel, teacher of a new law based on love, mediator of a new covenant, founder of a new Israel, the Church, and Savior of all people from their sins. While it has much in common with the Gospel of Mark, it also differs from it in many ways, especially as primarily a teaching Gospel. This will be evident as we examine the outlines of our Gospel, beginning next in this study of "Matthew."

II. Outlines of "Matthew's" Gospel

A. Concentric circles[93] outline

A climactic outline which features the repetition and broadening of certain key themes with a climactic ending to epitomize the rest

1. The authority of Jesus

   a) Jesus, messianic Son of David, like Moses (1–2)

   b) Jesus, messianic Son and Servant of God (3–4)

   c) Jesus, messianic teacher, mediator, founder (Sermon on the Mount, 5–7), miracle worker, greater than Moses (8–9)

2. Authority of the apostles

   a) To preach, heal, and cast out devils (10, missionary discourse)

   b) As nucleus of the new *Ekklesía* (Church, 11–13, parabolic discourse, 13)

   c) As promised full authority. Petrine/apostolic (14; 16; 18, ecclesial discourse)

3. Rejection of Jewish leaders

   a) Indirect rejection in parables, etc. (19–22)

   b) Direct rejection in woes! vs. scribes (23)

   c) Coming destruction of Jerusalem/world (24–25, eschatological discourse)

4. Universal salvation through Jesus' saving events

   a) Anointing, Eucharist, prayer-agony, arrest (26)

> *b)* Trials-denials, suffering-death-burial (26–27).
>
> *c)* Jesus' resurrection and appearances (28:1-15)
>
> 5. Commission of the apostles (Dan 7:13-14)
>
>> *a)* Jesus' authority shared with apostles (28:18-19)
>>
>> *b)* Universal mission of the apostles (28:19)
>>
>> *c)* Means of fulfilling mission: baptism/preaching (28:19-20)
>>
>> *d)* Condition of discipleship: observance of all Jesus' commands, especially love (28:20)
>>
>> *e)* Assurance of Jesus' presence always (Emmanuel, 1:23; 28:20)

B. Chiatmic[94] outline

Based on the Greek letter *Chi (X)* with parallels between the first and last points, in reverse order, under a central emphatic point:

parabolic (13) discourse
(nature of the kingdom)

Jews reject faith (11–12) (incredulous, hostile)	narrative	(14–17) apostles profess faith (Peter's unique authority)
missionary sermon (10) (the king's heralds)	discourse	(18) ecclesial sermon (the kingdom's leaders)
Galilee ministry (8–9) (authority lessons)	narrative	(19–22) Jerusalem journey (authority lessons)
montane sermon (5–7) (the kingdom's law)	discourse	(23–25) endtime sermon (the kingdom's future)
infancy prologue (1–4) (prep. for kingdom)	narrative	(26–28) salvation epilog (inauguration of k'dom)

C. Appendix: a tentative pentamerous[95] outline

1. Introduction

This tentative but complete outline features the number five (pentamerous) throughout, on the theory that the author was not content with five discourses but chose to arrange the entire Gospel around the number five. This is perfectly compatible with the outlines already provided.

2. Prologue

The Infancy Gospel (1–2, Jesus is like Moses)

a) The genealogy of Jesus, answering the question *who?*

b) The birth of Jesus, answering the question *how?*

c) The visit of the Magi, answering the question *where?*

d) The flight into Egypt, answering the question *whence?*

e) The move to Nazareth, answering the question *why?*

3. Book I

Proclamation of the kingdom (3–7)

a) Narrative: beginning of the ministry (3–4, Jesus prepares for the montane sermon)

   (1) John the Baptist: witness to and baptizer of Jesus

   (2) Jesus' forty days' fast and temptations by Satan

   (3) Establishment of missionary center at Capernaum

   (4) Call of the first disciples at the Sea of Galilee

   (5) Summary of Jesus' proclamation of the kingdom

b) Discourse: the Sermon on the Mount (5–7, greater than Moses, Jesus gives a new law)

   (1) The kingdom's challenge: Beatitudes, light and salt

   (2) Superiority of the kingdom's perfection over Mosaic Law

   (3) Interiority of the kingdom's perfection, e.g., in worship

   (4) Selflessness of the kingdom's perfection toward others

   (5) Three final warnings to summarize and conclude the sermon

4. Book II

Spreading of the kingdom (8–10)

a) Narrative: expanding ministry in Galilee and beyond (8–9, Jesus prepares for his missionary discourse)

   (1) Three miracle stories: leper, servant, mother-in-law

   (2) Three discipleship stories: scribe, disciple, storm

   (3) Two miracle stories: two demoniacs and a paralytic

   (4) Three discipleship stories: Matthew, sinners, fasting

   (5) Conclusion: need of shepherds and laborers

b) Discourse: the missionary discourse (10, Jesus empowers a new leadership)
  (1) Introduction: appointment of the twelve apostles
  (2) Jesus' original mandate to the apostles in Israel
  (3) Cautions about the hardships of the missionary task
  (4) Encouragement with a promise of presence and power
  (5) Conclusion: promise of rewards for all involved

5. Book III
   Revelation or catechesis of the kingdom (11–13)
   a) Narrative: pseudo-Israel rejected, true Israel called (11–12) Jesus prepares for his parabolic discourse
     (1) John the Baptist, Jesus, and the messianic kingdom
     (2) Pseudo-Israel: wayward children and impenitent towns
     (3) Jesus calls the humble to himself and his kingdom
     (4) Pharisees' narrowness vs. Jesus' mercy in three miracles
     (5) Blasphemy and impenitence of the Pharisees
   b) Discourse: parabolic sermon on the kingdom's nature (13, Jesus explains and challenges in parables)
     (1) Parable of the seed: crucial role of the hearers
     (2) Parable of the weeds: good and bad in the kingdom
     (3) Parables of mustard seeds and leaven (visible/invisible nature of the kingdom)
     (4) Parables of treasures and pearls: priceless kingdom
     (5) Parable of the net, metaphor of the scribe: good/bad, new/old

6. Book IV
   the Church and its leadership (14–18)
   a) Narrative: leadership lessons, mostly for Peter (14–17)
     (1) 1st quintet (14)
       (a) Nazareth rebuff
       (b) Baptist beheaded
       (c) First feeding
       (d) Walk on water
       (e) Peter's "walk"

     (2) 2nd quintet (15–16)

        (*a*) Pharisees dispute

        (*b*) Canaanite woman

        (*c*) Second feeding

        (*d*) Pharisees rejected

        (*e*) Peter's profession

     (3) 3rd quintet (16–17)

        (*a*) First prediction

        (*b*) Transfiguration

        (*c*) Demoniac boy

        (*d*) Second prediction

        (*e*) Peter's tax

  b) Discourse: the ecclesial or Church sermon (18, Jesus describes the Church and its leadership)

     (1) Teaching against ambition, especially among leaders

     (2) Teaching against scandal, especially toward the young

     (3) Teaching on pastoral concern and fraternal correction

     (4) Teaching on the power of communal prayer in Christ

     (5) Teaching on forgiveness, especially for the leaders

7. Book V
the future of the kingdom (19–25)

  a) Narrative: journey to and teaching at Judea and Jerusalem (Jesus prepares for his eschatological sermon)

     (1) 1st quintet (19–20)

        (*a*) Marriage/children

        (*b*) Riches & vineyard

        (*c*) Third prediction

        (*d*) Ambitious mother

        (*e*) Two blind men

     (2) 2nd quintet (21)

        (*a*) Messianic entry

        (*b*) Temple cleansed

        (*c*) Fig tree cursed

        (*d*) Jesus' authority

        (*e*) Two sons & tenants

       (3) 3rd quintet (22)
- (a) Wedding banquet
- (b) Caesar's tribute
- (c) Resurrection
- (d) Great command
- (e) David's son, Lord

   b) Discourse: the eschatological sermon (23–25, Jesus' judgment on Israel and the world)
- (1) Judgment on the scribes and Pharisees (seven woes)
- (2) Coming destruction of Jerusalem and Israel
- (3) Future hardships of the Church, the endtime, second coming
- (4) Parables on the need for watchfulness and preparedness
- (5) Parable on general judgment based on love of the needy

8. Epilogue
Saving events at Jerusalem and great commission (26–28)

   a) Narrative: saving events at Jerusalem (26–28:15, Jesus' sufferings, death, and resurrection)
- (1) 1st quintet (26)
  - (a) Preparations
  - (b) The Eucharist
  - (c) Agony & prayer
  - (d) Arrest, trial
  - (e) Peter's denials
- (2) 2nd quintet (27:1-44)
  - (a) Judas & the leaders
  - (b) Jesus before Pilate
  - (c) Scourging, crowning
  - (d) Way of the cross
  - (e) Crucifixion, taunts
- (3) 3rd quintet (27:45–28:15)
  - (a) Death, etc.
  - (b) Jesus' burial
  - (c) Priests' fears

(d) Resurrection

(e) Guards bribed

b) The great commission (28:16-20, Jesus commissions his apostles and Church)

(1) Gathering at a designated mountain in Galilee (Tabor?)

(2) Jesus' authority in heaven and on earth (Dan 7:13-14)

(3) Commission to make disciples of all the nations

(4) Commission to baptize and teach everything commanded

(5) Promise of perpetual presence (Emmanuel) until the end.

"MATTHEW'S" GOSPEL AND OUR LIFE

This final section of our exploration into the mind of "Matthew," like that of Mark previously, will give us the opportunity to detect the most relevant concerns in this Gospel and apply them to our lives. For as common sense teaches, it is not enough to understand the Bible, we must above all be able to live it,[96] not in some "ouija board"[97] fashion (closing our eyes and fingering a text to live by) but rather by absorbing the Word, inspired and incarnate, and letting our whole life be governed thereby.

For this purpose our exploration will focus on three principal points: (1) the portrait of Jesus as our teacher or master, (2) the portrait of Jesus as founder of the new Israel, the Church, with an in-depth study of that Church, and (3) the nature, meaning, and characteristics of Jewish Christianity in relation to our own lives.

Jesus the Teacher or Master

To appreciate the importance of this consideration we must first understand the absolute reverence[98] for the spoken and written word in the ancient world, particularly among the people of God. Today, living in a visual civilization, with television, movies, and videotapes readily available and even the ability to make our own, we have a natural tendency to discount anything we cannot see. Of course, it was not this way in the ancient world where these modern inventions were not even imagined. People hung on every word of orators, teachers, actors, and writers. In fact, so true was this that particularly in Israel, word and deed were virtually synonymous. Recall that the story of creation in the first chapter of Genesis is really that of a series of commands, and many events in the history of Israel are couched in terms of God's decrees. In Isa 55:10-11, NAB, this truth is lyrically expressed:

> For just as from the heavens
> the rain and snow come down
> And do not return there
> till they have watered the earth,
> making it fertile and fruitful,
> Giving seed to him who sows
> and bread to him who eats,
> So shall my word be
> that goes forth from my mouth.
> It shall not return to me void,
> but shall do my will,
> achieving the end
> for which I sent it.

This same reverence for the word understandably carries over into the New Testament which, while it is written entirely in Greek is nevertheless conceived and written according to a Semitic mentality. Thus the miracles of our Lord are accomplished by his mere word,[99] for example, in the healing of the leper and the centurion's servant in Matt 8:1-13.

But nothing appealed so much to the ancient mind among both Jews and Gentiles as an authentic teacher, one who spoke with authority[100] and did not have to content himself with quoting from some other teacher of his own time or earlier as was the practice of the rabbis of Jesus' time and since then. It is revealing to read ''Matthew's description of Jesus the teacher before, during, and after the great Sermon on the Mount:

> Jesus toured all of Galilee. He taught in their synagogues, proclaimed the good news of the kingdom, and cured the people of every disease and illness. As a consequence of this, his reputation traveled the length of Syria.[101] They carried to him all those afflicted with various diseases and racked with pain: the possessed, the lunatics, the paralyzed. He cured them all. The great crowds that followed him came from Galilee,

the Ten Cities, Jerusalem and Judea, and from across the Jordan (Matt 4:23-25, NAB).

This is followed by the Sermon on the Mount, prefaced by a very formal little introduction designed to give some idea of the importance of the sermon that follows: "But seeing the crowds, he went up into the mountain and, after he had sat down,[102] his disciples came to him and, opening his mouth, he began to teach them, saying . . ." (Matt 5:1-2, WFD). Jesus begins with the Beatitudes, his answer to the Ten Commandments. These had been revealed to the Israelites not as an end in themselves but clearly as a means, as a set of conditions, or specifications, for the keeping of the covenant,[103] an agreement establishing a bond of permanent relationship with himself, into which Yahweh had already invited the Israelites (through Moses) to enter with these touching words:

> You have seen with your own eyes what I did to Egypt, and how I have carried you on eagles' wings and brought you here to me. If only you will now listen to me and keep my covenant, then out of all peoples you shall become my special possession; for the whole earth is mine. You shall be my kingdom of priests, my holy nation (Exod 19:4-6. NEB).

Thus, it was the covenant of Sinai and the relationship with Yahweh that should have been central to Israelite life, while the commandments and all the other written and oral laws and practices, begun in the time of Moses but mostly drawn up in the course of Israelite history and all reducible to the Ten Commandments, should never have been anything more than means of keeping the covenant. Unfortunately, by the time of Jesus the commandments (especially that of the Sabbath observance), along with the innumerable written and oral laws, had become the unbearable burden of trying to be a good Jew. No wonder Jesus over and over again tried to recall his contemporaries to a loving relationship with Yahweh, first by reducing the Ten Commandments to the two relational commandments[104] of the love of God and neighber, and secondly by his own personal invitation to a loving relationship with the Father through him, an invitation gently expressed in the most beautiful passage of "Matthew's" Gospel:

> Come to me, all of you who are weary and loaded down with burdens [especially the legal burdens imposed on you], and I will relieve you [or give you rest]. Take upon yourselves my yoke[105] [my law of love which

will bind us together in a lasting union] and learn from me that [or because] I am gentle and humble of heart, and you will find rest for your souls [or lives], for my yoke is loving [or easy] and my burden light (Matt 11:28-30, WFD).

The reader may have noticed in the final sentence that I have changed the translation from "easy" to "loving." Why? Because the primary and more natural meaning of the adjective *chrestós* is kind, loving, good, merciful (how very appropriate for a word that sounds so much like *Christós*, "Christ!"), but above all because it reminds us that "love makes all things easy!"

It is mainly in his great Sermon on the Mount that Jesus spells out his "yoke," his law of love, more demanding by far but also much easier to fulfill because based on love. And so his answer to the Old Testament commandments is the far more demanding collection of Beatitudes, more demanding because open ended. While we may be able to say with the wealthy man, "Master, I have kept all these [commandments] from my youth" (Mark 10:20, WFD), who of us can ever claim to be perfectly humble, merciful, clean of heart, and the rest? The Beatitudes are really open-ended challenges which admit of ever-greater progress in their fulfillment. They truly do require a "holiness exceeding that of the scribes and Pharisees" (Matt 5:20), but love, the very love of Jesus himself living within us, enables us to fulfill them.

While time does not permit a complete commentary on the Sermon on the Mount, it certainly should be noted how Jesus speaks with such authority that in a whole series of antitheses, he does not hesitate to teach in his own name a far more demanding, interior, and spiritual morality than was ever required by Israelite laws, prophets, sages, or scribes (see Matt 5:17–7:14).

We must bring to an end this brief reflection on Jesus' greatest discourse, his "messianic manifesto," but not before calling attention to the crowd's reaction: "Jesus finished this discourse and left the crowds spellbound at his teaching. The reason was that he taught with authority and not like their scribes" (Matt 7:28-29, NAB).

From Jesus' first great discourse in "Matthew," namely the Sermon on the Mount, let us turn briefly to his last great discourse, which parallels the first in a chiasmic structure, namely the eschatological sermon and particularly the first part: the woes against the Pharisees and scribes. Here Jesus in a kind of brief general introduction gives us some unforgettable directives: first about how *not to be* and then how *to be* a good Christian teacher. Listen to the powerful words of Jesus the Master as we find them in Matt 23:1-12, RSV:

> The scribes and the Pharisees sit on Moses' seat; so practice and observe whatever they tell you, but not what they do; for they preach but do not practice. They bind heavy burdens, hard to bear, and lay them on men's shoulders; but they themselves will not move them with their finger. They do all their deeds to be seen by men; for they make their phylacteries broad and their fringes[106] long, and they love the place of honor at feasts and the best seats in the synagogues, and salutations in the market places, and being called rabbi by men. But you are not to be called rabbi, for you have one teacher, and you are all brethren. And call no man your father[107] on earth, for you have one Father, who is in heaven. Neither be called masters, for you have one master, the Christ. He who is greatest among you shall be your servant; whoever exalts himself will be humbled, and whoever humbles himself will be exalted.

These must have been shocking words to the apostles. How could Jesus say such things about the scribes and Pharisees? For that matter, how could he say such things in regard to himself and themselves? Yet they would not have been shocked if they had remembered those startling words of Jesus in Matt 11:25-27 revealing the source of his teaching authority in the Sermon on the Mount, in his other authoritative discourses, in his gentle invitation that follows, and in his future great commission. Since it is also found in Luke 10:21-22, Matthew must have discovered it with delight among the so-called Sayings of Jesus (*Q*). It reads thus:

> I praise you, Father, Lord of heaven and earth, because you have hidden these things from the wise and learned, and revealed them to little children. Yes Father, for this was your good pleasure.
>
> All things have been committed to me by my Father. No one knows the Son except the Father, and no one knows the Father except the Son and those to whom the Son chooses to reveal him (NIV).

Both these and Jesus' related words in Matt 23 are powerful indeed and deserve not only hearing but heeding, for it is always tempting to the highly educated and gifted teacher to develop an overweening regard for his or her abilities, forgetting that the ability to teach well is a gift,[108] no matter how much work one has devoted to developing it; and like all charismatic gifts it does not make the one gifted any better or greater but is intended for the good of others, as Paul clearly teaches in 1 Cor 12–14 and Eph 4:7-13.

In this context it is noteworthy that precisely in the Gospel according to "Matthew," the words "apostle" and "disciple" are used interchangeably,[109] as a cogent reminder that even apostles are still always learners or disciples.

Of course, Jesus the Teacher is no longer with us as he once was, so how do we now receive his teaching? Principally in two ways: through the New Testament and through the Church which he established. These are both means, not ends in themselves, and they are complementary to one another. God is the author of both, and it is contradictory to attempt to use the Bible against the Church or the Church against the Bible. The New Testament is, of course, written Church tradition, as the form critics[110] in particular have made abundantly clear, and conversely Church tradition is at least partly the ongoing interpretation of Scripture. In our vocation (*ekklesía*, "a people called") to live in a covenant relationship with Christ, to be united with and transformed into him, Scripture plays a crucial role not only in informing us about our call and destiny but also in helping us to achieve it. Every relationship absolutely requires communication, and Scripture is at least half of our communication with God, the other half being prayer. In the beautiful words of Vatican II,[111] borrowed from St. Ambrose,[112] "When we pray, we speak to God, but when we hear or read the divine oracles of Sacred Scripture, God speaks to us!" Now, however, it is time to reflect on the other great means of our hearing Jesus the Teacher, namely the Church which he established.

Jesus the Founder of the Christian Church

This is such an all-embracing subject that we cannot hope to do it justice in a broad treatment such as this. Hence we must confine our reflections about Christ and the Church to matters reflected in "Matthew's" Gospel, and even then in a summary fashion.

First of all, among the Gospels the name "Church" is found only in "Matthew." This appears surprising at first until we remember that "Matthew" is the only Jewish Gospel and that the Greek word for Church, *ekklesía*, is really Jewish in background and meaning, for it is nothing less than the Septuagint translation of the Hebrew word *Qahal* (assembly), referring to Israel primarily in her Exodus and desert wanderings. Literally meaning a people or group who are "called out," from *ek* (out or out of) and *kaléo*[113] (I call), it designates Israel as a people called out of Egypt to become God's chosen people, united with him by covenant at Mount Sinai. In the Christian dispensation of course, it refers to the Church, called out of all the nations of the earth to be God's new people, his new Israel, united with him through the new covenant[114] established by Jesus in his own blood at the Last Supper.

By using the word *ekklesía* then, our author places the Church in continuity with the Israel of the Sinaitic covenant and Law. And this is confirmed by those words of Jesus in the Sermon on the Mount (Matt 5:17-19, NAB):

> Do not think that I have come to abolish the law and the prophets. I have come, not to abolish them, but to fulfill them. Of this much I assure you: until heaven and earth pass away, not the smallest letter[115] of the law, not the smallest part[116] of a letter, shall be done away with until it all comes true. That is why whoever breaks the least significant of these commands and teaches others to do so shall be called least in the kingdom of God. Whoever fulfills and teaches these commands shall be great in the kingdom of God.

So much for the continuity with Israel, but to avoid any misunderstanding, Jesus quickly adds those words of discontinuity, that is, discontinuity with the pseudo-Israel of Pharisaic Judaism (Matt 5:20, NAB): "I tell you, unless your holiness surpasses that of the scribes and Pharisees you shall not enter the kingdom of God." Lest it be thought, however, that the choice and use of the word *ekklesía* was original with "Matthew," it must be pointed out that St. Paul,[117] writing entirely before A.D. 68, had used the word frequently both of individual Churches such as Corinth, Rome, and others as well as of the Church as a whole, though who originally made the happy choice of *ekklesía* for the Church if it was not St. Paul himself remains unknown.

In the above quotations we see the use of a special expression not just once but three times, namely that of "the kingdom of God." Translated from "Matthew's" Greek, *he basileía tōn ouranōn* (the kingdom of the heavens), so worded because Jews refrained from using the name of God, these few words represent one of "Matthew's" (and perhaps Jesus') favorite themes, as well as one of the most basic and significant ideas in the Bible.

Going back no further than the covenant at Mount Sinai, we see Yahweh inviting Israel to become his "kingdom of priests, his holy nation" (Exod 19:6). Hence the notion of "covenant" and "kingdom of God" were inextricably tied together throughout the subsequent history of Israel. In fact, over and over again the Israelites were reminded, especially by the prophets and psalmists,[118] that Yahweh was their king and they were his kingdom. This was true even when human kings were reigning but much more so when they ceased to rule at the time of the Babylonian Captivity and Israel began to look for an ideal king, the Anointed One, the Messiah or Christ. Thus, we see especially in Isaiah those graphic prophecies about the messianic king[119] and his kingdom, for example, in Isa 9:5-6, NAB:

> For a child is born to us, a son is given us;
>   upon his shoulder dominion rests.
> They name him Wonder-Counselor, God-Hero,
>   Father-Forever, Prince of Peace.
> His dominion is vast and forever peaceful.
> From David's throne, and over his kingdom,
>   which he confirms and sustains
> By judgment and justice both now and forever.
> The zeal of the Lord of hosts will do this!

But prophetic literature was not alone in emphasizing this idea of the kingdom of God. Apocalyptic literature[120] as well, both the inspired Book of Daniel and a host of Apocryphal[121] works, clearly continued the tradition, which would be fulfilled in Christ and the Church. For example, the famous "Son of Man" vision in Dan 7:13-14, which originally identified the son of man (human) figure[122] with Israel itself, came to be understood in the Apocrypha as the Messiah:

> As the visions during the night continued,
> I saw One like a son of man
>   coming on the clouds of heaven;
> When he reached the Ancient One
>   and was presented before him,
> He received dominion, glory, and kingship.
> Nations and peoples of every language serve him.
> His dominion is an everlasting dominion
>   that shall not be taken away,
> His kingship shall not be destroyed.
> (Translation from the NAB, but the rearrangement is mine.)

I have said that the expression *he basileía tôn ouranôn* is a pregnant expression, and rightly so. However, those who consciously or unconsciously apply the Greek penchant for distinctions to the interpretation of Scripture waste much time in arguing over whether the translation should be "kingdom of God" or "reign of God."[123] Why not both, in typical Semitic fashion? Does not Jesus himself, according to "Matthew's" Gospel, refer to the Kingdom of Heaven (God) as present in this life in the form of the church yet also future in the next life of heaven, as both exterior and interior? With this in mind then, there is no reason why we cannot regard *he basileía tôn ouranôn* as both the reign or rule of God over us and also the kingdom of his followers, particularly since we can hardly have the one without the other.

Having examined the importance in "Matthew" of those two expressions, "Church" and "Kingdom of Heaven" (God), let us now glance at the characteristics of God's kingdom of heaven on earth, the Church. These we will find mostly in the missionary, parabolic, and ecclesial discourses in Matt 10, 13, and 18 respectively.

From Matt 10 as well as from the great commission in Matt 28:16-28 and implicit in the very word *ekklesía* (Church), it is clear that Jesus intended and directed his Church to be a pilgrim Church, a missionary organization always on the move, always endeavoring to become the kingdom of heaven in heaven, and always assured of the powerful and peaceful presence of Christ the Founder.

From Matt 13 with its seven parables on the nature of the kingdom of God, we see from the parables of the seed, the weeds, and the net that the kingdom of heaven here on earth (the Church) is composed of a very disparate crowd: women as well as men, children as well as adults, saints as well as sinners, all races and nationalities, all social and economic classes. The Church is a means and a remedy, not an end and a reward. Consequently, as Jesus himself cautions[124] us and as common sense should alert us, because the Church is human in its leadership and membership, there will indeed be scandals[125] within her ranks. This phenomenon should never surprise or shock us but rather lead us to greater faith and fidelity, for it is the very presence of human scandals in the Church that confirms its divine origin and protection. With the scandals the Church has suffered through the centuries, any purely human organization would long ago have gone out of existence!

Continuing with Matt 13, we learn from the parables of the mustard seed and the leaven that the Church is destined to grow gradually and, as it were, imperceptibly,[126] spreading out as she has to embrace the whole world, and also gently, patiently, leavening society with her ideals. From the two parables of the treasure in the field and the pearl of great price, we learn that the "kingdom of heaven," both as the church on earth and as the church triumphant, is worth any sacrifice we may have to make to belong to it. Recall that enigmatic saying of Jesus: "The kingdom of heaven [both the church and heaven] suffers violence [or is subject to seige?] and the violent [or eager] take it by force [or capture it]" Matt 11:12, WFD.

Finally, from the ecclesial discourse in Matt 18 as well as from its preceding chapters we receive some important directives about the Church's members, but mostly about her leaders. For example, in Matt 16:13-20 we behold Jesus promising the "keys of the kingdom of heaven" to Peter, or Cephas.[127] Here, in spite of the traditional idea of St. Peter at the "pearly gates" (of heaven), the reference is clearly to the kingdom of heaven in the sense of the Church as is evident from what follows: "Whatever you [singular] bind on earth will be bound in heaven and whatever you [singular] loose on earth will be loosed in heaven" (NIV). Two chapters later however, we see Jesus conferring this power of binding and loosing in the plural on all the apostles (see Matt 18:18). Is this a contradiction? Or has Jesus taken back his promise to Peter and given it to all the apostles? Not at all! The two powers are perfectly compatible in what is known today as "collegiality"[128] in the Church, according to which all the bishops as successors of the apostles rule the Church but only in conjunction with the pope, the successor of Peter, and under his overall authority.

In Matt 18 all of us in the Church, but especially the leaders, learn the necessity of being humble, exemplary, and zealous, of having the fraternal charity to correct one another, to pray communally, and to forgive our debtors.[129]

The Ecclesial Gospel of "Matthew" is overflowing with important lessons regarding the Church in its characteristics as well as the requirements of its leadership and membership, but perhaps no verse is so worthy of reflection as the final verse of the Gospel, "And know that I am with you always[130] until the end of the world" (Matt 28:20b). The Church is meaningless and purely institutional until we realize that it is *Christ continuing to live and minister in the world today.*[131] Is that not echoed in the famous judgment scene in Matt 25, ''I was hungry and you gave me to eat, ...'' As in the case of the individual sacraments, ''carriers of divine life''[132] and particular aids to salvation, so also with the Church, the general means of salvation: it is the risen Christ who lives and works in and through them, giving them that power and authority which no merely human person or organization could ever supply. ''I assure you, as often as you did it for one of my least brothers, you did it for me!'' (Matt 25:40, NAB).

The Lost Treasures of Jewish Christianity

In our brief reflections on this little-known subject there is no intention to engage in anti-Hellenism. Not at all! I have the highest regard for Greek culture and the Greek language. In fact, I am even trying to promote the study of New Testament Greek with my book *Greek Without Grief.*[133] But I do recognize that Jewish Christianity has something precious to offer us in our personal and communal spiritual life if only we can recapture it.

In my treatment of Jewish Christianity I want to make clear that I am not writing for or about ''Jews for Jesus,'' nor am I writing about so-called Hebrew Christianity.[134] My concern is not so much that Jews come to know Jesus and accept him as their Messiah, desirable though that is, but that Christians and especially Catholics come to recognize the amount of Hellenism in our image of Christianity and open our minds to a different view of our beliefs, morals, and worship.

What then do I mean by Jewish Christianity? Perhaps the concept will be clearer if I call it Semitic Christianity or better still biblical Christianity, for that is indeed what we are basically speaking of: a Christianity which draws its knowledge of itself, not from Greek philosophy but from the Word of God in Sacred Scripture.

Why is this important? Because, in the words of St. Anselm, ''Theology is faith seeking understanding.''[135] And where do we find the faith but in Sacred Scripture and tradition, two streams from the same font of truth?[136] That is why the great constitution on divine revelation insists that Scripture, not philosophy, is the ''soul of sacred theology.''[137] In our brief treatment, then, of Jewish, or biblical Christianity, let us consider these three aspects: doctrine, morals, and liturgy or worship.

In the realm of doctrine Greek philosophy presents us with a picture of God as our prime mover, our grand designer, which impresses us, but purely in a cerebral way and hardly enables us to relate to him as we can in the personal, dynamic, existential, total manner characteristic of Jewish Christianity. There are, of course, historical reasons why Greek philosophy assumed such a prominent place in the Church's thinking. If I may summarize the process that occurred to cause this situation, let me begin by pointing out that to all intents and purposes all theology was biblical until Augustine's time in the fourth century. He himself was learned in Scripture and used it effectively in both his homilies and his other writings. However, when the Church came under attack from the Neoplatonists, led by Plotinus and various heresies of the age, Augustine, a Platonic scholar, decided to use the very tool employed by the enemies and "Christianized" Plato for that purpose. Little did he dream that this would become to a large extent the basis of the Church's theology for centuries to come.

Then in the thirteenth century, when the Church came under attack from Jews like Maimonides and Moslems led by Averroes and Avicenna, all using the newly rediscovered Aristotle whose thinking was far more precise than that of Plato, Thomas Aquinas proceeded to "Christianize" Aristotle, but I feel confident that he too, like Augustine, never dreamed that his Aristotelian-based theology would become normative for the Church until the Second Vatican Council. The great secret of Vatican II[138] was that for the first time in centuries everything was based on Scripture. Unfortunately many if not most priests did not realize that or, if they did, were not steeped enough in biblical knowledge to understand the Council, with the result that the laity (from *laós*, people, people of God) were left in the dark about the real meaning of the Council and were left confused by a whole series of changes without real explanations.

Now that the middle leadership of the Church is finally becoming aware of the laity's hunger for the Word of God in reliable interpretation, it is imperative that every effort be made to provide that interpretation, not drawn from Greek philosophy, which is the basis of our everyday thinking, but from some knowledge of the Eastern mentality according to which the Bible was written.[139]

One of the most glaring examples of this is the basic misinterpretation of such simple and often-used words as "flesh," "person," and "spirit," which constitute the three dimensions of our human nature according to Semitic thought. Flesh does not mean body and spirit does not mean soul! Rather, both are dimensions of our whole being, inclined to weakness and aspiring to union with God respectively. "The Word became flesh" (John 1:14), that is, human in all our human weakness, sin alone excepted. He did not become merely a body! The lifelong hostility between spirit and flesh in both Galatians and Romans is not between the soul and the body, as if the soul is good and the body is evil. How many extremes of bodily castigation might have been avoided with a proper understanding of these passages! Most absurd of all, Paul does not condemn the incestuous man of 1 Cor 5:1-13 to death when he declares in verse 5, NAB, "I hand him over to Satan for the destruction of his flesh, so that his spirit may be saved on the day of the Lord." No, he is merely excommunicating him temporarily, as he indicates more clearly in verse 13: "Expel the wicked man from your midst!"

Another fundamental difference between Jewish and Greek thought[140] is the tendency of the former to intend and understand in a single statement more than one human or literal meaning, while the latter with its penchant for definition, division, and distinction focuses on one meaning and discards other possibilities. An excellent example of this is Gen 1:26-28, the famous "image and likeness of God" text, where Greek thinking tends to see only one meaning, namely our creation with intelligence and free will, while Semitic thinking detects two additional meanings suggested by the context: dominion over creation (26, 28), albeit a dominion of stewardship only, and cocreativity with God through the proper use of sex (27-28). Besides these there are still two more possible meanings which would, I believe, qualify as spiritual senses, namely immortality (Wis 2:23) and, finally but most importantly, our destiny to be transformed into Christ, the perfect image of God (see Rom 8:29; 2 Cor 3:18; Col 1:15; Heb 1:3, etc.).

Now, having considered Jewish Christianity in relation to doctrine, let us turn briefly to the question of morality. In no way do we want to return to a morality of law, such as was required by Pharisaic Judaism. Paul makes that clear. After his conversion he had to rethink his entire idea of justification and salvation,[141] from a matter of earning them according to his Pharisaic background to an acceptance of them as a gift through the death and resurrection of Christ. Curiously, human nature being what it is, we have often through the ages and even today reduced religion to the externals of laws and practices and forgotten the essence, which is personal and communal relationship with God and with one another in God.

At the same time we have also, especially in our own day, tended to the opposite extreme of more or less tailoring morality to suit ourselves and presuming that God, who is all loving, kind, and forgiving, will readily approve. What blasphemy! Yes, God does indeed forgive the repentant sinner, but he does not and cannot condone sin. Perhaps that is one of the lessons of the so-called original sin described in the story of Adam and Eve. They ate "from the tree of the knowledge of good and evil" (Gen 2:17, NIV); they sought to be arbiters of their own morality, deciding for themselves what was right and what was wrong, which prerogative belongs to God alone because he is our maker and our supreme Lord. God alone knows everything perfectly, including our human nature (as we read in Ps 139) and the fateful consequences of our actions.

Through living the life of Christ we can and must keep a balance between the extreme of attempting to live by law alone (as if the more laws we have the more righteous we will be!) and the extreme of trying to live lawlessly and presuming on God's blessing on us anyway. Does not Jesus state categorically in his Sermon on the Mount, "Not everyone who says to me, 'Lord, Lord' will enter the kingdom of heaven, but only he who does the will of my Father who is in heaven" (Matt 7:21, NIV)? And this includes even those who have been accorded special gifts[142] if they fail to use them for God's glory instead of their own. "Many will say to me on that day, 'Lord, Lord, did we not prophesy in your name, and in your name drive out demons, and perform many miracles?' Then I will tell them plainly, 'I never knew you. Away from me, you evildoers!' " (Matt 7:22-23, NIV).

What we need today is that "fear of God"[143] in the sense of awe, reverence, and love of his will which has always characterized faithful Jews. In the words of one of my rabbi friends when we were all deeply concerned about a reported missile gap, "What we need most of all is to close the moral gap between knowing and doing the will of God!"[144] Finally, under the heading of liturgy, or worship, we need to capture that reverence and awe of the Lord that so characterized postexilic Judaism that to this day the Jews still refrain from even pronouncing the sacred name[145] of Yahweh. Yes, capture it and combine it with the grateful intimacy of Christians conscious of God's tender love for each of us as shown so unforgettably through the love and life, the death and resurrection, of his Son, our Lord and Savior, Jesus Christ.

What faith[146] was required of the Jews in Jesus' time and afterward to accept the humble carpenter of the despised village of Nazareth in the scorned area of Galilee as their expected triumphant Messiah, even as the very Son of their transcendent invisible God, whose name they would not say! What faith especially when they beheld him hanging lifeless on a cross of shame, condemned as false and criminal by the Jewish and Roman authorities alike! It is difficult for us, the heirs of twenty centuries of Christian belief, to place ourselves in their shoes and then make the act of humble and heroic faith that must have been required for them to become Jewish Christians. What we can do, however, with the help of our modern knowledge of astronomy and other sciences, is to develop a truly awesome realization of God's unlimited and indescribable greatness[147] and thus appreciate to some extent the incredible love that must have "possessed" the Son to "empty himself, taking the nature of a slave, becoming in the likeness of men!" (Phil 2:7, WFD).

In summary and conclusion, may the Gospel according to "Matthew" hold the revered place in our hearts and lives that it has always maintained throughout the history of the Church. These days there is a strong tendency to neglect "Matthew" in favor of the other Gospel writers. Indeed, "Matthew" is not as refreshingly candid as Mark, as lovingly compassionate as Luke, or as deeply mystical as John, but there are unique values in "Matthew" without which we would truly be the poorer, values which revolve around the portrait of Jesus the teacher, Jesus the founder of a New Israel, the Church, part of which is a precious heritage now largely lost to us, namely Jewish or biblical Christianity. If it is important to us to recapture our roots, then let the Gospel of "Matthew" help us to go back and recapture our Jewish roots and pair them with our Greek roots to form the one, whole body of Christ "built up in love to the full maturity of Christ the head" (Eph 4:15-16, NAB, but arrangement my own).

* * * * *

As with Mark, so also with "Matthew." It is not easy to say good-bye and pass on to Luke and Acts. Mark endeared himself to us by his straightforwardness and candor. He told Jesus' story as it was. "Matthew" is a far more careful writer, but he also invites our allegiance. Why? Because he too was writing in a period of crisis and stress, not a bloody persecution at the hands of Rome, true, but still for Jewish Christians a time of equal trauma: the proselytizing of resurgent Phariseeism and, worse still, the expulsion of Jewish Christians from the synagogues, to which they clung as tightly as children to their mother. Being weaned is never easy nor is being cast out of the nest. But providentially this very trauma afforded the occasion for the inspired writing of the Church's favorite "good news," The Gospel according to "Matthew."

NOTES

1. I refer to the author of the second Gospel as "masterful" for two reasons: (1) because he has constructed his Gospel in such a masterful, even meticulous way, and (2) because he pictures Jesus Christ as the teacher or master rather than as the wonder-working Son of God but suffering Son of Man, as we have seen in the Gospel according to Mark.

While this Gospel has been attributed to Matthew the apostle from ancient times, especially because of Bishop Papias of Hieropolis in the early second century as quoted by Eusebius in the fourth century (*Ecclesiastical History*, trans. Roy Deferrari, [New York: Fathers of the Church, 1953] 3:39), modern Scripture scholars of all persuasions almost unanimously discount this attribution and for these good reasons: (1) Papias was reporting hearsay and not very reliably; (2) he wrote that Matthew collected *lógia* (sayings, oracles) of Jesus in Hebrew, whereas the so-called Gospel of Matthew is neither mere sayings nor in Hebrew but an original, complete Greek Gospel; (3) this Gospel obviously depends on Mark, notably for its narrative including the call of Levi/Matthew the publican, and (4) it shows only a vague knowledge of the geography of Palestine. Essentially then, our second Gospel is anonymous. I have chosen to attribute it to a fictional person called Mattathias, whose name, "Gift of Yahweh," was fairly common and occurs biblically in at least three forms: Mattathias (see 1 Macc 2:1 ff.), Maththaios or Matthew (Levi) (see Matt 9:9; 10:3 ff.), and Maththias or Matthias (see Acts 1:23, 26). As described in my account of the composition of this Gospel, I feel that my fictional Mattathias exhibits all the characteristics required for the authorship of this superb inspired work.

I refer to the so-called Gospel according to Matthew as "the ecclesial Gospel" for three reasons: (1) It is the only Gospel containing the word *ekklesía*, or "church," in Matt 16:18 and 18:17; (2) it features the Church, usually under the designation of "the kingdom of heaven," e.g., in the sermon in parables of ch. 13; and (3) it has been the favorite Gospel used in the liturgy of the Church through the centuries, partly because it lends itself so well to public reading.

2. This expression is from Jesus' concluding words in his parabolic discourse, words which according to many actually describe the author of this Gospel: "Every scribe trained in the kingdom of heaven is like a householder who brings forth out of his storeroom new things and old" (Matt 13:52, WFD). It seems appropriate here as possibly a self-identification of the anonymous human author.

3. The designation of "the Great Sea" in ancient times indicated what we refer to now as the Mediterranean Sea.

4. The reference here is to the striking description of the sun in Ps 19:6-7 as a giant running a footrace.

5. See n. 1 above for the meaning of this name, chosen here for our anonymous author of this Gospel as a possible explanation of how it came to be designated as the Gospel according to Matthew (the apostle). There was always a tendency to ascribe New Testament books to apostles for the sake of greater authority. It must be remembered, however, that the titles or designations of the books are not part of the inspired text.

6. It was customary and expected among Jewish rabbis or scribes that they would work like others for their livelihood, as we see in the case of Paul, who was a tentmaker (see Acts 18:1-3; 20:34) and who, after becoming a follower of Jesus, continued the rabbinical practice of self-support and preaching free of charge. I have chosen to describe Mattathias also as a former rabbi continuing the rabbinical practice of self-support, and I have attributed to him the trade of saddle making, a picture of which can be found in *Everyday Life in Bible Times*, ed. Merle Severy (Washington: National Geographic Society, 1968) 401. For more on rabbis and work *see* Max Landsberg, "Rabbi," *The Jewish Encyclopedia*, 1916, (hereafter cited as *JE*).

7. The Seleucid agora seems to have been the oldest and principal one of three markets shown in reconstructions of ancient Antioch (*New Catholic Encyclopedia*, s.v. "Antioch," [hereafter cited as *NCE*]. *See also* Glanville Downey, *A History of Antioch in Syria* [Princeton, N.J.: Princeton University Press, 1961] illustrations at end after p. 752, or his abridged work, *Ancient Antioch* [Princeton, N.J.: Princeton University Press, 1963] illustrations after p. 295).

This market was named after King Seleucus I, Nicator (the Conquerer), who won control of Syria in 301 B.C. by his defeat of Antigonus at the battle of Ipsus (Issus) after the division of Alexander the Great's empire upon his death in 323 B.C. *See* Downey, *Ancient Antioch* 28–29.

8. Both Herod the Great and Herod Agrippa I contributed greatly to the construction and beautification of Antioch, as did Augustus, Tiberius, and Caligula. *See* Downey, *Ancient Antioch* 82–85.

9. Antioch-on-the-Orontes, Antioch of Syria, Antioch at Daphne, as well as Antioch the Great and Antioch the Beautiful, all of these were names given

to the capital city of Syria founded by Seleucus I in 300 B.C. some fifteen or twenty miles from the mouth of the Orontes River and the port of Seleucia Pieria, to distinguish it from some fifteen other cities similarly founded by Seleucus I and named after his father, Antiochus, or possibly his son, Antiochus Soter, or both. It was also called Tetrapolis by the geographer Strabo because of its four quarters or sections. See Jack Finegan, *Light from the Ancient Past* (Princeton, N.J.: Princeton University Press, 1946) 258, n. 12).

Interestingly, Antioch is no longer in Syria today but in Turkey and called by the Turkish name "Antakya." A most moving reminder of ancient times is the so-called Church of St. Peter, once a cave high on the slope of Mount Silpius overlooking all of Antioch and preserving the well-founded tradition that Peter lived some time at Antioch, whether or not he was its founding bishop as many claim (see Acts 12:17; Gal 2:11, and Downey, *A History of Antioch in Syria* 284).

But why locate the writing of "Matthew" at Antioch in the first place? For two complementary reasons: (1) No other place seems to qualify for various reasons; and (2) Antioch seems to have all the qualifications needed: an important Greek center, a Jewish minority, and an even smaller Jewish Christian subminority feeling itself squeezed between the burgeoning Greek and Greek Christian majority on the one hand and the Jewish minority, particularly militant Pharisaic Judaism, on the other. See Raymond Brown and John Meier, *Antioch & Rome: New Testament Cradles of Catholic Christianity* (New York: Paulist, 1983) 18–27.

10. Daphne, a plateau to the southwest of Antioch, was noted for its picturesque groves and springs which supplied fresh water by aqueduct to Antioch as well as for its delightful recreational surroundings, which in time turned into uninhibited and immoral conduct, based partly on the legend of Apollo's lustful chase after a nymph who managed to escape by turning into a laurel tree *(dáphne)*, as portrayed by magnificent mosaic flooring discovered there. See Downey, *Ancient Antioch* 19, 206.

In depictions of ancient Antioch there is a Jewish community shown within the city, not far from the Daphne Gate, and a Christian cemetery situated outside the city, also not far from the same gate. Did the Jewish Christians live in the Jewish sector but get buried in the Christian cemetery? The answer is not clear, so I left the question open regarding the location of Mattathias' home.

11. The mention of mustard plants is in obvious reference to Jesus' parable of the mustard seed in Matt 13:31-32 where it is symbolic of the Church's future external growth.

12. This luscious valley, which lies between the Lebanon and Anti-Lebanon mountain ranges in present-day Lebanon, is the source of the water both of the Orontes River that flows north and the Sea of Galilee and River Jordan whose water flows southward into the Dead Sea. It is the site of the famous shrine of Baalbek, originally pagan but later Christianized and now simply a tourist attraction.

13. Seleucia, at the mouth of the Orontes, was founded by Seleucus I (even

before Antioch) on the site of an older village called Pieria, whose name was attached to that of Seleucia. Once Antioch was founded by Seleucus and became the capital city of the Seleucid Empire, then Seleucia with its excellent harbor became the seaport of Antioch and in time the port of embarkation for the Christian missionaries, such as Paul and Barnabas, to the gentile world (see Acts 13:4).

14. A circus in the ancient world involved animals only as a racecourse for horsedrawn chariots, as depicted so dramatically in Lew Wallace's epic, *Ben Hur*.

15. Antioch in Syria was famous for its walls, which surrounded not only the city as a whole but each of its four unequal quarters, as described by Strabo. *See* Downey, *A History of Antioch in Syria* 612.

16. The Amanus mountains, which protected Antioch on the north, were actually part of the giant Taurus Range, passable only through certain crevices such as the famous Cilician Gates north of Paul's birthplace, Tarsus.

17. The Lebanon Range, source of the famous Cedars of Lebanon which were used in the construction of Solomon's Temple and palace (see 1 Kings 6–7), stretches all the way north into Turkey, and the twin mountains, Silpius and Staurin, protected Antioch on the south. With its mountains and walls, Antioch was thought to be virtually impregnable.

18. The word "acropolis" always conjures up an image of Athens, but it is well to remember that the word simply means "high city" and most ancient Greek cities possessed an acropolis, partly for defense, partly for worship of the gods. The Acropolis at Athens just happens to be the most beautiful, accessible, and famous of all.

19. Leadership in the Church at large and at Antioch in particular around A.D. 82 is not at all clear. In the lifetime of Jesus and continuing through time and eternity, he is of course the only supreme leader in his body, the Church. Yet as we will see in Matt 16:16-19; 18:18, and John 21:15-17, he first promises and then confers the visible leadership of his Church on Peter then, in union with him, on the other apostles, and in the course of time, on their successors. This is institutional leadership, which pertains to a conferred office or role in Christ's Church. Elsewhere in the New Testament, especially in Acts, we see the Church's apostolic leadership choosing additional helpers to assist them. For example, Acts 6:1-6 shows us the apostles authorizing seven other men whom we now call deacons to help them, especially in material matters, but the Holy Spirit lost no time in calling them to serve on a higher level as well: preaching, teaching, and baptizing.

We also see in Acts 14:23 and 20:17, 28 as well as 1 Pet 5:1-4; 1 and 2 Timothy, and Titus that the apostles, such as Peter and Paul, also have *epískopoi* (overseers, bishops) and *presbýteroi* (elders, priests) assisting them in the roles of preaching, teaching, administering sacraments, and governing the people of God. In the New Testament however, the words *epískopoi* and *presbýteroi* are often used interchangeably. Only later, in the writings of St. Ignatius of Antioch, do we find a clear distinction between bishops, priests, and deacons.

See "The Letters of St. Ignatius of Antioch," *Magn.* par. 13, p. 100; Phild., intro. par., p. 113, trans. Gerald Walsh, *The Apostolic Fathers*, The Fathers of the Church (New York: Cima, 1947).

In addition to these institutional leaders we see in Acts 13:1; 1 Cor 12–14; Rom 12:3-8, and Eph 4:7-13 what we may truly call inspirational leadership conferred on men and women by means of special charismatic gifts for use in the building up of the Church (*NCE*, s.v. "Charism").

Presumably in Antioch at this time both kinds of leadership were functioning, but with regard to institutional leadership I am portraying Ignatius as the resident bishop (overseer) of both Jewish and gentile Christians, then Mattathias as a presbyter (elder or priest) over the comparatively small Jewish Christian community, and finally I am leaving it to the reader's imagination to decide what kind of leadership is exercised by Mattathias" "fellow leaders." According to Josephus the Jewish community at Antioch was led by an *árchon* (ruler, governor) and several others called *gerousiárchontes* (rulers of the *gerousía* or assembly of elders), but he seems to be speaking of a semiautonomous civil governance, while we are concerned here with ecclesial leadership. *See* Flavius Josephus, *Wars of the Jews* VI, ch. 3, par. 3, *Complete Works*, trans. Wm. Whiston (Grand Rapids: Kregel, 1984).

20. The name "Isaac" represents the Hebrew *yishak* meaning "he laughs." It became the name of the "son of the promise" to Abraham and Sarah, the laughter being attributed to Abraham in Gen 17:17f., to Sarah in Gen 18:11-15, and to others in Gen 21:6. *See* John McKenzie, "Isaac," *Dictionary of the Bible* (New York: Macmillan, 1965) 396.

21. The Hebrew word *shalom* (peace) was so full of meaning that the Jewish Christians probably continued to use it as their principal greeting. The closest Greek equivalent would be *eiréne* (peace), but its primary emphasis is on freedom from war and disturbance whereas the Hebrew word signifies well-being, particularly as a gift of God flowing from a right relationship with him (*Theological Dictionary of the New Testament*, 1985, abr., s.v. "eiréně").

22. The reference here is to Jesus' promise in his great ecclesial or Church discourse, "For where there are two or three gathered together in my name, there I am in the midst of them" (Matt 18:20, WFD).

23. Josephus, *Wars of the Jews*, III, ch. 2, par. 4.

24. Josephus, *Antiquities of the Jews*, XII, 2, 1.

25. An excellent definition of "community" is "unity in diversity." Unity without diversity is only uniformity, diversity without unity is nothing but chaos.

26. The Seleucid kingdom of *Antiochus IV Epiphanes* (175–164 B.C.), who attempted in every way possible to destroy the religion and culture of the Jews but succeeded only in causing the revolt of Mattathias and his sons, of whom Judas, surnamed Maccabeus, became the first military leader of a guerrilla army that eventually won independence for the Jews that lasted until conquest by Pompey in 63 B.C. *See* the two Books of the Maccabees, which are regarded as Apocryphal by Jews and Protestants but as inspired by Roman Catholics.

See also the Book of Daniel, regarded by all as inspired, which was written as an apocalyptic (underground or resistance) work to encourage the Jews under persecution without tipping off the Graeco-Syrian persecutors. Later the Apocalypse or Book of Revelation, would be written in similar circumstances and for the same purpose.

27. This famous saying, which is hardly ever identified, can be found in Tertullian's *Apology*, ch. 39, par. 7, trans. Emily Daly (New York: Fathers of the Church, 1950).

28. Mark is almost universally thought to have written his Gospel before the destruction of Jerusalem in A.D. 70, while the so-called Gospel of Matthew and that of Luke are just as widely thought to have been composed after that tragedy. But how long after? Most commentators place Matthew somewhere between A.D. 80 and 85. I have chosen to fix the decision to write the gospel and the initial preparations in A.D. 82, with the completion of this meticulous work being dated somewhere between A.D. 83 and 85. My thinking is based not just on the biblical importance of the number twelve, which would be difficult to establish in the present context, but also on events at Jabneh which will be treated shortly.

29. The reference here, of course, is to Jesus' eschatological discourse in Mark 13; Matt 23–25; Luke 21.

30. The Zealots, who considered themselves the spiritual heirs of the Maccabees, apparently took their rise at the time of the census revolt in A.D. 6 and continued to harass not only the Romans but also suspected Jewish collaborators, using any means possible including assassination (such as threatened the life of Paul, see Acts 9:29; 23:12-15) and various other forms of terrorism, finally provoking the Romans into all-out war beginning in A.D. 66 and culminating in the destruction of Jerusalem in A.D. 70 and the suicide of over six hundred Zealots at Masada in A.D. 73. However, they surfaced once more in the abortive "messianic" uprising of Bar Kokhba (Son of the Star) in A.D. 132–35. *See* McKenzie, *Dictionary of the Bible* 947.

31. The Sadducees claimed descent from Sadoc, or Zadok, high priest at the time of Solomon (see 1 Kgs 2:35), but their actual origin is obscure. They were indeed the priestly aristocracy, who gained political as well as religious dominance in the time of the Persian rule and continued to maintain it until the destruction of the Temple in A.D. 70, which for all practical purposes put an end to priesthood in Israel, leaving Judaism totally under the Pharisees. *See* McKenzie, *Dictionary of the Bible* 758-59.

32. The designation of Pharisee, from the Hebrew word meaning "to separate," was and is worn proudly by Jews learned in the Law and determined to keep Judaism faithful to its obligations. Many, perhaps most, were highly dedicated and indeed can take credit for preserving Judaism through the ages, for the Jewish religion today is basically Phariseeism. Unfortunately, then as now there has always been the temptation to use religion for personal gain and glory, a temptation to which many Pharisees seem to have succumbed. It was these hypocrites (from Greek *hypócrites*, meaning "an actor") whom

Jesus condemned so scathingly in Matt 23. It is legitimate to wonder, however, how much of that condemnation was verbalized by Jesus himself and how much stemmed from the feelings of first-century Christians who saw themselves besieged by resurgent Phariseeism. For more information on the Pharisees see *JE*, "Pharisee."

33. *Jabneh, or Jamnia*, was originally a Philistine city, identified with Jabneel on the boundary with Judah, near Ekron (see Josh 15:11). Though not quite on the coast it had its own inland harbor and according to *the Geography of Strabo* bk. 16, p. 759, was so populous it could supply forty thousand warriors. According to 2 Chr 26:6 it was captured by King Uzziah of Judah and its walls destroyed. In the Book of Judith it is referred to as Jemnaan (see Jdt 2:28) but as Jamnia in Maccabees and Josephus.

Jabneh became a seat of Jewish scholarship even before the destruction of the Temple, for Rabbi Johanan ben Zakkai after predicting that Vespasian would become Roman emperor, asked him as a personal favor to spare Jabneh and its scholars, a favor which Vespasian evidently granted. After the destruction of Jerusalem the Great Sanhedrin moved to Jabneh, which became the religio-political center of Judaism.

The president of the Sanhedrin from about A.D. 80 until after the turn of the century was Gamaliel II, grandson of Gamaliel I, mentioned in Acts 5:34-39 and 22:3, who in turn was the grandson of the famous Rabbi Hillel. During his presidency Gamaliel II, an unyielding leader, managed to establish the Phariseeism of the liberal Hillel as the dominant school of thought rather than that of the conservative Shammai. In addition he led the condemnation and expulsion of Jewish Christians as *minim* (heretics) and added a prayer to the daily Jewish blessings for their destruction. Modern Yabna, south of Wadi Rubin, is generally assumed to be ancient Jabneh (*JE*, s.v. "Jabneh" and "Gamaliel II").

34. A mezuzah, derived from the Hebrew word for "doorpost," is a small parchment scroll containing the Shema (hear), the Jewish confession of faith and love from Deut 6:4-9, and Deut 11:13-21, written in twenty-two lines, the number of letters in the Hebrew alphabet. It is contained in a wooden or metal holder placed at the right outside doorpost (on entering), originally of residences but now also of public buildings. On the outside of the little rolled scroll and visible through a glass-covered aperture is the ancient name of God, *Shaddai* (Almighty? Mountain-Dweller?), which is found mostly in Genesis but also in Exodus, Psalms, and Ezekiel. Devout Jews kiss or touch the mezuzah in much the same way Catholics sign themselves with holy water (*JE*, s.v. "Mezuzah").

35. *See* Matt 23:15.

36. Judaizers is the name commonly given to those Jewish Christians who in spite of the decision of the Council of Jerusalem still insisted that to be a Christian one also had to be a Jew, which meant being circumcised and keeping the whole Jewish Law. The Judaizers plagued Paul and his missionary work, especially among the Galatians and the Corinthians. Of course, whether they were labeled Judaizers at the time of our story is questionable.

37. The decision at the Council of Jerusalem not to require Gentile converts to be circumcised and keep the Jewish Law (see Acts 15:6-12, 23-29). More on this when we study Acts.

38. *See* Matt 28:19, NAB.

39. Acts 9:2, JB.

40. *See* Acts 11:20-21, 24-26.

41. Acts 11:26. Some have thought that the designation of "Christian" was intended pejoratively, but that opinion is not well founded *(NCE*, s.v. "Christian [The Term]").

42. *See* Acts 12:1-17.

43. *See* Acts 13:1-3.

44. Greek, a word-rich language, is indeed more precise than Hebrew, a word-poor language. Indeed, it is more precise than almost any other language including English. For example, in English we have only one word for love between adults, while Greek has three: *éros* (romantic, physical love), *philía* (friendship), *agápe* (spiritual, divine love). Likewise, English has only one word for life, while Greek has three which are very carefully distinguished: *biós* (lifespan, manner of life) *psyché* (human, natural life), and *zoé* (spiritual, supernatural, eternal, divine life). See *Theological Dictionary of the New Testament*, 1985, abr., 7ff., 290, 294-95, 1347.

45. While Jesus never referred to Greek games or theater, Paul is prolific, especially in references to athletics as is evident from the following references: Acts 20:24; 1 Cor 9:24-26; Gal 2:2; Phil 2:16; 3:12, 14, 16; 1 Tim 1:19; 6:12; 2 Tim 2:5; 4:7. There are not as many references to Greek theater, but the few there are deserve our notice, e.g., Rom 13:14; 1 Cor 4:9; Gal 3:27.

46. In Paul as throughout the Bible, beginning with Gen 2:7, *flesh* (Hebrew *b'shar*, Greek *sárx*) is not the same as body but refers to the whole person in its dimension of human weakness, subject to sickness, accident, death, temptation, sin. "The Word became flesh" (John 1:14), that is, the Word became human in all our human weakness except sin. He did not just become a body! So also in Paul as in the Bible generally, spirit (Hebrew *rhuah*, Greek *pneûma*) refers to the whole person in its human dimension of aspiration and orientation to union with God. "The Spirit himself gives witness with our spirit that we are children of God" (Rom 8:16, NAB). And throughout the life of each person (Hebrew *nephesh*, Greek *sôma* meaning "body" or *psyché* meaning "soul" depending on the emphasis and context), there is a lifelong struggle between one's dimension of spirit, aspiring to union with God, and one's flesh, inclined to weakness and sin (see Rom 8:1-13; Gal 5:16-26). The reader can find treatments of the foregoing on love, life, and biblical anthropology (our human nature according to the Scriptures) in my book *To Live the Word, Inspired and Incarnate* (New York: Alba House, 1988) as follows: on love (174-76, 368-70), on life (12-13), on our human nature (29-34).

47. As helpful as Greek culture and especially the Greek language are in understanding and explaining truths, there is also an advantage and in a sense a greater one in the comparatively simple, straightforward, existential, holistic approach of the Semitic mind. Perhaps this is best and most simply

represented by their (mistaken?) belief that the heart is the seat of thought, which was echoed centuries later by Pascal: "The heart has its reasons that the reason knows nothing of" (Blaise Pascal, *Pensées de Pascal: Sur la Verite de la Religion Cretienne*, ed. Jacques Chevalier, 2nd ed. rev. [Paris: Boivin et cie, 1948] 278). It may be that this is what Mattathias has in mind when in Matt 11:25, NAB, he quotes a saying of Jesus: "Father, Lord of heaven and earth, to you I offer praise; for what you have hidden from the learned and the clever you have revealed to the merest children." A saying which is beautifully lived out at his entry into Jerusalem in Matt 21:15-16.

48. *See* Acts 17:22-33.

49. 1 Cor 2:2, WFD.

50. *See* Dicharry, *To Live the Word* 39–40, 52–53, etc.

51. This is true with the possible exception of television shows, especially situation comedies, which often are the result of brainstorming sessions. Even there however, it probably still takes some one individual to put it all together in an orderly fashion. I am inclined to believe this is somewhat true of what Stendahl calls "the school of Matthew." A "school" may indeed have brainstormed concerning the material in much the same way as I have tried to portray, but there was still need of someone like Mattathias to do the actual writing, probably even the planning. *See* Krister Stendahl, *The School of St. Matthew* (Philadelphia: Fortress, 1969).

52. *NCE*, s.v. "Hellenist." The fact that Mattathias was a Jew who spoke Greek as his principal language would explain the excellent Greek of his Gospel.

53. *See* Matt 13:52. The fact that Mattathias was a former Pharisaic scribe writing for Jewish Christians would explain why he rarely translates Semitic words or explains Jewish customs. And in that moving passage in Matt 11:25-29 from which I quoted in n. 47 above, is it not probable that Mattathias has his former Pharisaic colleagues in mind when he quotes Jesus in the final part, Matt 11:28-29, NIV: "Come to me, all you who are weary and burdened [under all these Pharisaic laws!] and I will give you rest. Take my yoke [my law of love] upon me and learn from me, for I am gentle and humble of heart, and you will find rest for your souls. For my yoke is easy and my burden is light."

54. In the introductory treatment on biblical inspiration I focused on the inspired human author himself but did not presume to critique an opinion that has become more popular in recent years among experts in inspiration, namely that the Church at large and particularly those who have been more closely involved in urging and aiding the human author to write were also inspired. This is truly a moot point. My inclination is to agree that others who helped the human author were indeed inspired, but is this called biblical inspiration or is it more like the inspirations we receive to do some particular good? Only God knows!

55. Careful research has convinced me that it was indeed the great St. Ignatius of Antioch who was shepherding the Church of Antioch at the time in question. The most solid tradition seems to be that Evodius, the first bishop

(or second if Peter was indeed bishop of Antioch) died in A.D. 63 or 64 and was succeeded by Ignatius, who was martyred at the arena in Rome in A.D. 110. Significantly, it was this same Ignatius who first alluded to the so-called Gospel of Matthew in at least three instances, namely, (1) Matt 3:15 in *Smyrn.* 1:1, (2) Matt 10:16b in *Pol.* 2:2, and (3) Matt 2:1-12 in *Eph.* 19:2-3. *See* Raymond Brown and John Meier, *Antioch & Rome* 24–25. It should also be noted here that not only was the Church first called Christian at Antioch but it was also first called catholic, or universal, at Antioch by Ignatius, its bishop, in his Letter to the Smyrnaeans. See "The Letters of St. Ignatius of Antioch," *The Apostolic Fathers,* Fathers of the Church, 121.

56. A *hallel* was a psalm of praise such as Ps 135 or 148. The word *hallel* means "praise" and *halleluia* means "praise to you, Yahweh!" It was probably a hallel that Jesus and the apostles sang before leaving the upper room for the Garden of Gethsemane the night before his death (see Mark 14:26).

57. Almost all historians and geographers mention the phenomenon of street-lighting at Antioch as something unique in the world. The question arises, however, as to whether there was street-lighting in Antioch at the time when our story takes place. I have chosen to indicate that there was, but the reader may prefer to discount the possibility.

58. That Mattathias was extremely conscious of being only a disciple of the Master, only a child of the Father, only an instrument of the Holy Spirit, is probably seen in his Gospel by the inclusion of those enigmatic words of Matt 23:7-12, NIV, which unfortunately are so often taken out of context and totally misinterpreted: "They [the Pharisees] love to be greeted in the marketplaces and to have men call them 'Rabbi,' But you are not to be called 'Rabbi,' for you have only one Master and you are all brothers. And do not call anyone on earth 'father,' for you have one Father and he is in heaven. Nor are you to be called 'teacher,' for you have one teacher, the Christ. The greatest among you will be your servant. For whoever exalts himself will be humbled, and whoever humbles himself will be exalted."

59. Mattathias' lack of personal acquaintance with Jesus helps to explain why the portrait of Jesus in his Gospel is not as clear and vivid as in the Gospel of Mark, which mirrors the eyewitness and enthusiasm of Peter. In the final part of this study of Mattathias, however, we will examine Mattathias' picture of Jesus as the great teacher and the founder of a new and true people of God.

60. While Mattathias during his years as a practicing Jew and Pharisaic scribe must have gone rather regularly to Jerusalem for the Passover and perhaps other major feasts, he does evidence only a vague knowledge of Israel, which would be in keeping with his never having lived there.

61. According to the two source theory, widely accepted in some form by most Scripture scholars, Matthew depends for the outline and narrative of Jesus' public life, death, and resurrection on the fast-moving, almost totally narrative Gospel of Jesus according to Mark. This is one reason why I have not attempted to probe sources such as the kerygma and the material

of form criticism, which have already been thoroughly examined in the study of Mark's Gospel.

62. I have used the expression "Sayings of Jesus" instead of the usual one in vogue among Scripture scholars, namely *Q*, the initial letter of the German word *quelle*, meaning "source." This is the designation of an anonymous source, written in Greek, mostly discursive rather than narrative, from which is apparently derived material that is common to the Gospels of Matthew and Luke but not found in Mark. So far as is known it is no longer extant but has to be reconstructed from Matthew and Luke. Whether or not it can be identified with the *lógia* (sayings) attributed to the Apostle Matthew by Papias of Hierapolis is a moot point. For further information see one or more of these books: Richard Edwards, *A Concordance to Q* (Missoula, Mont: Scholars Press, 1975); R. Edwards, *A Theology of Q* (Philadelphia: Fortress Press, 1976); Ivan Havener, *Q: The Sayings of Jesus* (Wilmington, Del: Michael Glazier, 1987).

63. *Koiné* or Common Greek, was that somewhat simplified form of Attic, or Athenian, Greek which had been spread and popularized throughout the Alexandrian Empire and which continued as the common international language all through the New Testament period. Thus it was the language used exclusively in the New Testament writings, with variations by different human authors depending on their individual backgrounds, education, and writing experience. For a brief, carefully organized introduction to Koine Greek *see* Warren Dicharry, *Greek Without Grief: An Outline Guide to New Testament Greek* (Chicago: Loyola University Press, 1989).

64. The phenomenon of Jews and Gentiles united harmoniously in one Church is a key emphasis in Paul's ecclesial letter, commonly called his Letter to the Ephesians. And "Matthew" managed to insert into his Gospel a number of references to the Gentiles, generally in very favorable terms, e.g., Matt 2:1-12; 8:5-13; 15:21-28; 22:1-14; 28:18-20.

65. In the Sunday liturgical readings especially before Vatican II, not only were most of the Gospel passages taken from the so-called Gospel of Matthew but a large number of them dealt precisely with the rejection of the Jews and call of the Gentiles. I tended to tire of hearing this same theme until it began to dawn on me that the Gospel and the Church were trying to remind us gentile Catholics not to make the same mistakes as the Jews with the same dire consequences. This important warning became clearly evident in the parable of the wedding banquet in which the man off the street (obviously a Gentile) is rejected for lacking a wedding garment, i.e., the right conduct and dispositions (see Matt 22:1-14). How would the Church be likely to repeat Judaism's mistakes? Well, one possibility would be (and has been, I'm afraid) by putting too much emphasis on Church, or canon, law and not enough on Scripture, prayer, and our personal and communal relationship with God and neighbor.

66. That the well-known Sermon on the Mount is from the Sayings of Jesus known as *Q* becomes evident when we compare "Matthew" with Mark and Luke, noting that Mark has no such sermon while Luke has a similar though

shorter discourse which he situates on a plain instead of a mount to emphasize the accessibility of Jesus as the universal and compassionate Savior (see Matt 5–7, Luke 6:17-49).

67. The missionary discourse seems to come both from Mark and Q because Mark also contains it, but there is much in Matthew and Luke which is not found in Mark (see Matt 10:1-42; Mark 6:1-6; Luke 9:1-6; 10:1-20).

68. The parabolic discourse also seems to derive from Mark and Q, as we see in Matt 13:1-53; Mark 4:1-34; Luke 8:4-21.

69. The ecclesial discourse is mainly unique to "Matthew," but there are some segments in common with Mark and Luke, those in Luke probably derived from Q, e.g., Matt 18:1-9 has parallels in Mark and Luke, while Matt 18:10-18 and 21-22 have limited parallels in Luke, presumably from Q, and Matt 18:19-20 and 23-35 are unique to "Matthew."

70. The eschatological discourse proper (see Matt 24–25) has close parallels in both Mark 13 and Luke 21, but the woes against the scribes and Pharisees in Matt 23, which are usually considered part of the eschatological discourse, are almost entirely unique to "Matthew," probably because only the Jewish Christians felt threatened by resurgent Phariseeism.

71. Matt 28:52.

72. There may even be a double parallel between Jesus' authority (see Matt 5–9; 21–22) and that of the apostles (see Matt 10; 16–18; 28).

73. There is a clear and presumably intended inclusion-conclusion between the name "Emmanuel" (God with us) in the beginning of "Matthew's" Gospel (see Matt 1:23) and the end, where Jesus promises to be always with his Church (see Matt 28:20).

74. The term "concentric circles" is modeled on the well-known phenomenon that when one drops a pebble into water, ripples go out from the place of the pebble in ever-widening circles. In modern literature perhaps the only common use of this structure is seen in journalism, where the writer usually provides the heart of the story in the first paragraph and then keeps returning to it throughout the article in order to flesh it out with more details. In the ancient Eastern world, however, this was a favorite type of development and seems to occur in several places of the Old and New Testament, e.g., possibly the Song of Songs, the Gospel of John, and in particular, Jesus' final discourse.

75. Chiasmus is a structure dear to the biblical mind but almost totally foreign to our thinking and development. It derives its name from the Greek letter *chi* which looks a lot like our capital X. However, the structure really uses only the lower half of the "X" and does so in such a way that there are parallels between the beginning point and the ending point, then between the next-to-beginning point and the next-to-ending point to a midpoint of the structure which stands alone as the emphatic point of the entire structure. Our Gospel definitely seems to be built in this fashion as will become more evident when the outlines of the Gospel are presented.

76. First of all, it is important to bear in mind that the Oriental mentality tended to use such things as genealogies, etymologies, etc. not for historical

or biographical purposes but in a symbolic way in order to teach something. For example in Matt 1:1-17 the genealogy of Jesus, which like all biblical genealogies is traced through the father (in this instance the foster father, Joseph), helps to portray Jesus as the son of David and son of Abraham. Even more than that, his genealogy is neatly divided into three segments of fourteen generations each. Why? Because the name of David adds up to the number fourteen. How? By a cherished process which they called *gematria*. The biblical writers did not have arabic numerals, which had not yet been developed, nor did they like to use the cumbersome Roman numerals except perhaps on monuments. So what did they use? Both Jews and Greeks employed the letters of their respective alphabets, which had much in common, since the Greek alphabet is derived from Phoenician or Canaanite, and Hebrew is a form of Canaanite. *Gematria* is the process of switching from letters to numbers or vice versa. And according to *gematria*, the numerical values of the letters in David's name add up to the number fourteen.

77. It is a curious phenomenon in "Matthew's" Gospel, probably because of a preoccupation with community in this ecclesial work, that singulars in Mark become plurals, or at least duals, in "Matthew." For example, where Mark has one demoniac at Gerasa (see Mark 5:1-20), Matt 8:28-34 has two demoniacs. Where Mark has one blind man at Bethsaida (see Mark 8:22-26) and again at Jericho (see Mark 10:46-52), we find two blind men in Matt 9:27-31 and 20:29-34. Of even greater interest and somewhat humorous is the fact that while Mark pictures Jesus riding into Jerusalem on one donkey (Mark 11:1-11), "Matthew" incredibly has him riding on two donkeys in Matt 21:1-11! Note v. 7 which reads, "They [the apostles] led the donkey and her colt and put their cloaks on them, and he sat on them" (Matt 21:7, WFD)!

Along with the number two, the number three is also emphasized in "Matthew." For example, does not Jesus make his emphatic declaration in Matt 18:20, WFD, "For where there are two or three gathered together in my name, there am I in the midst of them"? In addition, looking only at threesomes in "Matthew" but not in Mark, we see the Magi present three gifts in Matt 2:11, Jesus tempted three times in Matt 4:1-11, and giving special instructions in the Sermon on the Mount about three things: almsgiving, prayer, and fasting (see Matt 6:1-18).

Finally as we might expect, the ideal biblical number, seven, is likewise featured in "Matthew" though not as much as we will see in John and Revelations. "Matthew" has seven Beatitudes in 5:1-12 (omitting bracketed 5:3 and combining 10-12, which really form one Beatitude), seven petitions in the Lord's Prayer (Matt 6:9-13), seven parables of the kingdom in Matt 13, seven woes against the Pharisees in Matt 23, and seven parables that stress preparedness in Matt 24:32-25:46. It should also be noted that in his inherited love of symbolism, "Matthew" mentions no fewer than seven mountains, both the number seven and the phenomenon of mountains being highly symbolic.

78. Just a few examples of how the Gospel of "Matthew" softens expressions in Mark to show Jesus and the apostles in a more favorable light: (1)

In Mark 4:11-12 Jesus appears to speak in parables so that (Greek *hína*) the hearers may not understand and become converted (actually Jesus is only using a quotation from the call of Isaiah in Isa 6:9-10), but "Matthew" softens *hína* (so that) to *hóti* (because). (2) In Mark 6:5, Mark reports that Jesus "could not" work any miracle at his hometown of Nazareth, whereas "Matthew" changes the expression to "did not" in Matt 13:58. (3) Of course Matthew completely omits the strange episode in Mark 3:21 which seems to imply that Jesus appeared to his relatives as "out of his mind."

79. Cf. Mark 10:35-45 and Matt 20:20-28.

80. Matt 13:52, WFD, in a fairly free translation.

81. "The kingdom of heaven" (Greek *basileía tôn ouranôn*, Hebrew *malkuth shamaim*) is a typical Jewish circumlocution for the kingdom of God or the kingship of God. We will examine this concept more closely in Part III.

82. While Mark does have a number of Old Testament quotations and Luke (as we will see) has Old Testament allusions, especially in his Infancy Gospel, "Matthew" literally abounds in Old Testament quotations, which he often prefaces with words referring to the fulfillment of prophecy, e.g., Matt 1:22-23; 2:17-18; 3:3; 4:14-16, etc. In Matt 2:23 we seem to have an Old Testament quotation with the usual fulfillment preface, but actually there is no text in the Old Testament which predicts that "he shall be called a Nazorean." Is "Matthew" making it up out of the whole cloth? Not at all! Rather, in typical rabbinical use of Scripture, he is putting together several words which seem to add up in sound and meaning to the equivalent of a prophecy.

The words that he seems to have had in mind, all of which bear some resemblance to the word "Nazareth" and carry a meaning appropriate to the figure of the Messiah, are these: *neser* (shoot) from Isa 11:1 (a messianic prophecy); *nazir* (consecrate) referring to a nazirite consecration such as that of Samson and Samuel (see Judg 13:4-5; 1 Sam 1:11), both consecrated as saviors of God's people and thus types of Jesus; and *nasr* (prince), a term used by the patriarch Jacob in his oracle (see Gen 49:26) about his son Joseph, who like Jesus was not only a prince (prince of peace) but also a savior of his people.

83. In Isa 11:1 Yahweh is definitely referring to Israel, but "Matthew" applies it beautifully to Jesus, the Son of God. Here also we could use the example employed in Matt 2:23 which I have explained in the foregoing note.

84. "Matthew" is indeed an anti-Jewish Gospel in the sense that it is certainly a polemic against the Pharisaic Judaism under Gamaliel II after the destruction of Jerusalem. It is not, however, a polemic against all Jews of that time or now, and therefore we the readers must be very careful not to allow the anti-Pharisaic feelings of this Gospel to lead us into anti-Semitism. Quite the opposite! As Paul points out in Rom 11:29, NAB, etc., "God's gifts and his call are irrevocable!" The Jews are still his chosen people. So are we Christians. If ever, then, there should be one people loving another, it should be Christians and Jews. Unfortunately that has not always been the case in Judeo-Christian history. Far from it! But with the impetus of Vatican II and its statement on the Jewish question, hopefully the relationship will continue to improve.

85. The term for "church," *ekklesía* (called out), will be rather fully explained in Part III.

86. As indicated in Part I, I have placed the conception of "Matthew's" Gospel around A.D. 82, about two years after the beginning of Gamaliel II's presidency of Jabneh, for it was he above all who in effect outlawed any kind of Judaism except that of Hillel's Phariseeism, which labeled all others, especially Christians, as *minim*, or heretics, and who had them expelled from Jewish synagogues. It was perhaps this expulsion, so traumatic for the Jewish Christians who continued to glory as both Jews and Christians, that brought about the writing of the Gospel according to "Matthew."

87. The ruins of the ancient city of Hierapolis (Priestly City) can be found today not far from those of Laodicea, the famous city in Revelations which was condemned for its lukewarmness (see Rev 3:15-16). It was a favorite of many in the ancient world because of the high alkaline content of its stream which seemed both to fix the dye in cloth and to maintain the health of its devotees. Centuries of alkali have left it looking very much like Niagara Falls, in gleaming white sediment.

88. There seem to be no geographical indications in this Gospel which could not have come from Mark's Gospel, in contrast with John where there are very specific descriptions characteristic of an eyewitness, the most notable of which would be his description in John 5:2-3 of the sheep pool with five porticoes, which has been confirmed by archaeology.

89. If the Apostle Matthew did not write this Gospel, and it seems almost certain that he did not, then we really do not know who did. I have simply chosen a name which is another form of Matthew to help explain how it might have come to be called "The Gospel according to Matthew," and more importantly, I have endowed this fictitious person with the background and characterisics that the author of this Gospel would seem to have had. There is no intention to deceive but simply to provide as much of a story for the conception and writing of this Gospel as possible in the circumstances.

90. Since the description of the "scribe of the kingdom" in Matt 13:52 is thought by many to be autobiographical and since the very content of the Gospel would seem to require a personal knowledge of Pharisaic Judaism, I have chosen to describe the author as a former rabbi and now a Christian presbyter (elder) or priest, responsible for the Jewish Christian minority in the largely gentile Christian Church at Antioch-on-the-Orontes.

91. To see the difference between a *lógion* (saying) and a pronouncement story, simply compare Jesus' teaching about divorce and remarriage in Matt 5:31-32 (a *lógion* in the Sermon on the Mount) with the pronouncement story on the same subject in Matt 19:3-12. In the latter instance we see the historico-religious setting of Jesus' statement, namely the division between the liberal Pharisaic school of Hillel which permitted almost any imperfection in the wife as justification for divorce, and the conservative Pharisaic school of Shammai which restricted justification for divorce and remarriage to adultery only. It would be tempting to delve into the entire controversy about the meaning of the "exceptive expressions" in Matt 5:32 and Matt 19:9, but that would lead

us beyond the scope of this examination. Instead let me refer the reader to three articles expressing three divergent opinions on this very thorny question: Bruce Vawter, "The Divorce Clauses in Mt. 5:32 and 19:9," *The Catholic Biblical Quarterly* 16, no. 2 (April 1954) 155–67; Joseph Fitzmyer, "The Matthean Divorce Texts and Some Palestinian Evidence," *Theological Studies* 37, no. 2 (June 1976) 197–226; Don Smith, "The Matthaean Exceptive Clauses in the Light of Matthew's Theology and Community," *Studia Biblica & Theologica* 17, no. 1 (April 1989) 55–82. I would only add for the sake of clarity that, according to the general consensus of scripturists, Jesus himself did prohibit divorce and remarriage with no exceptions, as is clear from the apostles' reaction (Matt 19:10) as well as from the parallel passages in Mark 10:2-12; Luke 16–18; and 1 Cor 7:10-11. The so-called exceptive clauses in "Matthew" had to be his own additions. And the predominant opinion, at least among Catholic scholars, is that the *porneía* (uncleanness) permitting divorce and remarriage is a union within forbidden degrees of kinship according to Jewish Law (Acts 15:20, 29; 1 Cor 5:1). Only "Matthew" includes the exceptive clauses because his alone is a Jewish Gospel. *See* John Meier, *The Vision of Matthew: Christ, Church, and Morality in the First Gospel* (New York: Paulist, 1979) 248–57.

92. As an example of how widely the Infancy Gospels of "Matthew" and Luke differ, in the former Jesus is born at Bethlehem because Joseph and Mary obviously live there and later move to Nazareth only because Herod the Great's cruelest son, Archelaus, now reigns in Judea; in Luke Jesus is born at Bethlehem because of the universal census ordered by Augustus, and the Holy Family returns to Nazareth because Joseph and Mary obviously live there. What must always be borne in mind, however, is that the Infancy Gospels are not part of the kerygma, which begins with John the Baptist as we see in Mark, and therefore they are somewhat like Gen 1–11, a brief theological and spiritual overture to set the stage or mood for the largely eyewitness but interpreted account that follows.

93. For a reminder about concentric circles see n. 74 above.

94. For a reminder about chiastic structures see n. 75 above.

95. I present this "pentamerous" outline of "Matthew," that is, one which features the number five, not as a definitive solution to the question of structure and development in this masterful Gospel but simply as an interesting possibility which offers some intriguing quintets. To my knowledge no one else has suggested this arrangement, so I must take full responsibility for it myself.

96. This profound truth is the major reason for my writing, *To Live the Word*.

97. There are actually Bible readers who make important decisions by praying and then opening the Bible at random, being guided by whatever verse their finger or eyes first rest upon. This is not necessarily to be condemned. After all, is it not better than leaving God out of decisions altogether? The problem is that it can so easily become a kind of superstition not unlike the practice of the people of Jesus' time, especially the scribes and Pharisees, who were constantly demanding a special sign (see Matt 12:38-42; 16:1-4).

98. This reverence is what is often referred to as "fear of the Lord" (Isa 11:2-3, etc.), but the word "fear" has taken on a far more negative meaning in our English language today. Words like "reverence," "awe," "love," "respect," "filial obedience," come much closer to capturing the meaning intended in the sacred text.

99. Perhaps the ease with which in "Matthew" Jesus performs all kinds of miracles by his mere word may explain why "Matthew" either omits or tones down the so-called process miracles in Mark 7:31-37 and 8:22-26, which seem to require more effort and can only be done in stages.

100. In Greek there is a very careful distinction made between *exousía* (authority) and *dýnamis* (power). The former normally indicates legitimate authorization from above, usually involving the full use of human faculties (Matt 28:18), whereas the latter normally implies force of some kind, either from God (especially the Holy Spirit) enabling us to act beyond our normal human capabilities (see Luke 1:35; 24:49; Acts 1:8; 1 Cor 2:4) or from Satan and other evil spirits (see Acts 8:10; Eph 6:12).

101. Does the surprising mention of Syria here indicate that "Matthew" does indeed emanate from Antioch in Syria? Not necessarily, but it may be a clue. "In the New Testament, the name Syria designates the Roman province of Syria, erected in 64 B.C. and governed by an imperial legate who resided in Antioch (Matt 4:14; Luke 2:2; Acts 15:23, 41; 18:18; 20:3; 21:3; Gal 1:21). The province of Syria included Palestine . . ." (John McKenzie, *Dictionary of the Bible* 860).

102. Jewish rabbis always taught sitting down rather than standing, perhaps because they rarely spoke briefly, but more seriously because "they were official expounders of the Law" (Matt 23:2; Luke 4:20). *See* H. L. Ellison, "Matthew" *The International Bible Commentary*, rev. ed., ed. F. F. Bruce (New York: Guideposts, 1986) 1144.

103. For more on the central importance of the covenant *see* Dicharry, *To Live the Word* 4-6, 71-72, 78-79.

104. *See* Matt 22:34-40; Mark 12:28-34; Luke 10:25-37; Rom 13:8-10, etc.

105. In the context, the word *zygós* (yoke) evidently refers to the yoke, or burden, of the innumerable laws required by the scribes and Pharisees, which made the service of Yahweh almost impossible. However *zygós* may contain another meaning. In 2 Cor 6:14, WFD, it clearly refers to marital union: "Do not become yoked (or mismatched) with unbelievers." Is Jesus in this passage also inviting us into a deep spiritual union with himself? I like to think so, particularly because there are other passages which carry the same thought, e.g., John the Baptist's tender expression in John 3:29, NAB: "It is the groom who has the bride. The groom's best man waits there listening for him and is overjoyed to hear his voice. That is my joy, and it is complete."

And again in 1 Cor 6:16-17, NAB: "Can you not see that the man who is joined to a prostitute becomes one body with her? Scripture says, 'The two shall become one flesh.' But whoever is joined to the Lord becomes one spirit with him." This, of course, is but an application to the individual of the centuries-old tradition, according to which the covenant of Sinai was regard-ed from the time of Hosea on as a spiritual marriage between Yahweh the (faith-ful) bridegroom and Israel the (faithless) bride, a theme repeated in Isaiah, Jeremiah, and Ezekiel and carried over into the New Testament with Jesus Christ as the bridegroom and his body the Church as the bride (see Matt 22:1-14; Rom 7:4; 2 Cor 11:2-3; Eph 5:22-32; Rev 19:7-9; 21:2).

106. Phylacteries (from Greek *phylásso*, I guard) were small leather boxes on the forehead and arm containing certain texts: Exod 13:1-10, 11-16; Deut 6:4-9; 11:13-21. Fringes or tassels were worn on the edges of outer garments in accordance with Num 15:37-40 and Deut 22:12 (see Mark 6:56).

107. This text has given rise to countless challenges and even condemna-tions of priests for allowing themselves to be called "father." However, the context makes it quite clear that Jesus is simply warning his apostles (and in-deed all the leadership of his Church) that their authority comes from God and they are not to pride themselves as rabbis, fathers, or teachers in their own name. That Christian leaders have every right, under God, to be called spiritual fathers is evident from 1 Cor 4:15 and 1 Thess 2:11.

108. The reference here is to charismatic gifts as distinguished from the seven sanctifying gifts of the Holy Spirit. The former, which Paul lists variously in 1 Cor 12, Rom 12, and Eph 4, do not make us any better or holier, for they are given not for ourselves but for the good of others and the building up of the Church. Now just as we are guilty of pride if we use these gifts for our own self-glorification, so we are guilty of sloth and false humility if we ne-glect to develop them and use them for others (see Luke 19:11-26).

109. That the words "apostle" and "disciple" are interchangeable is most evident in a comparison of Matt 10:1 and 10:2.

110. As the Catholic Church has been declaring for centuries and as the form critics, after Bultmann and Dibelius, have insisted, not only did the Church exist before the New Testament was written, but she contributed much if not most of the material or tradition incorporated into the New Testament. This is spelled out in the familiar three-stage development proposed by the form critics, i.e., *sitz im leben Jesu* (the life situation of Jesus), *sitz im leben kirche* (the life situation of the Church), and *sitz im leben evangelisten* (the life situation of the evangelist).

111. A rather free translation of *Vatican Council II: The Conciliar and Post Con-ciliar Documents*, ed. Austin Flannery (Collegeville: The Liturgical Press, 1975) 764.

112. *See* "Duties of the Clergy," *Some of the Principal Works of St. Ambrose*, bk. 1, ch. 20, par. 88, trans. H. De Romestin, The Nicene and Post-Nicene Fathers (2nd ser.), ed. Schaff and Wace (Grand Rapids: Eerdmans, 1969).

113. *Theological Dictionary of the New Testament* 1985, abr. s.v. "kaléo."

114. *See* Matt 26:28; Mark 24:24; Luke 22:20; 1 Cor 11:25, 2 Cor 3:6; Heb 8-9; and 1 Pet 2:9-10, an obvious allusion to Exod 19:5-6.

115. The smallest letter in Greek is *ióta* (*i*), corresponding to Hebrew and Aramaic *yod* (׳), sometimes written *jot*.

116. The smallest part of a letter in Greek is a small stroke *(keraía)* such as we see at the bottom of *ióta,* but the reference is probably to the Hebrew *tittle* (small sign) such as distinguishes the letter *daleth* from *resh.*

117. Paul uses *ekklesía* of individual Churches, e.g., in 1 Cor 1:2 and similar greetings, but also of the whole Church, e.g., in Eph 5:22-32 and elsewhere.

118. The kingship of Yahweh is emphasized above all in the Coronation Psalms, which are found in Ps 92 and following.

119. The very word "Messiah" (Anointed One) implies kingship, which is why Jesus tries so hard, mainly in Mark, to keep his messiahship secret until his triumphal entry into Jerusalem and why he insists before Pilate that his kingdom is not of this world (see John 18:36).

120. Apocalyptic literature, which is a different literary form from prophetic writing is seen in the Book of Daniel in the Old Testament and the Apocalypse, or Book of Revelation, in the New. It is best described as "underground or resistance literature," written in a time of persecution to encourage the victims without alerting the persecutors.

121. Apocryphal literature refers to pious and edifying writing, Jewish or Christian, which is not considered inspired or canonical. The difficulty, however, is that the Pharisees under Gamaliel II at Jabneh, or Jamnia, as part of their "regrouping" drew up their own canon of sacred books (of the Old Testament) along lines much stricter than that of the Septuagint translators three centuries earlier, omitting some seven books that were commonly accepted at the time of Jesus, namely, (1) among historical books, 1 and 2 Maccabees, Tobit, and Judith; (2) among prophetic books, Baruch; and (3) among wisdom literature, Ben Sirach, or Ecclesiasticus, the Wisdom of Solomon, and parts of the Books of Daniel and Esther.

Later when Martin Luther translated directly from the Hebrew Bible in the 16th century A.D., those books simply were not there in the Hebrew Bible. Thus, those seven books which Catholics consider inspired and canonical are called "Apocrypha" by Jews and Protestants, while other books which neither they nor Catholics consider inspired or canonical are called "Apocrypha" by Catholics, "Pseudepigrapha" by others.

122. In the context in which various kinds of animals represent various empires, the figure of "one like a son of man" clearly symbolizes Israel, which will receive dominion over all others. However, when messianic expectations began to develop more intensely under Babylonian, Persian, Greek, Syrian, and Roman domination, the "son of man" figure came to be identified more and more with the Messiah in noninspired literature, notably the Book of Henoch.

123. "Kingship" and "kingdom" are correlative terms, as are "rule" or "reign" and "realm." While in different contexts the expression *basileía toû theoû* or *tôn ouranôn* seems to stress God's kingship over us more than his kingdom to which we belong, it would be a disservice to this pregnant expression to identify it with either kingship or kingdom to the exclusion of the other.

124. *See* Matt 13:24-30; 18:7.

125. This is not, of course, to condone or welcome scandals in the Church but to recognize that ours is a Church of sinners as well as saints, a remedy not a reward, human as well as divine. Nor does this in any way affect the infallibility of the Church or of the pope speaking in the name of the Church, for infallibility does not guarantee impeccability; that is, God's protection of the Church, the body of Christ, from solemnly teaching error in matters of faith and morals does not protect the same teachers from falling into sin, sometimes even heinous, scandalous sin. What an additional motive for love and gratitude toward Jesus that he not only "became flesh" (John 1:14), "died for our sins and rose for our justification" (Rom 4:25), but continues "to be always with" (Matt 28:20) and identify himself with (see John 15:1-8) his and our Church of saints and sinners.

126. This gradual, almost imperceptible, yet amazing growth and influence of the Church is mirrored in the only parable unique to Mark (see 4:26-29): the seed growing of itself.

127. Impartial scholars recognize in Matt 16:13-20 Jesus' promise of the primacy in his Church to Peter, as they see the fulfillment of that promise in John 21:15-17. However, there are preachers who insist that Jesus did just the opposite, denigrating Peter as a little rock (*pétros*) and building his Church on the bedrock (*pétra*) of himself or Peter's faith or something else. Such an interpretation first of all violates the context, in which Jesus is obviously rewarding Peter for his profession of faith in his messiahship (and in "Matthew" his divine sonship) and proceeding to confer on him "the keys of the kingdom" (the symbol of authority), closing with the incredible promise to ratify in heaven whatever he will bind or loose on earth.

In addition, it ignores the fact that Jesus was speaking Aramaic, not Greek, and in Aramaic (as in Syriac, which is Aramaic written in different lettering: either Jacobite or Nestorian) the selfsame word, *kepha*, is used in both places: "You are rock and on this rock I will build my Church." This, of course, is confirmed by the prominence of Peter in the New Testament, heading every list of apostles and, in Acts, leading the apostolic choice of Matthias, speaking for the Church on Pentecost, receiving the first Gentiles into the Church, and deciding the issue at the Council of Jerusalem.

128. From a comparison of Matt 16:19 and 18:18 it should seem obvious that Jesus intended his Church to be governed in a collegial fashion, that is, by all the apostles and their successors in union with and under the primacy of Peter and his successors. However, at different times in Church history varying events have intervened to disturb that balance, at least temporarily. One of those times involved Vatican I in A.D. 1870. Two historical events occurred to force an abrupt dispersal of the Council Fathers, namely the outbreak of the Franco-Prussian War and the Battle of Rome for the unification of Italy, a battle which took place on the Janiculum Hill overlooking the Vatican itself. Because of this premature dismissal the Council was unable to discuss the role of bishops, priests, religious, and laity in the Church. Only the role of the pope and particularly his infallibility was thoroughly discussed and debated, with

the result that, between the two Vatican Councils the role and prerogatives of the pope received an undue amount of emphasis, to the detriment of the bishops and others in the Church. It was only at Vatican II and thanks largely to the firm guidance of Pope Paul VI that genuine collegiality was emphasized in the governance of the Church.

129. The striking parable which concludes the ecclesial discourse is a powerful reminder to Church officials or leaders that we are all in deep debt to God, which, in his mercy (and through the salvific grace of Christ), he readily forgives provided we forgive whatever (paltry) debt is owed us by others. In this connection the Greek of the Lord's Prayer in the Sermon on the Mount is very revealing. According to the traditional translation, we normally say "Forgive us our debts [or trespasses] as we forgive our debtors [or those who trespass against us]" (Matt 6:12). But in the Greek the second verb is not *aphíemen*, in the present tense, meaning "we forgive" but rather *aphékamen*, in the perfect tense, which in Greek has a very specific use, describing what began in the past and continues in the present. What we should be saying, then, or at least meaning is this: "as we have already forgiven and continue to forgive our debtors [or those who trespass against us]."

130. Recall that this is a major emphasis in "Matthew," as is clear from the inclusion-conclusion structure involving the name "Emmanuel," a name which means 'God is with us' " (Matt 1:23, NAB) at the beginning and at the end, Jesus' promise to his Church: "And know that I am with you always, until the end of the world" (Matt 28:20, NAB).

131. Besides the above promise of Jesus there are many other indications of Jesus' presence and operation in his Church, perhaps the most impressive of which (when it is properly translated) is the first verse of Acts: "I wrote my former account, O Theophilus, about all those things that Jesus began to do and to teach until the day when, after instructing his chosen apostles through the Holy Spirit, he was taken up [into heaven]" (Acts 1:1, WFD). Notice the key word "began" (*erxato* in Greek, the imperfect of *árchomai*, meaning "I begin"). Jesus only began in his earthly lifetime. Now in his risen state *he continues to do and teach in and through the Church and its individual members*, particularly those who surrender themselves totally to him, namely the saints. When we honor them we are really honoring Christ living and loving and serving through them.

132. This apt description of the sacraments can be found in George Maloney, *The Breath of the Mystic* (Denville, N.J.: Dimension, 1974) 49.

133. Warren Dicharry, *Greek Without Grief*, see n. 63 above.

134. On Jews for Jesus and Hebrew Christianity *see* Moishe Rosen, *Jews for Jesus* (Old Tappan, N.J.: Revell, 1974); Arnold Fruchtenbaum, *Hebrew Christianity: Its Theology, History, and Philosophy* (Washington: Canon, 1974); B. Z. Sobel, *Hebrew Christianity*, (New York: Wiley, 1974).

135. St. Anselm, *Proslogian: Fides Quaerens Intellectum*, Opera Omnia, vol. 158 (Paris: Migne, 1863) 1:225.

136. *See* Constitution on Divine Revelation, *Vatican Council II* ed. A. Flannery (New York: Costello, 1975) 117.

137. *Ibid.* 764.

138. *See* Dicharry, *To Live the Word*, introduction, xiii.

139. For more on what follows regarding the Eastern mentality, *see* Dicharry, *To Live the Word*, 29–34. I would like to call attention particularly to two other remarks of Jesus: (1) "Watch and pray that you may not enter into temptation; the spirit indeed is willing but the flesh [is] weak" (Matt 26:41, WFD, and parallels) and (2) "The spirit is life-giving, the flesh profits nothing; the words which I have spoken to you are spirit and life" (John 6:63, WFD). In other words, Jesus is not denying that he will truly give himself to us in the Eucharist but rather that we cannot understand or accept this great gift except on a spiritual rather than a natural level.

140. Not all Scripture scholars agree on the possibility of more than one literal meaning, but *see* St. Augustine, *Christian Instruction*, trans. John Gavigan, Fathers of the Church, 147.

141. There is no way that we in our natural state can merit justification. No, it is gratuitous, a pure gift or grace received through faith and baptism. However, once justified, once in the state of what we call "sanctifying grace," then we can live with some confidence about our ultimate salvation. Paul clearly distinguishes between the two: "Since we have now been justified by his blood, how much more shall we be saved from God's wrath through him!" (Rom 5:9, NIV). And although we cannot merit anything in our natural state, once justified we can truly merit or "store up treasures in heaven" (Matt 6:20, NIV). For Jesus' words about heavenly rewards, particularly in the Sermon on the Mount, "Matthew" does not hesitate to use the Greek word *misthós*, meaning "a wage or salary." How can this be? Because once we are justified Christ lives in us. Our virtues, then, are his virtues; our works are really his works in and through us. And his virtues and works are meritorious of themselves because of who he is. For a full discussion of justification and salvation *see* app. C, pp. 425–37, of my book *To Live the Word*.

142. None of us can judge the state of soul of any particular person as Jesus insists in Matt 7:1-5 (but note at the same time the interesting hyperbole [exaggeration] in vv. 3 and 5). Yet how often have we seen gifted people become so enamored of their own gifts and accompanying applause that they "have turned aside from their early love" (Rev 2:4, NAB), namely the love of Christ himself. This is a prostitution of God's gifts. The more gifted we may be, or think we are, the more conscious we should be of Jesus' warning: "From everyone who has been given much, much will be demanded; and from the one who has been entrusted with much, much more will be asked" (Luke 12:48, NIV).

143. *See* Isa 11:2-3.

144. The quotation is an approximate one from Rabbi Robert Kahn, now rabbi emeritus of Temple Emanu El in Houston, Texas.

145. The sacred name revealed to Moses in Exod 3:14 is the tetragrammaton (four-letter word) best pronounced "Yahweh," (I am who am), which in the context probably means "I am the only God who truly is!" However, particularly after the Babylonian Exile, Judaism developed such a transcendent

image of God that they would not pronounce his sacred name. Instead they would substitute the word *adonah* (Lord). When the Jewish (Masoretic) scribes added vowel points to the Hebrew text some six centuries after Christ, they used the vowel points of *adonah* with the letters of "Yahweh" whenever the tetragrammaton appeared in order to remind the reader not to say "Yahweh" but rather *adonah*. Unfortunately, careless translators construed the two words together, resulting in the non-word "Jehovah."

146. Because faith as the very foundation of the spiritual life is so indispensable, Jesus places special emphasis on it throughout the Gospel, for example in Matt 21:21-22, NIV: "If you have faith and do not doubt, not only can you do what was done to the fig tree, but also you can say to this mountain, 'Go, throw yourself into the sea,' and it will be done. If you believe, you will receive whatever you ask for in prayer." And it is no mere coincidence that the anonymous author (Apollos?) of the magnificent Epistle to the Hebrews, faced with a crisis similar to that of "Matthew," namely the very real danger of apostasy on the part of Jewish Christians, also places special emphasis on faith, notably in Heb 11.

147. Please see my brief treatment of this matter in *To Live the Word* 46–47.

RECOMMENDED READING LIST

Brown, Raymond, and Meier, John. *Antioch & Rome: New Testament Cradles of Catholic Christianity.* New York: Paulist, 1983.

Ellis, Peter. *Matthew: His Mind and His Message.* Collegeville: The Liturgical Press, 1974.

Havener, Ivan. *Q: The Sayings of Jesus.* Wilmington, Del.: Michael Glazier, 1987.

Meier, John. *The Vision of Matthew: Christ, Church, and Morality in the First Gospel.* New York: Paulist, 1979.

Schnackenburg, Rudolf. *God's Rule and Kingdom.* New York: Herder and Herder, 1968.

QUESTIONS FOR REFLECTION AND DISCUSSION

1. What do we know about the authorship of The Gospel according to "Matthew"?

2. What seem to have been the circumstances that led to the writing of this Gospel?

3. Why is the Gospel according to "Matthew" called the ecclesial, or Church, gospel?

4. What seem to be the principal lessons for life that we can draw from the Gospel according to "Matthew"?

5. What is "Jewish Christianity" and what relevance may it have for Christianity today?

PHILIPPI

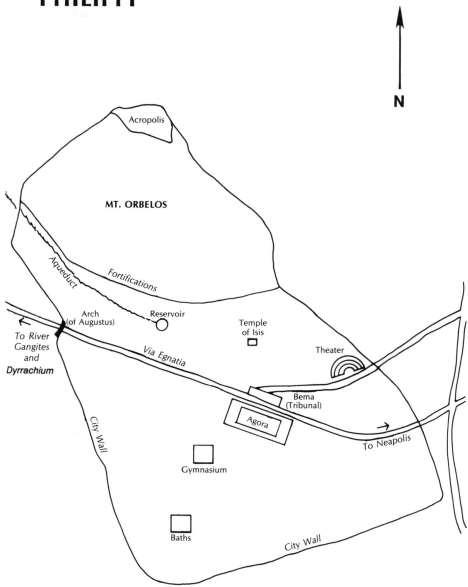

N

Acropolis

MT. ORBELOS

Aqueduct

Fortifications

Reservoir

Arch
(of Augustus)

To River
Gangites
and
Dyrrachium

Via Egnatia

Temple
of Isis

Theater

Bema
(Tribunal)

City Wall

Agora

To Neapolis

Gymnasium

Baths

City Wall

3
Luminous Luke[1] and the Parallel Gospels[2]

THE STORY OF LUKE

A light of revelation for the nations (Luke 2:32)

It was the kind of fall morning that one would like to bottle and save for midwinter: serene blue sky above, white pillars all around gleaming under a brilliant sun, the air crisp and invigorating. How satisfying to be back again in the jewel of Philippi![3] This was the happy thought bringing a warm smile to Luke's gentle face[4] when he heard his name called in a deep, resonant voice. Ah! He would know that sound anywhere. He turned just in time to receive a hearty embrace from his cherished friend Theophilus.[5] What a welcome surprise! They had not seen each other in three whole months, and now, Luke's first morning back, who would show up to join him in his daily constitutional but his excellency, the chief administrator of Philippi and his esteemed fellow Christian, General Theophilus!

"*Chaîre, Theóphile!*[6] How in the world are you, my friend? I've missed seeing you this summer!"

"And I, you, my dear Luke! Life has been boring here without you and your stimulating conversation! Where have you been all this time?"

Luke lowered his eyes. "I know, my friend. It must have seemed careless of me not to apprise you of my whereabouts, but I had to leave in such a hurry that there was no time to inform you. My dear aged mother was dying in our home city of Antioch-on-the-Orontes,[7] and I had all I could do to reach her in time, both as a son and as a physician."[8]

147

"I fully understand, my dear Luke," Theophilus assured him, "but did you reach her in time, and did she recover?"

"No, Theophilus, that was more than I could expect, yet I was at least able to be with her when the Lord took her to himself, and that was a great consolation for us both."

"I'm deeply sorry, Luke. Please accept my very sincere condolences. I've long admired your filial affection[9] for her and only wish I could have known personally the object of such devotion. She must have been an extraordinary lady to have a son like you, so full of love and compassion.[10] May she rest in peace with the Lord as she certainly deserves!"

"Amen!"[11] added Luke. "And thank you, Theophilus, for your sympathy and support. As much as I know she's better off with the Lord, I can't help missing her very deeply. She was all I had left in the world, since my father died many years ago and I have no brothers or sisters.[12] I would gladly have remained with her in Antioch these many years, but the demands of my double vocation as physician and as presbyter[13] have necessitated my presence and dedication here in Philippi. After all, it was blessed Paul himself who not only recruited me for Jesus in Troas[14] but also had me accompany him here and commissioned me as leader of this Church. Thank God, my mother understood and rejoiced that I've been able to serve the Lord and his people in this dual role."

"Well said, my dear friend and spiritual father. What a blessing your presence and ministry have been to me and all our Christian brothers and sisters in this area! What love and peace have pervaded this rough military colony because of you! No, wait! Hear me out! I know that you consider yourself 'an unworthy servant,'[15] but believe me, as the special instrument of the Lord's compassion, you've brought both physical and spiritual healing to an extraordinary number of people, and we'll always be grateful to you and to God because of it."

Luke fell silent. He was embarrassed at these generous and obviously sincere words of his friend, for he knew so well from Paul that it is God alone who "makes things grow."[16] But he also realized that his good friend Theophilus would only continue along the same lines unless he changed the subject, so he quickly did just that. As they continued on the Egnatian Way,[17] leaving the city's impressive Arch of Augustus[18] well behind them and approaching the River Ganga or Gan-

A view of Philippi, where Luke may have written his parallel works.
A view of Mt. Tabor from the ruins of Naim, (where Jesus raised the dead boy in Luke's Gospel).

gites[19] (where Paul and his companions had made their first European convert, the Lady Lydia),[20] he turned to his walking partner and eagerly queried, "What's the news here in Philippi since I left?"

Theophilus thought a moment. The question had caught him off-guard, and as he rummaged around his memory for something to report, he realized that nothing very newsworthy had happened at Philippi in the entire summer. Everything had just gone along as usual but at a slower pace, as so often happens in the summertime. Shaking his head almost apologetically, Theophilus gave his brief account. "I hope you believe me, Luke my friend, when I tell you that nothing very noteworthy has occurred this entire summer. Oh! A few babies were born, and their mothers called for you, but the midwives did a good job of bringing them into the world. A few deaths, but a lot fewer than ever before, come to think of it. No epidemics, no heresies or schisms, no rebellions against Roman rule. Just a nice, quiet, and very hot summer. But what about you? As they like to say in Rome, *Quid nunc?*[21] What news do you bring from your summer away? Knowing you, I feel very confident that taking care of your dying mother in no way prevented you from learning what was going on in the great city of Antioch itself as well as on the journey there and back. So tell me, please, I'm anxious to hear everything."

Luke sighed, not with sadness but with the problem of not knowing just where to begin. As they turned back toward Philippi, dominated by Mount Orbelos with its lofty acropolis[22] rising majestically above the surrounding Plain of Drama,[23] like Mount Tabor[24] over the great and fertile Valley of Esdraelon, he was instantly reminded of something he had learned in Antioch that he couldn't help regarding as uniquely important to the Church.

"I had a most inspiring conversation," he began, "with the blessed bishop of Antioch, Ignatius,[25] who received me with great warmth as he always has and brought me up to date on conditions in the area. Things are going well in the Church there, except for the Jewish Christians.[26] It seems that the Pharisees at Jamnia (you remember I told you about them?) have now gone all out to win them back from Christianity to their own form of Judaism under pain of expulsion from the synagogue as heretics. For me as a Graeco-Syrian and for you as a Graeco-Roman, this might not seem like much of a tragedy, but for our fellow Christians of Jewish origin it's nothing short of catastrophic. They've always felt so much at home, so secure in their attendance at the local synagogue in addition to their worship and life as Christians, followers of the Messiah of the Jews, that having to choose like this is something that cries out for our compassion.''

"I'm truly sorry to hear that," Theophilus assured him, "but surely there's something that can be done to assist them in this wrenching situation, isn't there?"

Luke glanced at him sharply, surprised that he seemed to be anticipating what he, Luke, was going to say next. "As a matter of fact there is indeed something, and I feel it will not only help Jewish Christians but all of us 'followers of the way,'[27] so I'm pretty excited about it. Bishop Ignatius tells me that the leaders of the Jewish Christians at Antioch have gotten together and decided to compose a Jewish gospel to meet the current threat. A Jewish gospel, emphasizing Jesus as Messiah, teacher, and founder of the Church, the new and true Israel, rather than the pseudo-Israel of the Pharisees! Not only that but Ignatius assures me that at his personal request the Jewish Christian presbyter, one Mattathias, a former Pharisee himself, has agreed to write the work in Greek so that it will be available to us all. I just can't tell you, Theophilus, how happy that makes me. I'm as full of admiration for Mark's Gospel as I am for Mark himself, whom I got to know very well when I traveled with Paul to his first Roman imprisonment.[28] But I really think that we could use another gospel, perhaps more refined[29] than Mark had time to make his and with a broader scope. After all, Mark's Gospel, excellent as it is, was written in very special circumstances, Nero's Roman persecution. It's basically a narrative Gospel, with precious little of Jesus' actual teaching. So a gospel which contains a lot of Jesus' teaching and a great deal of emphasis on the Church ought to be a real boon to all of us Christians, Gentile as well as Jew. Don't you think so, Theophilus?"

"Oh! What did you say, Luke? I'm sorry, but I guess my mind was wandering."

"That's not like you, my friend. You must be thinking about your beautiful wife and family, and I don't blame you, for you're a very lucky man indeed. If I didn't have these two vocations which keep me so preoccupied as well as the compelling example of Paul and Jesus himself, I too might have married and reared a large family.''[30]

"Now stop needling me, Luke. I admit I'm terribly devoted to my wife and family, and you would be too if, as you say, you weren't already so taken up with the 'things of the Lord'[31] and the needs, both physical and spiritual, of his people. But that's not what distracted my mind from our interesting conversation. No, it was actually something you yourself said just a few moments ago that caused me to think along certain lines which had never occurred to me before, at least not so clearly as now.''

"Well, well!" kidded Luke, "What have we here? Don't tell me that the head of our Roman colony at Philippi is taking to daydreams and reveries. I know it's a spectacularly beautiful day, especially with the sun now highlighting the entire forum[32] as well as the bema,[33] and certainly the theater[34] (even though we can't see it from here), but these things have never affected you in this way before. Why now? Come on, tell me what's on your mind.''

"All right, Luke, you asked for it, so I'll tell you straight out just what it is that's gotten hold of my mind and won't let go. I think we need yet another gospel in addition to Mark's and this new one being written in Antioch, and moreover, you're the man who ought to write it! There! Now what do you think of that?''

Luke stopped in his tracks as if struck by a lance. "What? Still another gospel? Why? Aren't two enough—Mark's Gospel for Gentile Christians and this new one for Jewish Christians? Let's not overdo a good thing! And what makes you think I have the time, the information, and the inspiration to write a gospel? Please, my friend, I appreciate your confidence, but leave me out of all this!''

"Now wait a minute, Luke," countered Theophilus. "Believe me, I'm the last one who'd want to burden you any more than you've already burdened yourself. I know how dedicated you are, how hard you work, how little rest you allow yourself. But that having been said, let's look at this idea as objectively as we can. First, as you yourself pointed out, Mark's Gospel was written to fill a very particular need, that of our fellow Christians persecuted in Rome by the tyrant Nero. To me that hardly qualifies it as a Gentile gospel in the sense I'm thinking of. And the same is even more true of this new gospel. You yourself called it a 'Jewish gospel,' and I'm sure it'll be just that even if it's written in Greek.

"But that still leaves the need of a truly Gentile gospel or, better still, a truly Greek gospel, one that appeals to cultured people[35] with the accuracy of its history and the cogency of its teaching, yet one that portrays Jesus just as he is, Savior of the whole world and of all kinds of people in the world.[36] And you, Luke, my modest friend, are the one perfectly suited to write it. Syrian you may be, and therefore able to understand the Eastern mentality,[37] but in Greek knowledge, culture, language, and style[38] you have no equal. No one can explain the Lord's teachings as lucidly as you or recount his parables as vividly as you. In addition, you've had the matchless advantage of being the traveling companion of Paul himself. You even have a complete set of his Letters[39] as well as scrolls of Mark's Gospel[40] and the Sayings of Jesus.[41] I even suspect you've got your own collection of Jesus' parables[42] that you've been gathering for some time now. All of us who've been privileged to hear your challenging sermons over the years are most grateful for both their content and their presentation, and for that very reason I feel (no, we feel!) that you ought to draw up in a permanent form with universal appeal, a reliable and inspiring account of Jesus and the Church; reliable because of your sense of history, and inspiring because you're filled with the Holy Spirit. There, I've said it! The Lord must have helped me, for I honestly hadn't given all of this a single thought until now.''

Luke began once more to voice his objections, based on his humble opinion of his worth and abilities as well as the demands of his dual role at Philippi, but Theophilus held up his hand to stop him, for he knew that he had ''shot all his arrows''[43] and would have to leave it to Someone greater than he to ''win the battle'' of convincing and persuading his humble friend. As they entered the monumental arch and strode along the Egnatian Way between the forum on the right and the tribunal with its prison on the left (probably where Paul and his friends had been scourged, imprisoned, and miraculously released, bringing Theophilus and his family[44] the most wonderful life and happiness they had ever known), the administrator stopped, turned to Luke, and in his most earnest voice suggested, ''Look, I know this whole idea is quite a shock to you, my friend, so I'm not asking you to make a decision right now. All I ask is that you think about it and pray over it, then whatever the Lord and his guiding Spirit move you to do will be perfectly acceptable to me. When this idea came to me during your account it must've come from God himself, who knows I'm not the kind of man that could think of something like this on my own. Maybe I'm wrong and it's just a delusion. I just don't know. So all I ask of you, my friend, is to pray and reflect on the idea, then please let me know what you've decided. Will you do that for an old friend, or rather for the Lord himself and his people?''

"Well, since you put it that way, how can I refuse? I make no promises, not even to you, except to do as you ask, namely to pray for guidance on what to do in view of the needs and possibilities. So give me some time.[45] How much time I have no idea, but I'll get back to you as soon as I'm clear in my own mind and heart about what the Lord is asking of me in this matter. In the meantime, have a good day, give my best to your wife and family, pray for me, and let me get started on my twin duties for the day."

"Fine, my esteemed friend," replied Theophilus, "and may you also have a peaceful day. *Kaleméra!*"[46]

After the departure of his friend, Luke hastened to take care of his daily duties, but even in the midst of his most pressing obligations one thing kept clamoring for his attention—the urgent suggestion of Theophilus. By midafternoon the dedicated physician-presbyter found himself so enmeshed in the whole idea that he decided to postpone the remainder of his day's work and concentrate his energies on prayer and reflection regarding the subject.

Feeling the need of being totally removed from distractions and of devoting himself exclusively to prayer and union with Christ, he hastened to climb Mount Orbelos to the acropolis, where he could sit undisturbed and completely open to the voice of God revealing his holy will. Unlike the more famous Acropolis of Athens, that of Philippi was only a collection of fortifications, unused since the famous Battle of Philippi in 42 B.C., but from its perch atop Mount Orbelos a thousand feet above the plain it afforded the visitor a majestic view of all the surrounding area. Here Luke was accustomed to find refuge from the problems and preoccupations below so that, like Jesus[47] himself, he might be able to commune with the Father in deep contemplation. Particularly at sunset he felt one with the Lord and attuned to his guiding Spirit—almost as if he could reach up and touch the face of God!

As Luke settled himself in this ideal locale and with artistic appreciation,[48] gazed out over the peaceful beauty surrounding him, he could not help thinking how natural and appropriate it was for Moses, Elijah, and above all Jesus[49] to have their mystical experiences of union with God on or at a special mountain like this. Imperceptibly the words of young Samuel formed themselves in his open mind and heart: "Speak, Lord, for your servant is listening!"[50]

Then, like Elijah at Mount Horeb,[51] he endured in quick succession a storm of mixed emotions, an earthquake of uncertainty beyond control, and even a fire of deep resentment over the added burdens he was being asked to assume. Hadn't he "left all things"[52] to follow Jesus? And wasn't his entire life a total service to God and neighbor? The Lord knew him inside and out;[53] how could he possibly seek from him such an onerous service as that of writing a gospel? Instinctively however, he knew that "God was not in the storm, nor in the earthquake, nor in the fire."[54] No, only in the "gentle whisper"[55] that followed did he find rest, peace, and sure awareness of God's loving presence and unquestionable will.

Without a word Luke surrendered himself[56] to that will, certain that the Lord was indeed calling him to the difficult task of writing a gentile gospel and would as surely make it possible for him to complete it. In the words of Paul, his incomparable mentor and cherished friend, he was able to declare with complete confidence, "I can do all things in him who gives me strength!"[57]

More than this momentous decision Luke was simply incapable of handling that evening. He would leave until another time such burning questions as How will this gospel differ from those of Mark and Mattathias? Which of my scrolls should I use as the main source or sources of this gospel? Do I even have enough source material to write a work worthy of being called a gospel? If not, where can I find further material? Ephesus? Rome? Jerusalem? Antioch? But I've just returned from Antioch! How can I possibly get away again so soon?

Then there would be such further questions as: how to develop his gospel, what the overriding theme and subthemes would be, and what structures to use. No, all of this was entirely too much to wrestle with that evening. The sun was already setting and there was only enough daylight left for him to find his way home and get some much-needed rest.

Sleep came to Luke that evening with unusual swiftness (the Lord be blessed!). But even in sleep his mind kept on functioning, with the result that upon arising in the morning, he found to his surprise that many of his questions had already been answered, that he had somehow acquired a far clearer vision of what to do and how to do it. At first he tended to discount this vision. It seemed to resemble so much the dream analyses of the Aesculapian physicians at Epidaurus and Pergamum,[58] whose methods he had rejected as a student at the Hippocratic school of medicine on the island of Cos.[59] The more he thought about it, however, the more he was able to discern the differences, to consider, at least, what his semiconscious mind had produced.

First of all, his main focus would center on Jesus, the universal and compassionate Savior. He certainly felt right at home with that theme because he had learned it so well from Paul, the great Apostle of the Gentiles, as well as from his daily medical ministrations. Thus, for example, while Mark had used the miracles of Jesus to paint his portrait of Jesus Christ, the powerful Son of God, who nevertheless became the Suffering Servant of Yahweh, and while Mattathias (so he had heard) was using the miracles primarily to introduce the discourses of Jesus, he, Luke, would show Jesus using his miraculous powers even without being asked,[60] thus exemplifying his boundless compassion for all, particularly the most neglected and rejected[61] of the society in which Jesus lived: Gentiles and Samaritans, sinners and slaves, the sick and the maimed, women and the poor. What a demonstration that God's ways are not like our ways![62]

This portrait of Jesus, albeit central, would then lead to another focus: the Church which he had founded, for this also needed to be emphasized. But how? Above all, by showing clearly that it was founded precisely to continue the life, ministry, and suffering of Jesus[63] himself throughout the ages. "And how," Luke wondered, "can I accomplish that effectively? I have it! By composing not just one but two gospels: one of Jesus in his life, death, and resurrection, and one of Jesus continuing to live, teach, and sanctify in and through the Church!"

This of course was nothing new, for Luke had learned it from Paul, who had learned it the hard way from Jesus himself: "I am Jesus whom you are persecuting!"[64] And in all of Paul's Letters, so cherished by Luke, that theme of the union of Christ and his Church remained central explicitly or implicitly. "But wait! Isn't there more?"

"Yes, of course, there's the place of the Church in salvation history. With the destruction of Jerusalem in A.D. 70, it had become clear that Jesus would not return anytime soon. In fact, he might not return in triumph for a long, long time. Meanwhile, he would be with his own in and through his Church.[65] Which means that in salvation history there are really three epochs:[66] that of Israel, beginning with the call of Abram; that of Jesus the Christ or Messiah of Israel and Savior of the world; and finally that of the Church, 'the fullness of Christ,'[67] until his return.

"But here," thought Luke, "a salutary caution is in order. The risen Christ continues to live and serve in his Church, yes, but the Church is composed of human members. And where humans are involved, as Jesus himself warned, there will be sins and scandals.[68] In particular, humans are prone to sins and scandals of pride, greed, and sensuality.[69] A gospel that is truly relevant should therefore help Christians remain true to their pristine fervor and grow in the humility, poverty, and purity which Jesus exhibited throughout his life, both in example and teaching. So, while I am portraying Jesus in the gospel as the universal, compassionate Savior, I must be careful to picture him also as the most demanding of masters, especially in these three areas, which make up the principal dangers to Christian, indeed, to human life."

Thanks to his fruitful slumber Luke awoke already filled with a multitude of ideas that would serve well in developing his Gentile gospel. But he still had to face questions about such important matters as sources and structures. In the matter of sources, thank God he already had the Gospel of Mark, based on the kerygma and tradition of the Church as well as the testimony of Peter, and he could certainly save some time and effort by following Mark's already accepted lead and hanging the portrait of Jesus on the four pegs of the baptism and witness of John the Baptist, the Galilean ministry, the journey to Jerusalem, and the saving events in Jerusalem.

"But," thought Luke, "if I'm writing twin gospels, one showing Jesus in his public life and the other revealing him in his ecclesial life, perhaps it would be well to distinguish them clearly by confining the earthly ministry of Jesus to Israel itself and waiting until the second book to show him ministering to the gentile world through his Church, in fact, through his two greatest leaders and missionaries, Peter and Paul. In this arrangement, of course, I must consciously omit those sections of Mark[70] which place Jesus outside of Israel, but that won't be too difficult.

"All right, so much for Mark, but I will certainly need more than his Gospel or my efforts will be narrow indeed. Well, there's also that collection of the Sayings of Jesus which I understand Mattathias is using quite extensively, since his focus is on Jesus the teacher. As Theophilus perceived, I've used much of that material in my sermons apparently with good effect, so it should also provide a helpful source for the gospel. And then of course, I'll try to keep my eyes and ears open for other sayings and parables of Jesus,[71] a few of which I've already been fortunate enough to gather little by little for some time now, particularly while I was at Caesarea Maritima[72] in Judea during blessed Paul's imprisonment there. What a glorious opportunity that was to visit the places where the Lord had lived and labored, suffered and died! And what a treasure of additional sayings and parables, few in quantity but invaluable in quality, did I discover at that special time, when I had the chance to interview various disciples who had walked and talked with but above all listened to the Lord! Now I begin to see how the providence of God works! I thought I was making that collection for my own knowledge, or at most for use in preaching and teaching. Little did I dream that I was doing it to paint a vivid portrait of Jesus in a gospel!"

Luke stopped the rapid flow of his thoughts, strangely puzzled over what he vaguely perceived to be a lacuna in the source material he needed for his twin gospels. "What could it be? I think I do have more than enough of Jesus' words and deeds for an inspiring gospel. And I've been blessed in my life to know both Peter and Paul, from whom, as from others in Jerusalem, Judea, Samaria, Galilee, and Antioch, I have a rather complete picture of the early life of the Church in those areas. What then? I honestly don't know, but I believe I do know how to find out! Why not pay a visit to the venerable Apostle John at Ephesus?[73] I've a feeling that he can supply some additional information, perhaps about the blessed mother of Jesus, or maybe about Jesus himself but known only to Mary and through her to John. Yes, that's what I'll do! The first chance I get, I'll make the short trip to fabulous Ephesus.

"Now, what about structures, those careful arrangements of materials which can make such a difference in the clearness and coherence of any writing? Well, to begin with, if I'm writing twin gospels, one of Jesus in himself and one of Jesus in the Church, then I already have the setting for parallels.[74] I can see a running parallel between Jesus and the Church. Yes, and what about a parallel between the story of Peter and the story of Paul in the second work?

"Secondly, it might help if I include the structure of inclusion-conclusion[75] in both books, making sure that each work has its own distinctive theme at the beginning and end. And I'm confident that it won't be too difficult to fit in some of the other characteristic structures that help to make writings clearer and more readable, such as triplets,[76] concentric circles,[77] and chiasmus.[78] But I'd also like to add a structure which is part of my very nature, one that I can best designate simply as a 'journey structure.'[79] As a physician and later as a presbyter I see journeys as part of the very fabric of my life, and the Lord has enabled me to make 'a virtue of necessity'[80] by seeing journeys in a spiritual way as a mirror of my very life. We are all on a mystical journey with Jesus to the life of glory. We are all pilgrims on the way,[81] the road, of salvation. Then why not expand the journey segment[82] of the kerygma to comprise all those lessons and virtues that should characterize Christians in following Christ to the heavenly Jerusalem? And why not make the whole story of the early Church a journey from Jerusalem to 'the ends of the earth,'[83] symbolized by Rome, the center of the known civilized world? But that's only the external journey, so to speak. In addition, there's also an internal journey, as the Church under the guidance of Jesus and his Spirit slowly but surely finds its way from a purely Jewish matrix to the universal, integrated 'body of Christ'[84] that Jesus intended: the new 'people of God, ekklesía,'[85] called out of all the nations of the earth to be the whole Christ, continuing his life and ministry until the end of the ages!

"Whew! I can't believe I've gotten into this whole idea so quickly and completely. Won't Theophilus be surprised when I report to him that I've not only agreed to follow his suggestion but I've also gone a long way toward visualizing what this gentile gospel (rather, these twin gospels) will look like. In fact, I've even caught much of his enthusiasm,[86] as our gracious Lord has enabled me to picture the possibilities. Thank you, my loving Savior, for your generous graces and gifts. May these gospels truly be the work of your Holy Spirit for your greater glory and the inspiration of your holy people!"

Theophilus was completely astonished when after such a short time Luke was able to give him a positive report which went far beyond what he had initially envisioned. Not one but two gospels! Twin gospels! What an inspired idea! He was filled with awe at the way the Lord was so evidently working, even through him but especially in the mind and heart of his good friend Luke, to provide his followers with still another gospel, in fact two gospels, which promised to be extraordinary indeed. He realized, of course, that deciding on and planning these gospels constituted only the beginning. Inspired or not, writing was no easy task,[87] even for someone of Luke's talents. It would still be some time before even the first of Luke's gospels would be finished, but Theophilus had to confess that he could hardly wait for that moment. In the meantime, he fully concurred in Luke's proposal to visit the venerable John, and he promised to help in any way he could to enable Luke to make the visit sooner rather than later.

As luck or Providence would have it Luke had to wait only a month before a favorable opportunity presented itself, and he immediately took advantage of it, embarking on an Egyptian ship departing from Neapolis,[88] the port of Philippi, and sailing by the coastal route[89] to the port of Ephesus.[90] It had been years since Luke had beheld the fabled beauties of that illustrious city, one of the four principal centers of the Roman Empire, and then as now his visit was of necessity a brief one. As his vessel navigated the narrow Cayster River[91] into the protected harbor of Ephesus, Luke promised himself that someday, God willing, he would really do the metropolis justice. But for now he was determined to see the Apostle John as quickly as possible and then be on his way back to Philippi, his dual ministry, and the additional project of his twin gospels.

With that in mind he disembarked, strode rapidly up the monumental Arcadian Way,[92] turned right at the great theater[93] (where Paul had occasioned the riot of the silversmiths), and hurried up to where he hoped to find John. His hope was not dashed, for (blessed be the Lord!) John was exactly where Luke was told he could find him. There he was, the last living apostle, engaged in teaching a group of young people about Jesus. Of course! What else would he be doing? Mary, his blessed charge,[94] had passed on to reunion with her Son in heaven about twenty years before, and since then John, sedulously avoiding administration,[95] had dedicated himself to preaching, teaching, and personal guidance of both clergy and laity.

Luke held back, unwilling to interrupt the patriarch's loving lesson and frankly enjoying his saintly presence. But as if alerted by some inner voice, John turned and acknowledged Luke's presence with a smile that lit up the eyes of all around him, including Luke's. What a face! Aged, yes, but somehow still youthful, preserved in the love of Jesus and his holy mother. Recognizing in Luke a kindred soul, John dismissed his young students with a gentle smile and blessing, then turned to his visitor with a gracious "The Lord be with you,"[96] to which Luke eagerly responded, "And also with you!" Arm in arm they repaired to John's quarters where Luke introduced himself rather timidly, sensing that somehow John already recognized him—a sense confirmed by the recognition in his deep-set eyes.

After some preliminary questions about the state of the Church in Philippi and its surrounding area, John opened his hands and his heart with a simple question. "How may I serve you?" Luke was not sure and said so but explained his twin project insofar as he could and left it to John, with his inner vision, to suggest how he might be able to contribute to it. The "beloved disciple"[97] knew immediately what Luke was seeking. "You want to know about Mary and about the early years of Jesus,[98] don't you?"

"Yes, of course," sputtered Luke. "If I'm to draw up parallel gospels of Jesus and the Church, and the latter will of necessity include the Church's infancy,[99] then I need an "infancy gospel"[100] for the story about Jesus, don't I?" And a radiant smile suffused his face, for his quandary was over and he knew exactly why he had come. Then a cloud erased the smile and he remarked apologetically, "But I don't want to pry into anything that may be confidential. Has blessed Mary even divulged to you her story and that of Jesus in his infancy and youth? And if so, are you free to share that information with others?"

John's relaxed face was reassuring. "In answer to your questions, dear Luke, yes, Mary did indeed tell me in all simplicity and humility her beautiful story—before, at, and after the infancy of her divine Son. But no, I cannot tell it to others as a general rule. Only to someone like yourself, who obviously love Jesus with your whole being and have been chosen to spread his story far and wide now and for ages to come. I will therefore gladly tell the story, for (as you might imagine) it is a joy to do so, and I leave it to you under the guidance of the Holy Spirit to use it as you think best.

"I trust that in planning and writing your twin gospels you will use all of God's gifts to you, natural and supernatural. Do not hesitate to reword accounts[101] in ways that will best serve your overall purpose and plan. This is why the Lord has given you an education and talents granted to very few people. Someday he may indicate that he wants me, yes, even me, to write a gospel. So far he has not, and therefore I very gladly share what I know with you for his greater honor and glory." Then he proceeded to tell the beautiful story of Mary, Joseph, and the child Jesus, all the while with an angelic smile that indicated more than words ever could how much he enjoyed recalling not only his three short years with Jesus but also his longer years with Mary, whom Jesus had entrusted to his care.

When he finished there was silence in the room for a long time. John had completed his account, and Luke was too overcome to put his feelings into words. Eventually John broke the silence. "Do you have any questions about the story, or is there anything else you need to know?"

Luke pondered a few minutes. What an opportunity! He must not let it pass, for never again would he be in the presence of such a saint and such a treasury of personal knowledge of the Savior. So he did make bold to ask John about the additional stories and parables of Jesus that he had collected over the years, in order to ensure that they were authentic. They were. And not only did John authenticate them, but he also added details and even some entire stories and parables that Luke had never heard before.

Finally Luke decided to ask a general question that had been bothering him. He fully intended to make references to the Hebrew Testament not only in quoting Jesus (who was immersed in the Scriptures) but also in drawing connections on his own between the story of Israel and the story of Jesus and the Church. The question was, did he have to make direct quotations, which he might find difficult and sometimes even impossible because of literary demands, or could he simply allude to ideas, events, words,[102] and the like from the Hebrew Testament, a practice that would permit many more references and still not unduly extend the length of his twin gospels?

John's patience, the first quality of Christian love,[103] knew no bounds as he assured Luke that the practice of allusions instead of direct quotations would not only be perfectly permissible but even desirable at times for the very reason proposed, namely not to extend the account too long. Luke's relief was evident in his face. He felt more confident than he ever had, and as he took leave of the venerable John after a light repast, his step was far lighter and more buoyant than when he arrived.

Since the splendid city was such a commercial, artistic, and religious center, there was a multitude of ships ready to sail, and Luke was fortunate to find one bound for Neapolis almost at once. Boarding it with a sense of relief and gratitude to God, he found a somewhat private and comfortable corner where he was able to drop his bag and stretch out for a rest. What a rest! He had forgotten how long it had been since he had enjoyed a good night's sleep and how tense he had been at the prospect of a private conversation with the most revered person[104] in the Christian world. No sooner had he settled himself than a deep sleep enveloped him and restored all the energies that he had been expending without fully realizing it.

Upon arrival back at Neapolis and then Philippi, Luke sought out his friend Theophilus and wasted no time in reporting to him about his inspiring visit with John, to the delight and even the envy of his faithful friend. The rest is history or, better still, "His Story," known to us as The Gospel according to Luke, and the parallel first history of the Church, known simply as Acts of Apostles.[105]

ANALYSIS OF LUKE'S WRITINGS

We will follow the same order of treatment that we did with the Gospels of Mark and "Matthew" with one very obvious difference: With Luke we are involved with two books, twin Gospels, the parallel Gospel according to Luke and his Acts of Apostles. In all other ways, however, we shall endeavor to take up the same considerations and in the same order that we did with Mark and "Matthew" so that the reader may more easily make comparisons[106] and also remember the material involved. Our treatment of Luke's works will be divided into two segments: first, an overview in outline form for the sake of clarity, understanding, and memory; and secondly, some outlines of the twin Gospels so that in reading them we may more easily derive the depth of riches which they contain.

I. **Overview**

    A. General impression

        1. These twin works of Luke constitute the largest block of literature by any New Testament author, larger even than

all the writings attributed to either Paul or John. Obviously, then, a good understanding and appreciation of these parallel books helps us to grasp a good portion of the New Testament as a whole.

2. Written in impeccable Greek,[107] these works clearly manifest themselves as addressed to a primarily gentile readership, in fact, the widest possible readership, including the highly educated as well as the less educated but more neglected and rejected, those who are the special objects of the compassion of Jesus, the universal Savior, and of Luke himself.

3. Similar to Mark in begin written for Gentile Christians and to "Matthew" in its strong emphasis on the Church, its careful arrangement, and its wide use of structures, it nevertheless differs from both in its historical perspective, its stress on universalism, its multiple allusions (especially in the "Infancy Gospel"), its portrait of Jesus as totally compassionate but also totally demanding, and its picture of the Church as continuing the life, ministry, and sufferings of Jesus until he comes again.

4. Twin works featuring journeys, real and symbolic; multiple adventures, particularly in Acts; plus fascinating parables more dynamic, challenging, and memorable than those in Mark and "Matthew." In addition, scrupulously refined in softening many of Mark's hurried and rough-hewn expressions.

5. Like Mark and "Matthew," containing many miracles, but Luke does not recount Jesus' miracles, like Mark, to establish his divinity (despite which he freely chooses to die for us) or, like "Matthew," to establish his authority to teach in the name of God and even in his own name as in Matt 5:21-48. No, in Luke, Jesus' miracles are worked out of compassion by the universal Savior of all, particularly in favor of the most rejected and neglected by fellow human beings.

6. In addition to the main theme or themes such as Jesus, Divine Physician and Good Shepherd who out of loving compassion personally or through the Church feeds the hungry, heals the wounded, and rescues the lost, Luke's twin works

(above all, the Gospel) contain several subthemes that cause them to be referred to as the Gospels of the Holy Spirit, of women, of prayer, and of joy.[108]

B. Composition

1. Circumstances

   After the destruction of Jerusalem, the delay in Jesus' return, and the spread of the Church among Gentiles, there was need of a genuine gentile gospel portraying Jesus as the universal, compassionate Savior, especially of the neglected, and of the Church as continuing the life, ministry, and sufferings of that Savior, compassionate yet vigorously combating the tendency of her members to succumb to pride, greed, sensuality.

2. Authorship

   a) Who was better suited to write such a gospel, (rather, twin gospels) than Luke, compassionate physician, companion of Paul, and as his appointed presbyter, leader of the Church at Philippi and friend of the chief magistrate?

   b) There is virtually no dispute about Lukan authorship of his Gospel and Acts. Luke was no more an apostle or major Church official than Mark, and so the only logical reason for attributing these parallel works to him is that he actually wrote them.

   c) That having been said it must be added that outside of a virtual consensus on the general date of composition (A.D. 80–85) there is no agreement on where Luke wrote or what caused him to write. However, because of the Scriptures which seem to indicate that Luke stayed at Philippi[109] after going there with Paul and that he dedicated both books to one Theophilus whom he addresses as "Your Excellency," I have chosen to see the latter as a friend of Luke and magistrate of Philippi,[110] urging him to write what eventually became the twin works.

3. Purposes

   a) To provide a thoroughly gentile, universal, and historical portrait of Jesus Christ as compassionte Savior of all, especially the most neglected and rejected

    b) To provide a thoroughly Gentile, universal, and histori-
cal portrait of the Church as continuing the life, ministry, and sufferings of Jesus until the end of time

    c) To combat the natural temptation of the Church and its
members to lose their pristine fervor and fall victim to the
temptations of pride, self-indulgence, and greed

    d) Possibly also to provide an apologetic which would help
Christians and non-Christians to understand and accept
the innocence of Jesus and the Church of any subversion
against Jewish or Roman authority and the gradual evo-
lution whereby Christianity, born in a Jewish milieu,
quickly became a largely gentile religion

4. Sources

    a) Like "Matthew," Luke's Gospel depends on the Gospel
of Mark for most of its narrative content and order and
on the Sayings of Jesus, or *Q*, for much of its discourse
material.

    b) Underlying the Gospel of Mark and therefore Luke as well
are the Church's kerygma[111] (baptism, Galilean ministry,
journey to Jerusalem, and saving events in Jerusalem) and
also the segments, or forms, of tradition[112] that had developed in the Church largely in response to questions
and problems arising in the Church's life, all of which occasioned reminiscences about the words and deeds of
Jesus.

    c) An unknown source or sources, oral or written, from
which Luke derived the material unique to his Gospel
(and Acts of Apostles) as hinted at in his dedication to
Theophilus

        (1) Of particular interest is the origin of the unique ac-
tion parables[113] in the long journey section of Luke's
Gospel. Are they from a distinct source or sources?
Or from *Q*, but omitted by "Matthew" because more
personal than ecclesial? In any case, do they draw
their excellence of storytelling composition from Jesus
or from Luke himself? The answer is not clear, but it
may involve a combination of possibilities.

(2) Where did Luke draw the material for his history of the early Church, known as his Acts of Apostles?

    (a) Did he have one or more Palestinian sources, for example, Paul, John, Mark, Cornelius, Philip and other deacons?

    (b) Did he have one or more Antiochean sources, for example, Paul, Silas, and others who are named in Acts 13:1?

    (c) His own diary for the "we sections" of Acts 16:10-17; 20:5–21:25; 27:1–28:16?

5. Structures

    a) As a Graeco-Syrian, probably born at Antioch in Syria but well educated and well traveled, Luke must have been thoroughly familiar with literary structures of both the East and West.

    b) Like "Matthew," he does seem to use such structures as inclusion-conclusion, concentric circles, and chiasmus,[114] as we will see in the following outlines.

    c) But the structures he favors are not the prime favorites of "Matthew," rather parallels and journeys[115] (plus triplets) as will be clearer in the outline segment of this analysis.

II. Outlines

A. Preliminary remarks

1. Out of several possible outlines of Luke's works, I have chosen to include the following ones as most likely to provide the reader with a clear picture of the unfolding of Luke's twin Gospels.

2. Specifically, the following outlines include

    a) one of Luke's Gospel highlighting material unique to Luke, which gives us an "x-ray" picture of Luke's thought and structures;

    b) an outline of Luke-Acts showing the parallels between Christ and the Church and, in Acts, between the acts of Peter and the acts of Paul;

       c) an outline of Acts revealing the development and spread of the Church in concentric circles.

   3. Not included are complete, detailed outlines of Luke-Acts, obtainable from any good commentary.

B. Outline of the Gospel according to Luke

   1. Prologue (1:1-4)
      Dedication to Theophilus

   2. Infancy Gospel (1:5–2:52)
      An overture of Lukan themes in a diptych of seven scenes comprising seventy weeks, in probable allusion to Dan 9:24[116]

     a) Annunciation diptych (1:5-56)

       (1) Annunciation of John at the Temple (1:5-25)

       (2) Annunciation of Jesus at Nazareth[117] (1:26-38)

       (3) Complementary episode: visitation at Ain Karim[118] (1:39-56)

     b) Birth diptych (1:57–2:52)

       (1) Birth of John at Ain Karim (1:57-80)

       (2) Birth of Jesus at Bethlehem[119] (2:1-20)

       (3) Circumcision, Temple presentation[120] (2:21-40)

       (4) Complementary episode: finding of Jesus in the Temple,[121] his obedience and growth (2:41-52)

   3. Preparation for ministry (3:1–4:13)

     a) Historical setting[122] (3:1-2)

     b) John the Baptist at the River Jordan[123] (3:3-20)

     c) Baptism of Jesus, Son and Servant of God[124] (3:21-22)

     d) Genealogy of Jesus, Savior of all[125] (3:23-38)

     e) Jesus' temptations, ending at the Temple of Jerusalem (4:1-13)

   4. The Galilean ministry (4:14–9:50)

     a) Opening of Jesus' messianic ministry (4:14-44)

       (1) Messianic manifesto at Nazareth[126] (4:14-30)

       (2) Preaching, miracles at Capernaum (4:31-44)

     b) Galilean ministry (5:1–9:50 seven Lukan events)

       (1) Disciples called,[127] apostles chosen (5:1-11, 27-32; 6:12-16)

(2) Sermon on the Plain[128] (6:17-49, cf. Matt 5-7)

(3) The widow's son raised at Naim (7:11-17) ⎤ All

(4) Mercy to the penitent woman (7:36-50) ⎬ about

(5) Ministry of the women[129] to Jesus (8:1-2) ⎦ women

(6) Mission of the Twelve, Peter's profession, conditions of discipleship (9:1-6, 18-27)

(7) Transfiguration, second prophecy (9:28-36, 43-45)

5. Journey to Jerusalem[130] (9:51–19:27, Christian life)

   a) Events involving Samaritans: inhospitality, mission of the seventy-two,[131] good Samaritan (9:51–10:37)

   b) Teachings on prayer: Martha/Mary, Our Father, prayer parables (10:38–11:13)

   c) Teachings on trust (12:1-34), penance and preparedness (12:35–13:9, 22-20, 34-35)

   d) Teachings on humility (14:1-11), charity: (14:12-24), renunciation (14:25-35)

   e) Teachings on sin/repentance/mercy: lost sheep, lost coin, lost son[132] (15:1-32)

   f) Teachings on the right use of material goods: unjust steward, rich man/Lazarus (16:1-31)

   g) Miscellaneous teachings: forgiveness, faith, humility, gratitude (17:1-19), persevering prayer (18:1-8), pride and humility (18:9-14)

   h) Events at Jericho: blind man, Zacchaeus, parable of the money (18:35–19:27)

6. The Jerusalem ministry (19:28–21:38, messianic entry,[133] lament, controversies, eschatological discourse)

7. Salvation at Jerusalem

   a) Preliminary events: (22:1-38, betrayal, Passover and Eucharist, ambition, promise and prediction to Peter[134])

   b) Passion events: (22:39–23:56, agony and arrest, trials and denials, way of the cross and crucifixion, death and burial)

   c) Resurrection events: (24:1-53, women at the tomb, two disciples of Emmaus,[135] commission, ascension,[136] return to the Temple at Jerusalem)

C. Parallel outlines I: Jesus in himself and the Church

Gospel of St. Luke	Acts of Apostles
1. Prologue to Theophilus (1:1-4)	1. Prologue to Theophilus[137] (1:1-3)
2. Jesus' infancy (Temple), beginning at Jerusalem (1:5-2:52)	2. The Church's infancy (kingdom), beginning at Jerusalem (1:4-26)
3. Jesus anointed with the Spirit at his baptism (3:1-4:13)	3. The Church anointed with the Spirit at her baptism (2:1-13)
4. Jesus' Galilean ministry: preaching, miracles (4:14-9:50)	4. The Church's Palestinian ministry: preaching, miracles (2:14-11:18)
5. Journey to Jerusalem of Jesus and Christians (9:51-19:27)	5. Journey to "the earth's ends" of Paul and the Church (11:19-21:14)
6. Jesus: Savior of all by the cross (19:28-24:51)	6. Paul/Church: witnesses to all by the "cross" (21:15-28:28)
7. Epilog: Temple (24:52-53)	7. Epilog: Kingdom (28:30-31)

D. Parallel outlines II: the acts of Peter and Paul[138]

1. Peter's authority in the Church (1:15-26)	1. Paul's authority in the Sanhedrin (8:3; 9:1-2)
2. Peter empowered by the Holy Spirit (2:1-4)	2. Paul empowered by the Holy Spirit (13:2-3)
3. Peter's first discourse (2:14-41)	3. Paul's first discourse (13:16-43)
4. Peter's crucial vision (10:9-23; 11:1-18; 15:5-12)	4. Paul's crucial vision (9:1-9; 22:5-16; 26:9-17)
5. Peter sees the Spirit come upon Gentiles (10:34-48)	5. Paul sees the Spirit come upon Gentiles (19:1-7)
6. Peter's miracles	6. Paul's miracles

a) General
     Shadow cures (5:15-16)
	a) General
	     Cloth cures[139] (19:11-12)

b) Special	*b)* Special

(1) Cure of a lame man (3:1-10; 9:32-35)	(1) Cure of a lame man (14:8-18)
(2) Raising of the dead (9:36-43)	(2) Raising of the dead (20:7-12)
(3) Defeat of a magician (8:9-24)	(3) Defeat of a magician (13:6-12)

7. Peter's persecutions

    a) Before the Sanhedrin (4:5-22)

    b) Scourging by the Jews (5:40)

    c) Prison and release (5:18-19; 12:6-11)

    d) Persecuted by Herod Agrippa I (12:1-5)

7. Paul's persecutions

    a) Before the Sanhedrin (22:30–23:11)

    b) Scourging by the Romans (16:22-23)

    c) Prison and release (16:25-26)

    d) Hearing before Herod Agrippa II (25:13–26:32)

E. Ecclesial Outline of Acts of Apostles, showing the Church's growth and development in concentric circles after Jesus' commission in Acts 1:8 (Note: In this broad outline, chapters only are given.)

  1. The Church in Jerusalem (1–5): A.D. 30

    a) Before Pentecost: commission, ascension, election of Matthias (1)

    b) During Pentecost: outpouring (baptism) of the Spirit, Peter's discourse (2)

    c) After Pentecost: ideal community (summaries), encounter with Judaism (3–5)

  2. Church growth beyond Jerusalem (6–12): A.D. 30–46

    a) Appointment and apostolate of seven deacons (6–8)

    b) Conversion of Paul, Apostle to the Gentiles (9; also 22; 26)

    c) Vision of Peter, conversion of Cornelius (10; also 11; 15)

    d) Ministry to Gentiles at Antioch; Christians (11)

    e) Herod's Palestinian persecution; Peter imprisoned, released, goes elsewhere. Antioch? Rome? (12)

3. Apostolate to the Gentile world (13–28): A.D. 46–62/63

   a) Paul's 1st Mission: Cyprus, South Asia Minor (13–14)

   b) The Council of Jerusalem: pro-gentile "dogma" (15)

   c) Paul's 2nd Mission: Asia Minor and Greece (16–19)

   d) Paul's 3rd Mission: Asia Minor and Greece (19–20)

   e) Paul's Jerusalem arrest, Caesarean imprisonment (21–26)

   f) Paul's voyage to Rome in chains, shipwreck. Rome: two-year house arrest, preaching, teaching[140] (27–28)

LUKE'S WORKS AND OUR LIFE

In this third and final segment of our study of Luke and his writings, we will do well to consider the following subjects: (1) Luke's portrait of the compassion of God and his Son, Jesus Christ, the universal Savior, with special emphasis on the portrait of Jesus and Mary in the annunciation and visitation accounts; (2) Luke's portrait of the Church as continuing the life and ministry of Christ in its leadership and membership; and (3) Luke's subthemes and conditions for the "followship" of Christ in our journey to the heavenly Jerusalem. These biblical, theological, and spiritual reflections should enable us to extract much of the "sweetness and light" in which Luke's writings abound.

Our Compassionate God

The word "compassion" has a very instructive etymology, being derived from the Latin word *compassio*,[141] which in turn is composed of *cum* or *con* (with) and *passio* (suffering) from the verb *patior* (I suffer). Thus it means nothing less than "suffering with" someone, as does the related word "sympathy" from the Greek *sympátheia*,[142] composed of *syn* (with) and *páthos* (suffering) from the verb *páscho* or *pathéo* (I suffer). Perhaps even more instructive, however, is the Hebrew word for compassion, *rahamim*,[143] the plural of *raham*, meaning the womb! How beautifully this relates to those tender, feminine, nurturing expressions of Yahweh in the Old Testament and of Jesus in the New, especially in the Gospel of Luke (see Isa 49:15-16; Matt 23:37-39; Luke 13:34-35; 19:41-44).

All of these expressions help us to get away from the abstract image of God as the great unmoved mover above and beyond any possibility of involvement in our pain and suffering. That is the picture that many of us received from Thomistic philosophy and theology, which maintains that we relate to God but he does not relate to us[144] because, if he did, he would somehow be dependent on us, which of course would involve an impossibility. Fortunately the process theologians today have discovered what was clear in the Bible all along, that God does relate to us with the relationship of love,[145] which is a perfection, not an imperfection. In fact, God is love itself, as John tells us so beautifully in 1 John 4:8, 16.

It is precisely the compassionate dimension of God's love for us that preoccupies Jesus in Luke's writings, especially the Gospel. "Be compassionate as your Father is compassionate!" (Luke 6:36, NAB). And both before and after that powerful statement in Jesus' Sermon on the Plain, we find examples of how we can best practice that compassion: "Love your enemies" (6:27 ff.), "give to all who beg from you" (6:30), "lend without expecting repayment" (6:35), "do not judge or condemn, but pardon" (6:37), "give and it shall be given to you in good measure" (6:38). And as if we need a concrete example of God's compassion, Jesus and Luke provide it in that magnificent parable of the prodigal son in Luke 15:11-31, whose merciful father is the perfect picture of our compassionate God, as well as in the compassion of Jesus himself to the suffering (Luke 7:11-17), to sinners (7:36-50), to all (8:22-56; 9:37-43).

The question arises then, with Luke's Christlike compassionate concern for the underprivileged, is he rightly regarded by liberation theologians[146] as a patron saint for their movement? Well, yes and no! He certainly advocates justice, equity, and charity for the poor and oppressed of the world as is evident even in Mary's Canticle, which is generally and rightly considered largely a Lukan creation (see Luke 1:52-53), so that it is easy to see him as a patron saint of nonviolent liberation of the oppressed. If, however, it is a question of violent overthrow of institutions or governments in order to obtain justice, whether one considers this justifiable or no one would be hard pressed to find approval in Luke's writings. For example, in the just-mentioned Canticle of Mary it should be noted that it is God who will set things right.

Let us turn now to those profound portraits of Jesus and Mary, so rich in symbolic allusions, which Luke gives us in his annunciation and visitation accounts in his inspiring "Infancy Gospel." First, the annunciation story in Luke 1:26-38. Was it real? Did it physically and visibly happen, or is this Luke's concretization of what may have occurred entirely in Mary's mind and heart by an inner vision? I have no problem with recognizing Luke's hand in the many details involved, but I find it hard to believe that the God who had sent angelic messengers[147] on so many occasions of lesser importance would not have arranged an angelic annunciation on this greatest of all occasions. Besides, how would Mary in her profound humility have been able to accept it had it not been overwhelmingly clear to her in something she could see and hear?

Whether the annunciation visibly and historically happened is not the important consideration for us. Rather, we should be eager to garner the theological and spiritual riches contained in the account so that thereby we may derive a more complete picture of Jesus as well as of his holy mother.

First, let us notice that the account is actually a dialogue of three statements by the angel and three responses by Mary, which constitute a double addition to our list of Lukan triplets. And I might add that the angel's statements in particular form a continuous deepening and broadening of his announcement in a structure of concentric circles. With that brief preface let us examine as concisely as possible the content and connotations of this biblical jewel.

As previously pointed out in note 6, the angel's greeting and initial announcement *(chaîre kecharitoméne*, Rejoice, O most highly favored one!) recalls the similar invitations to the "Daughter of Zion" to rejoice in view of messianic announcements (see Zeph 3:14-18; Zech 9:9-10). Then the greeting which is still used liturgically, *ho kýrios metà soû* (the Lord is, or be, with you), echoes the angel's greeting to Gideon in Judg 6:12 as well as that of Boaz, the ancestor of David, to his workers in Ruth 2:4. The third part of the initial announcement, in keeping with more reliable manuscripts, is *eulogeméne sù en gunaixín!* (Blessed are you among women!), a clear reference to the fulsome praise of Judith, one of the women instrumental in the salvation of Israel from defeat and oppression (see Jdt 13:18).

Mary's first response is one of deep humility. "She was troubled by his word and wondered what kind of greeting this might be" (Luke 1:29). In other words, why should she, a lowly teenaged girl of Nazareth, be greeted in this extravagant manner? And just as her response resembled that of Gideon in Judg 6:15, so the angel's next words also resemble those of the angel to Gideon in Judg 6:23, "Do not fear, Mary," followed by an expression too frequent in the Old Testament to require textual reference, "You have found favor with God." Then comes the heart of the annunciation in clear allusion to the famous Emmanuel prophecy in Isa 7:14: "And behold, you will conceive in your womb and bring forth a son, and you will call his name Jesus" (Luke 1:30-31, WFD). And before Mary can respond again the angel goes on to describe what this child will be like, "He will be great," an echo of the Coronation Psalms (see Pss 93–99), thus identifying the child as king and equal to Yahweh, an incredible idea which is confirmed by the words "and he will be called Son of the Most High!" Finally, an allusion to another clear messianic prophecy, that in which Yahweh promises David an everlasting dynasty (see 2 Sam 7:11-16): "and the Lord God will give him the throne of David his father and he will be king over the house of Jacob forever, and of his kingdom there will be no end"[148] (Luke 1:32-33, WFD).

What must have been Mary's astonishment at this unmistakable prediction that she was chosen to be the mother of the long-awaited Messiah! Her response this time, perhaps out of virginal purity, is a request for information: "How will this be since I do not know man," that is, since I do not have relations with a man? (Luke 1:34, WFD). A strange question indeed in view of the fact mentioned by Luke earlier that while she was indeed a virgin, she was betrothed to be married to Joseph (see Luke 1:27). Why did she not assume that she was to marry Joseph and the Messiah would be born of their union? Had she vowed to remain a virgin for life, and had she and Joseph planned a virginal marriage? Perhaps, but such a decision would have been truly extraordinary in that time and place. Does Luke place the question in her mouth in order to give the angel an opportunity to explain how the Messiah would be conceived and born? This literary explanation, proposed by Raymond Brown,[149] may be more likely in view of the whole arrangement of the annunciation account in twin triplets of announcement and response, which smacks of a Lukan literary device. We may never know for sure, but we are certainly alerted to hear the angel's answer as he provides the key explanation of what will happen and how.

"The Holy Spirit will come upon you and the power of the Most

High will overshadow you, and therefore the holy [one][150] to be born will be called Son of God'' (Luke 1:35, WFD). In this one sentence we have a wealth of allusion and meaning. The first part, "the Holy Spirit will come upon you," seems to be an allusion to the very first chapter of Genesis in which "the [creative] spirit of God was hovering over the waters" (Gen 1:1, NIV, RSV, JB) shaping and filling the earth, which was until then "formless and empty" (Gen 1:1, NIV, etc.).

A powerful allusion indeed, but not more so than the parallel one which follows immediately: "and the power of the Most High will overshadow you." The Greek verb for "overshadow" is *episkiázo*,[151] which happens to be the Septuagint translation of the Hebrew verb *shakan*,[152] whose noun form, *shekinah*, is the term used to describe the luminous cloud symbolic of God's special presence that had overshadowed the Israelite tabernacle (containing the ark of the covenant) in the desert. In other words, the angel assures Mary that nothing is required of her except her consent because the child will be miraculously conceived in her womb by the power and presence of God. And for the sake of added assurance he informs her about the miraculous pregnancy of her cousin, the barren and aged Elizabeth, now happily in her sixth month "because nothing is impossible with God!" (Luke 1:37, WFD).

Completely convinced, in fact, overwhelmed, Mary's third response is one of total loving self-surrender to God's holy will: "Behold the maidservant of the Lord; let it be done to me according to your word"[153] (Luke 1:38, WFD). Then the angel left her. The announcement or, better still, the proposal, was made and accepted, and the Messiah, the divine Savior, could now begin his earthly sojourn in Mary's womb. But what a magnificent dialogue has just taken place, perhaps historically *and* in Luke's masterful literary arrangement! A dialogue commemorated not only in the great Feast of the Annunciation and Incarnation[154] but also in the splendid Basilica of the Annunciation in Nazareth where an ancient altar is still visible in the lower grotto,[155] on whose face are the moving Latin words *Verbum caro hic factum est*, meaning "The Word was made flesh here."

Immediately after the annunciation Luke's "Infancy Gospel" continues with the story of the visitation: "Rising in those days, Mary went in haste into the hill country to a city of Judah,[156] entered the house of Zechariah, and greeted Elizabeth" (Luke 1:39, WFD). Then a strange thing happened. "When Elizabeth heard Mary's greeting, her child moved in her womb, and Elizabeth, filled with the Holy Spirit, exclaimed with a loud cry, 'Blessed are you among women and blessed is the fruit of your womb. And how can it happen to me that the mother of my Lord should come to me? For behold, when the sound of your greeting came to my ears, the child in my womb leaped for joy! And blessed are you who have believed [or blessed is the believer] that [or because] there will be fulfillment for the things told her from the Lord" (Luke 1:41-44, WFD). Mary's response of course is her canticle of praise, commonly called the "Magnificat," which is most probably a Lukan composition from Old Testament allusions, especially the famous Canticle of Hannah in 1 Sam 2:1-10, after which, according to Luke 1:56, WFD, "Mary remained with her [Elizabeth] about three months [surely until the birth of John] and returned to her house [in Nazareth]."

What a touching story, exemplifying Mary's loving concern for others and the recognition by her cousin Elizabeth of her role as mother of the Messiah. But there is more, much more, in the allusions involved. In 2 Sam 6 we read that David, having captured the strategic city of Zion, or Jerusalem, from the Jebusites (see 2 Sam 5), determined to make it his capital not only politically but religiously. For that purpose he decided to bring the ark of the covenant into the city. Where was the ark? Well, by way of flashback to 1 Sam 3–7, let us recall that as revealed beforehand to the child Samuel, the sinfulness of the priestly sons of Heli, the high priest, and his own failure to correct them resulted in the defeat of Israel and the capture of the ark by the Philistines. However, Yahweh had his own means of retrieving the ark. Not only did its presence in Philistine territory cause the statue of their god Dagon to topple over but it also caused among the people the twin plagues of hemorrhoids and deadly mice, which forced the Philistines after seven months to return the ark to Israel with a guilt offering of golden hemorrhoids and mice. The oxen bearing the ark headed straight for the land of the Israelites, arriving at Beth Shemesh,[157] whose inhabitants were soon filled with fear and beckoned the nearby people of Kiriath-jearim[158] to come and take the ark to their town. There its presence led to a great reform and it remained at least twenty years,[159] until David made up his mind to bring it into Jerusalem.

Now come the allusions. When the ark was being brought up to Jerusalem "while David and all the Israelites made merry before the Lord," the ox-cart on which it rested began to tip, and Uzzah, son of

Abinadab in whose home the ark had been kept, reached out to steady it, whereupon he was struck dead. David, shocked and fearful, exclaimed, "How can it happen[160] that the ark of my Lord will come to me?" (2 Sam 6:9, WFD). He therefore had the ark diverted to the nearby house of Obededom where it remained three months and greatly blessed his household. When David learned of this blessing he rightly interpreted it as a sign from Yahweh to bring the ark into Jerusalem, which he did, "leaping and dancing before the Lord" (2 Sam 6:16). Notice the similarity between the exclamations of David and Elizabeth, the three months at the home of Obededom and that of Elizabeth, and the leaping for joy by David before the ark and by John the Baptist in Elizabeth's womb before Mary and her child.

A series of coincidences? I think not. Rather a series of allusions on Luke's part to honor Mary, because of the divine child in her womb, as the "Ark of the Covenant." And we are reminded of this when we visit Kiriath-jearim in Israel, for there we find a large statue of Mary (rare in Israel) surrounded by olive trees and entitled "Ark of the Covenant." But that is not all. In the Apocalypse, or Book of Revelation, chapter 12 presents that inspired vision of the "woman clothed with the sun" (Rev 12:1), and the scene preparatory to that vision is none other than that of the ark of the covenant (see Rev 11:19)! About this we will see more when we take up the Apocalypse, but for now we need to proceed to our reflections on the Church and the other matters that I have indicated.

Luke's Portrait of the Church

It is said that repetition is the mother of education.[161] Perhaps, then, the reader will forgive me if I presume to repeat something already expressed in note 137. My reason for doing so is simply that what I am repeating is nothing less than the key that unlocks the door of the understanding of Luke's Acts of Apostles and, in fact, all of Church history. I refer to Acts 1:1, WFD.

When properly translated, it should read something like this: "I wrote my former account, O Theophilus, about all that Jesus began to do and to teach until that day when, having instructed the apostles whom he had chosen through the Holy Spirit, he was taken up [into Heaven]." The key word is "began" (*érxato*, the imperfect of *árchomai*), whose translation, unfortunately, is totally missing in the New American Bible and not well done in the Jerusalem Bible.

What the proper translation of this verse accomplishes is to emphasize that the Church, on which Acts of Apostles is focused, is nothing less than *the continuation of the life, ministry, and suffering of Jesus Christ.* According to Luke, Jesus in his earthly lifetime simply "began to do and to teach!" He continues to do so in Acts but now in and through his Church and, more specifically, through his two great apostles, Peter and Paul.

"But," one may rightly ask, "is it not risky to base an entire thesis on the translation of one verse?" Yes, it would be if there were not confirmation from a number of other factors in both Luke and Acts, such as (1) the basic parallel between Luke and Acts, the journeys in both, and the special emphasis on the "way" in Luke 9:51–19:27; Acts 9:2; and elsewhere, where it was the first designation of Jesus' followers until at Antioch they began to be called Christians[162] (see Acts 11:27); (2) the "great Markan omission" (see Mark 6:45–8:26) comprising the temporary sojourn of Jesus and his apostles outside of Jewish territory which is missing in the Lukan account between Luke 9:17 and 9:18, clearly because Luke has decided to delay Jesus' Gentile mission until Acts when he can show him accomplishing that mission through the Church and especially through Peter and Paul; (3) in Luke's Gospel also, the emphasis on Jesus' speaking through his apostles, for example, in Luke 10:16, WFD (confirmed by but far clearer than Matt 10:40 and John 13:20): "The one who hears you hears me, the one who rejects you, rejects me; and the one who rejects me rejects the one who sent me"; (4) the prayer of Peter and the Christian community to Jesus in Acts 1:24-25, WFD: "You, Lord, the reader of hearts, show which one of these two you have chosen to take the place of this ministry and apostolate, from which Judas turned away to go to his own place"; and (5) the identification of Jesus with his suffering followers revealed to Saul/Paul on the road to Damascus: "Saul, Saul, why are you persecuting me?" and "I am Jesus whom you are persecuting!" (Acts 9:4-5, WFD).

If such has been the case with the early Church, thus it has remained throughout history and will continue to do so until the end of time, for has not Jesus himself promised his Church in Matt 16:18, WFD, that "the gates of Hades [hell or death] will not prevail against her" and in Matt 28:20, WFD, that he would be with her always "until the end of the age"?

This continues to be particularly manifest in the saints, whom God is constantly raising up to reassure the faithful and combat the evils of each age. We honor the saints because Jesus Christ lived and lives in these chosen persons who have surrendered themselves to him. If we fail to honor them, we fail to honor Christ. And this honor is especially due to Mary, the queen, mother, and model of all saints, and, indeed, of all of us that we may become saints. As Leon Bloy expressed it in the emphatic final line of his famous book, "There is only one misery, and that is—not to be saints!"[163]

But what is this Church like in which Jesus continues to live and minister and suffer? Luke answers this fair question succinctly in his four masterful summaries of the life of the early Christian community in Acts which, somewhat like the four Gospels, combine to give us a powerful, four-dimensional portrait of the pristine Church.

The first and most comprehensive ecclesial picture, in Acts 2:42-47, describes in idyllic terms the early Christians' hunger for instruction, fidelity to communal life, devotion to the Eucharist, and immersion in prayer. They were in awe of the wonders wrought by the apostles, or rather by Jesus through them. They practiced community of goods and ate their meals in common. And while they were daily at the Temple worshiping and sharing their faith with others, they used their homes for the "breaking of bread," that is, for their Eucharistic meals.

The second summary (Acts 4:32-35), perhaps in a kind of concentric circles arrangement, returns to and expands the idea of unity in the early Christian community: the internal unity of mind and heart and the external unity of voluntary communism, while the apostles continued to manifest the power of the risen and living Christ by their performance of miracles.

The third summary, Acts 5:12-16, maintains its continuity with the first summary by way of concentric circles, returning to and expanding the practice of meeting at the Temple, specifically at Solomon's Porch,[164] to preach the good news of Christ and to heal the sick who (along with the possessed) were brought even from the towns roundabout, especially to Peter whose very shadow[165] often cured them.

For our fourth summary I like to combine two short ones, separated by the brief story of the institution of assistants, whom we commonly identify with deacons. In Acts 5:41-42 the apostles, having been scourged by order of the Sanhedrin, rejoiced in their suffering for Christ and continued preaching the good news without interruption, while in Acts 6:7 the word of God continued to spread, bringing many converts into the fold, including even many priests.

These are the summaries whereby Luke, in his second work, places before the eyes of Christians the ideal of Christian community: learning, praying, worshiping, celebrating the Eucharist, living a communal life in goods and meals, sharing their faith, love, and compassion by preaching the good news, healing the afflicted, and suffering for Christ.

At the same time, Luke realistically includes the manifestations of fallen human nature which, as he is completely aware, will plague the Church throughout her existence, since she is divinely founded and protected but still composed of human members.[166] Thus we have the tragic story of Ananias and Sapphira, husband and wife, who pretend to join wholeheartedly in the Church's community of goods but hold back some of their funds and compound their offense by lying about it (see Acts 5:1-11). We also see the phenomenon of human competition in the daily distribution of food, the Hellenists[167] (Greek-speaking Jews) complaining that their widows are being neglected in favor of the Hebrew (Aramaic-speaking Jews) widows. Happily this leads to the institution of assistants (deacons)[168] who will take care of such material matters so that the apostles can devote themselves to prayer and preaching (see Acts 6:1-6).

Another aberration in the early Church is that of the famous (or infamous) Simon Magus, who attempts to buy the apostles' supernatural power, thus lending his name to the sin of simony for all time (see Acts 8:9-24). One of the most distressing human problems because it involves such good people is the falling out between Paul and Barnabas over the latter's cousin, John Mark (see Acts 15:36-40).

But by far the greatest turmoil in the Church is the result of the fundamental difference between many Jewish Christians attached to the Mosaic Law on the one hand and, on the other hand, both Jewish and gentile Christians who feel no need to continue the practice of that Law, notably in the case of gentile converts. This leads to the tug of war between the two positions reflected in the challenges to Peter and Paul in Acts 11:1-18 and 15:1-2, which is settled only by the decision of the Council of Jerusalem under the supreme leadership of Peter and the Jewish Christian leadership of James (see Acts 15:3-35). Unfortunately, as we see in Paul's Letters, especially Galatians and probably Second Corinthians, there are Jewish Christians who refuse to accept the Jerusalem decision and, becoming known as Judaizers, continue to dog the steps of orthodox missionaries like Paul and his companions for many years.

There are those who maintain that in its early years the Church was very democratic or congregationalist, if you will, and that it was only later, probably under the influence of Imperial Rome with its penchant for law and administration, that it became "catholic" in the sense of being governed by a monarchical hierarchy. Yet the New Testament really does not bear that out. We have already seen the authority promised Peter alone in Matt 16:13-20 and that given the Church as a whole and the apostles in particular in Matt 18:15-18. We will see when we study John 21:15-17 the conferral of Church primacy on Peter. And in our beloved Luke we see Peter's special position in such passages as Luke 6:14 where Peter is named first among the apostles (as he always is, although in different Gospel lists the order of the others is never the same), Luke 9:20 where Peter makes his profession of faith in Jesus' messiahship for all the apostles (as he does also in the other three Gospels, Mark 8:29; Matt 16:16; John 6:68), and Luke 22:31-32 where Jesus singles Peter out for special prayers which will enable him to be converted and strengthen the others.

In Acts 1:13 Peter is again named first in the list of apostles, and in Acts 1:15-26 he authoritatively leads the election of Matthias to replace Judas. On Pentecost, while the Holy Spirit descends on the entire Church assembled in the upper room, including Mary, and other women—about one hundred twenty in all—again it is Peter who speaks for them all, explaining the meaning of the Spirit's outpouring. And in the chapters that follow, even after the conversion of Paul it is Peter who is always the leader, especially in the reception of the first Gentiles, for which he is instructed by a heavenly vision (see Acts 10), and in the crucial Council of Jerusalem in Acts 15 where it is Peter who settles the issue (see Acts 15:6-12) with James then or later simply adding some recommendations to avoid scandalizing the Jews (see Acts 15:13-21).

Before leaving the question of Church authority it may be helpful if I point out the parallel between authority in the Old Testament and the New. For example, just as Core, Dathan, and Abiron are summarily swallowed up because they oppose the authority of Moses and Aaron in Num 16, so Ananias and Sapphira are struck dead because, as Peter says, they have not lied to men but to God (see Acts 5:1-11). By the same token, however, just as Moses and Aaron are refused entry into the Promised Land because they fail to reflect the mercy and patience of Yahweh (see Num 20:2-13), so also the authorities in the Church, including Peter and the apostles, are to exercise their leadership with the compassion and patience of Christ himself, as we see Jesus teaching over and over again both directly (see Mark 10:35-45; Matt 18:1-4; 21-35; Luke 9:45-48; 17:7-10; 22:24-30) and indirectly, through Paul (see Acts 20:28, etc.) and Peter (see 1 Pet 5:1-4).

Finally, it should never be forgotten that the authority shared by Christ with Church leaders was never intended to be exercised over the faithful without any input from the faithful. After all, the laity are the people of God (*laòs toû theoû*) whom the hierarchy are called to serve, after the example of Jesus, who came "not to be served but to serve" (Mark 10:45) and who is in our midst "as one who serves" (Luke 22:27). Hence, especially in Acts, we see the laity fully involved before and at Pentecost (see Acts 1:12–2:4), in thanksgiving and "little Pentecost" after the apostles' release from detention (see Acts 4:23-31), in the choice of the deacons (see Acts 6:1-6), in the commissioning of Barnabas and Saul for their missionary work (see Acts 13:1-3), in the preparations for the Council of Jerusalem (see Acts 15:2-4), and elsewhere. It should be noted, however, that only the apostles and presbyters (bishops/priests) participate in the Council itself, as we read in Acts 15:6.

From the remainder of Acts, one of the most beautiful and instructive incidents occurs when at Ephesus Paul's dear lay friends Aquila and Priscilla do not hesitate to complete the instruction of the brilliant preacher Apollos, and to the latter's credit he evidently receives it with humility and gratitude (see Acts 18:24-26). Which brings up one final point regarding leadership in the Church. Just as in the Old Testament there was the institutional leadership of priests and kings but also the inspirational leadership of judges and prophets, the latter often far outweighing the former in importance especially where the salvation of Israel was concerned, so also in the New Testament there is clearly more than one kind of leadership.

We find, of course, that of Peter and the apostles, as well as of bishops/priests (epískopoi/presbýteroi), understood interchangeably in New Testament times but distinguished by the end of the first century, and finally, that of deacons (*diákonoi*). That was and is institutional leadership in the Church, but in addition there was and is inspirational leadership, and the latter can be even more important in salvation history than the former. Examples in Acts are such prophets as Agabus in 11:27-30 and 21:10-12, "certain prophets and teachers" at Antioch in 13:1-2, the three prophesying daughters of Philip the deacon in 21:8-9, and many others who play important roles without the mention of charismatic gifts, for example, Tabitha in 9:36, Mary, Mark's mother in 12:12, Lydia of Thyatira in 16:14-15, and Aquila and Priscilla in 18:2-3, 18-19, 26-27.

Not all are called to institutional leadership, but all can be called to inspirational leadership simply by exercising the natural and supernatural (charismatic) gifts that God gives us. As I like to put it in modern terms, how many of us know the names of priests in India today? But we all know the name of that wonderful inspirational leader, Mother Teresa! Would that all who are called to inspirational leadership were willing to exercise it and that all institutional leaders were inspirational as well!

One final note on the sacraments in Luke-Acts. *Baptism*, of course, is quite prominent as we see in Acts 2:38, 41; 8:12, 16, 37-38; 9:18; 10:48; 16:15, 33; 19:5. So also is the *Eucharist*, first in Luke 22:14-20 and at least symbolically, in Luke 9:10-17; 24:13-35, and perhaps 41-45, then in Acts 2:42, 46; 20:7 under Luke's preferred expression, "to break bread." Likewise, what came to be the sacrament of *reconciliation* is rather prominent in both Luke and Acts, for example, Luke 5:20; 8:48; 15:1-32; 18:13; 23:43; 24:47 and Acts 5:31; 13:38; 26:18.

Reception of the Holy Spirit through the sacrament of *confirmation* may also be intended or at least hinted at in Luke 3:22 and Acts 2:1-4; 10:44-48; 19:6-7, but particularly in Acts 8:14-17. In this last-named passage the Samaritans have already received the sacrament of baptism at the hands of Philip the deacon, but in order to receive the Holy Spirit it is necessary for Peter and John to come from Jerusalem to impose hands on them, whereupon they do receive the Holy Spirit. Is this the so-called baptism of the Spirit, or the sacrament of confirmation, or both? It is not easy to say, but certainly the main elements of the sacrament are there. When it comes to *holy orders*, however, the picture is clearer, for not only are the apostles in effect ordained at the institution of the Eucharist in Luke 22:14-20, but at least in a primitive way there seems to be the ordination of deacons in Acts 6:6 and of presbyters or priests in Acts 14:23.

Luke's Subthemes and Conditions

In this final section of our study of Luke-Acts I will have to be as brief as possible in order not to extend our study beyond reasonable length. For that purpose I shall confine my remarks to certain key points and leave it to the reader to pursue the study further, if desired, by means of references to other works including my own and above all by means of prayer and the reading of Scripture.

Our brief treatment will consist of two parts: (1) the subthemes of women, the Holy Spirit, prayer, and joy, all of which receive special emphasis in both Luke's Gospel and Acts; and (2) those conditions for following Christ to the heavenly Jerusalem which are most prominent in Luke's long journey account.

That the four subthemes I have delineated receive a great amount of emphasis both in the Gospel of Luke and in Acts is so obvious from their reading that I shall not insult the reader's intelligence by listing references. Just read the twin works themselves. What I am more concerned about is this: Why did Luke single these out? And is there some insight about each of these we need to discover in order to derive the riches from Luke's writings that we should? In responding to these questions, I hope with the Lord's help to avoid mere subjectivism and sentimentality.

Taking up Luke's emphasis on women first, I have already speculated in our story section that Luke was particularly devoted to his own admirable mother, whose image he perhaps saw in other women. But I cannot help thinking that somewhere in that picture was an extraordinary devotion to the mother of Jesus, the Virgin Mary. Whether Luke ever met her or not (and in my story I have him learn about her from John), he must have come to recognize in her not only the chosen one through whom the Savior entered our world but someone with a very special role in our sanctification and salvation. In a sense, I have come to appreciate that role myself by contemplation of the annunciation and visitation accounts, particularly the former.

In the interest of time and space let me focus just on the threefold responses of Mary which, as I have mentioned already, express her deep humility, her spotless purity, and her selfless love. Are those not precisely the virtues that we need to cultivate so that Jesus may truly dwell in us, take full possession of us, and continue his life and ministry through us? Not that acquiring these virtues is easy, especially in our current milieu so preoccupied with building our own image, transforming the sacredness of sex into self-indulgence, and making ourselves the end-all of our existence.

Sheer force of will and repeated practice will never accomplish the task, for these are supernatural virtues, and no amount of stoic effort will ever enable us to gain them. No, they can come only from God, indeed they are ultimately the virtues of Jesus himself, and she in whom the Savior was formed by the power of the Holy Spirit has a choice role in enabling him to be formed in us as well. The words of Paul to the Galatians seem to fit Mary even more than the apostle: "My children, with whom I am in labor again until Christ be formed in you!" (Gal 4:19, WFD).

But if those touching words suit Mary so well, how much more do they fit the Holy Spirit, the creative, transforming Spirit of God, the sigh of love between the Father and the Son! He it was who formed Jesus physically in the womb of Mary, and he it is who longs to form him spiritually in us. And that he can and will do to the extent that we learn from Mary to be emptied of self through humility and purity and selfless love.

I have spoken of the Holy Spirit in masculine terms because that is the traditional terminology, but I could as well have used feminine expressions. After all, there is no sex or gender in God, but the Holy Spirit, if we wish to speak in those terms, exhibits more feminine, nurturing characteristics than masculine ones. It is true that the Latin word *spiritus* is masculine, but the Greek word *pneûma* is neuter, and the Hebrew word *rhuah* is feminine. So the choice is ours, but personally I prefer the feminine designation, and I have a feeling that Luke would have inclined that way as well.

Now, if we are attuned to the Spirit, prayer, which is so necessary to our spiritual life, comes easily, as Paul makes clear in Rom 8:26-27. By our very nature we are destined for union with Christ[169] and, through him, with the Father in the Holy Spirit. But that union is impossible without communication, and our communication with God is what we call prayer. And as Paul indicates, we really do not know how to pray as we ought, so the Holy Spirit assists us[170] in this essential means of union. The more we are determined to live the life of the spirit (our whole being aspiring to union with God) rather than the life of the flesh (our whole being inclined to temptation and sin), the more attuned we are to the Spirit of God and the more surrendered to his guiding and transforming action, the more also we are filled with and submerged in peace and joy.

Luke's fourth subtheme, that of joy, is one that is probably the most easily misunderstood. The reason is that we tend to live so much on the surface of our lives that we think of joy in terms of emotional or, at most, intellectual enjoyment, but neither one compares with joy in the spirit of our being, which is really joy in the Holy Spirit. It makes no difference what happens to us: illness or accident, rejection or failure, loss of a loved one through death or divorce—if we have spiritual joy, it remains. Nothing and no one can take it away. We are at peace in the center of our being that nothing but God can touch.[171]

That does not mean that we are insensitive to others. Not at all! We are more sensitive and concerned than we would otherwise be. But because we retain our serenity, our rootedness in Christ, we are freer to help others in their pains and sorrows. That is joy in the Spirit!

In our consideration of Luke's subthemes I have been speaking in terms of our personal spiritual life, and for an important reason. Before Vatican II much if not most of our emphasis was on individual salvation. After Vatican II the emphasis has to a great extent passed to communal, ecclesial Christian living. This, of course, has been good and necessary, but as so often happens with our human nature, we have tended to go from one extreme to the other and missed the *via media*. The Church is composed of persons, and therefore we must never neglect our personal spiritual life. In fact, our baptism was first of all an incorporation into the body, that is, the Person of the risen Christ himself and, by that very fact, into the corporate body of Christ, the Church.

Just as in Luke's Gospel it is primarily with our personal spiritual life that Jesus and Luke are concerned, so also in Luke's Acts of Apostles it is above all with the spiritual growth of the Church, internally and externally, that Jesus and Luke are preoccupied. We see this to be true throughout Acts, particularly at all the key points of Jesus' life and ministry in the Church. In Acts the Holy Spirit is mentioned no less than fifty-two times, more than twice the amount in Luke, which contains the second largest number of uses. This is no accident. At every turn the risen Christ is guiding, protecting, and renewing the Church through the presence and power of the Holy Spirit, often in very extraordinary ways.

Finally, let us take a brief look at the principal conditions for the "followship" of Christ to the heavenly Jerusalem, as we find them emphasized in Luke's famous journey account of his Gospel, (see Luke 9:51-19:27).

The first and most basic condition, of course, is that of humility. Basic because the absolute requirement for any salutary action of the risen Christ and the Holy Spirit in us is that we renounce ourselves (Luke 9:23). Taking a cue from Mary and Jesus himself, we see Mary's clear humility in her first response to the angel's greeting in the annunciation (see Luke 1:29) and in her Magnificat (see Luke 1:48); and we see Jesus' incomparable humility in his very incarnation, described by Paul in Phil 2:5-8.

Jesus' teaching on humility occurs in several passages of the journey account: Luke 10:21-22; 14:1-11; 18:9-17. Clearly then, both in example and in teaching, Jesus challenges us to embrace humility as the indispensable condition of any growth in the spiritual life. We can never wholly be rid of self-love in this life, for our most basic instinct is self-preservation, but through the humility of Mary and Jesus we can be so emptied of self that Christ can truly continue his life and ministry in us.

A second condition, which I like to include under the general heading of purity, comprises not only chastity according to our vocation but also detachment from material things or from anything in our lives that presents an obstacle to our union with our risen Lord. Again, the perfect examples are those of Mary and Jesus, the former in her virginal purity as reflected in her second response to the angel at the annunciation (see Luke 1:34); the latter in the celibate purity of his life and, more explicitly, in his example and teaching about detachment.

Jesus' example consists mainly in the poverty of his birth and life (see Luke 2:7; 9:58) and of his death and burial (see Luke 23:34,53), all of which are epitomized cogently in Paul's unforgettable description in 2 Cor 8:9, WFD: "You know the graciousness of our Lord Jesus Christ who, though he was rich, became poor for you, so that by his poverty you might become rich!"

Instances of Jesus' teaching on detachment, poverty, and trust in God are if anything more frequent in Luke's journey account than any other instructions, even those on humility, for example, 10:4; 12:13-34; 14:12-14, 25-26; 16:1-15, 19-31; 18:18-30.

On our way to the heavenly Jerusalem we must be willing to travel lightly, unencumbered by this world's material goods and pleasures, as Paul, that great tricultural missionary who was also Luke's model and mentor, expresses it in 1 Cor 9:25, NAB: "Athletes deny themselves all sorts of things. They do this to win a crown of leaves that withers, but we a crown that is imperishable."

Finally, the essential virtue of love toward God and our neighbor without which we are spiritually naked is taught especially in the touching parable of the good Samaritan, which in Luke's account flows naturally from Jesus' teaching on the greatest of the commandments. It is well to remember, as is evident also from events in the New Testament, that by the time of Jesus the Law had become far more important in Judaism than the covenant for which the Law was instituted. And in the Law, by far the most important commandment in Jewish eyes was that of the Sabbath rest. That is why we see Jesus in the Gospels trying so often to raise people's minds from the legalism of the Sabbath rest to the relationalism of the twin commandments of love, to which all the Ten Commandments are reducible.

* * * * *

Such is the background of Jesus' response to questions about the greatest commandment in Matt 22:34-40 and Mark 12:28-34 and about the works needed for salvation in Mark 10:17 and Luke 10:25. Only in Luke, however, do we find the added universal and practical teaching (featuring as hero a Samaritan, despised by Jews as a half-breed and a heretical worshiper of Yahweh) that anyone in need is our neighbor and that our loving charity must be unconditional and universal, extended to all regardless of race, color, nationality, creed, sex, or status. This is what is meant by Christian charity, so movingly expressed in "Matthew's" judgment scene (see Matt 25:31-46), inculcated by Mary in her third annunciation response and visitation to Elizabeth, and exemplified by Jesus throughout his life and death. For it is love, above all, that characterizes Jesus our blessed Savior and his beloved witness, St. Luke.

NOTES

1. For St. Luke, the accepted author of the Gospel according to Luke and the Acts of Apostles, I have chosen the adjective "luminous" for three reasons: (1) The name itself, *Loukâs*, seems to be a Greek version of Latin *Lucius*, which in turn is derived from *lux, lucis* meaning "light"; (2) the writing of Luke in its clarity of expression and dramatic vigor certainly deserves the description "luminous"; and (3) the prophecy of Simeon quoted after the title depicts Jesus as "a light of revelation for the nations" (Luke 2:32, WFD), which light Luke helped to spread both as a missionary-companion of Paul (converted by the risen Christ in a flash of light to be the Apostle of the Gentiles, see Acts 9:3-5, 15) and as an evangelist-historian.

2. The "parallel Gospels" referred to here are The Gospel according to Luke and his Acts of Apostles, which certainly parallel each other as will be clear later.

3. Philippi was founded by King Philip II of Macedonia, father of Alexander the Great, in 358 B.C. on the site of an older settlement named "Krenides" (Child of Springs) from the many springs in the area. It was likewise known for its nearby gold mines, which provided Philip and Alexander their means of national and world conquest. In history and drama, however, it is more famous as the site of the famous Battle of Philippi in 42 B.C., when the triumvirate of Octavian, Anthony, and Lepidus defeated Brutus and Cassius, the chief assassins of Julius Caesar. At that time Philippi became a Roman colony with special rights and privileges, inhabited largely by veterans of the famous battle. Then and later, after Octavian's defeat of Anthony and Cleopatra in the decisive naval Battle of Actium in 31 B.C., the city was enhanced with many monuments and ornaments, all contributing to the descriptive title of "jewel." Such was Luke's evident pride in Philippi that in Acts 16:12 he refers to it as "a leading city of the district of Macedonia, and a Roman colony." Today, however, nothing remains of the once proud city except ruins, identified in Turkish as *Felibedjik*, or "Little Philippi."

We do not know for certain just where or when Luke wrote his parallel works. I have chosen Philippi as the place primarily because two of the three "we sections" of Acts (see 16:10-17; 20:5-22:19) connect him with that city. For the date of composition I have chosen a period after A.D. 70 because of the more detailed prophecy of the seige and destruction of Jerusalem in Luke 13:34-35; 19:41-44; 21:20-24. How long after? And what was the chronological relationship between "Matthew" and Luke? I have attempted to solve or circumvent that longstanding debate by placing them around the same time (A.D.

82–85), with Luke following "Matthew" by several months both in conception and completion and occasioned by but not dependent on the latter. For
more information on Philippi *see* F. F. Bruce, *Jesus and Paul: Places They Knew*
(Nashville: Nelson, 1983) 85–94.

4. To my knowledge there is no reliable portrait of Luke, nor is that of
great importance, but I cannot help feeling that his gentleness and loving compassion would certainly have shone in his face. If one desires a more physical
description, I picture him as tall, slender, and healthy, about sixty to sixty-
five years of age with a full head of naturally curly "salt-and-pepper" hair
and a serene visage featuring luminous brown eyes and a short, trimmed beard.

5. Both Luke's Gospel and Acts of Apostles were composed for one *Theophilus,* referred to by Luke as "Your Excellency" (Luke 1:3-4; Acts 1:1). Many
regard the name as fictitious and symbolic, much like the Philothea of St. Francis
de Sales, but they seem to find it difficult to cite examples of such symbolic
dedication in the ancient world. To me it is more reasonable, then, to accept
the name "Theophilus" as that of a real person. But who was he and why
was he addressed as "Your Excellency?"

First, the title of "excellency" would imply the position of a magistrate or
some equally important person. I think it perfectly fitting to see a close bond
of friendship between Luke, the ecclesial head in Philippi, and a Christian convert (of Luke's or Paul's?) who is also the chief magistrate or civil head of Philippi. Moreover, as a Roman military colony, Philippi's magistrates happened
to be *strategoí* (generals) as we see in Acts 16:20-22, 35-38. Nor is this an accident, for a careful examination of Acts reveals that Luke's usage of the titles
of the magistrates in various Greek cities is always historically accurate, from
strategoí (generals) in Philippi to *politárchai* (city rulers) in Thessalonica (see Acts
17:6) and *Asiárchai* (rulers of Asia, i.e., the Roman province) in Ephesus (see
Acts 19:31). This is an important confirmation of Luke's overall historicity as
exemplified in the historical setting of Luke 3:1-2 and elsewhere, especially
in Acts, which is replete with accurate historical data.

Ironically, however, there are two famous historical problems in Luke 2:1-2
and Acts 5:34-37 whose solutions, because of time and space considerations,
I must leave to reliable commentators on Luke and Acts, e.g., Raymond Brown,
The Birth of the Messiah (Garden City, N.Y.: Doubleday, 1977) 547–55; Joseph
Fitzmyer, *The Gospel Acccording to Luke* (Garden City, N.Y.: Doubleday, 1981)
1:393–95; Johannes Munck, *The Acts of the Apostles* (Garden City, N.Y.: Doubleday, 1967) xlvii–xlviii, 48–51; Ernst Haenchen, *The Acts of the Apostles* (Philadelphia: Westminster, 1971) 254–58.

In these admirable works one can find all the details of both the problems
and the possible solutions. For my part I just want to remind the reader of
what I mentioned about biblical history in the introduction, p. 9, namely that
it was in effect the remembered past, subject to human limitations in memory
and reporting, hence subject to material error, especially because the concern
of the biblical writers was not about history as such but rather about salvation
history, or simply "His Story!"

6. "Hail, Theophilus!" or better still, "Rejoice, Theophilus!" This is virtually the same greeting that was spoken to Mary by the angel in the annunciation account, *Chaîre, kecharitoméne!* (Hail or rejoice, most highly favored one!), with clear messianic reference to Zeph 3:14 and Zech 9:9, both of which begin with the words "Rejoice, O daughter Zion!"

7. Most early writers and current Scripture scholars are in general agreement that Luke was most probably a Graeco-Syrian from Antioch-on-the-Orontes, or Antioch of Syria, to distinguish it from the other fifteen cities named Antioch by Seleucus I Nicator. This background would help explain his understanding of the Eastern mentality, as we see in his Infancy Gospel (Luke 1–2), as well as his knowledge of Greek culture and language.

8. Luke is clearly referred to by Paul in Col 4:14, WFD, as "my beloved physician" (in Greek, *hiatrós*), which profession enabled him, like Paul, to "preach the gospel free of charge" (1 Cor 9:18, NAB) but above all fitted him to minister to persons as a whole, practicing what we call today holistic medicine, and to exercise fully his Christlike compassion.

9. Luke must have been very devoted to his mother to have developed such a reverence and concern for women, beginning with Mary the mother of Jesus, especially in his Infancy Gospel and continuing with other women: holy, prayerful, ministering (e.g., Luke 8:1-3; 10:38-42; 23:27; Acts 9:36-42; 16:13-15), or sick, suffering, sinful (e.g., Luke 7:11-17, 36-50; 8:43-48; Acts 16:16-24). Luke seems to have been that rare type of man who is both strong and courageous on the one hand but gentle and caring on the other, the perfect example of whom is Jesus himself. It is evidently true to say that one of the best examples of Jesus' continuing to live and minister in and through his followers exists in Luke himself, the author of Luke-Acts.

10. Besides what has just been mentioned, which also refers to compassion, it is instructive to note that where "Matthew" has Jesus declare in his Sermon on the Mount, "You will then be perfect as your heavenly Father is perfect" (Matt 5:48, WFD), Luke quotes him in his Sermon on the Plain as demanding, "Become compassionate just as your Father is compassionate" (Luke 6:36, WFD).

11. This familiar expression, "Amen," is, along with the almost equally familiar "Alleluia" or "Hallelujah," a beautiful remnant of the Hebrew origins of Christianity. "Amen" is from the Hebrew verb *Aman* (to stand) and can be translated "Let it stand" or "Let it be," thus expressing agreement with what is said or done. The verb *aman* occurs frequently, especially in the Old Testament, in its two most common meanings, "to be faithful" or "to believe." In the New Testament Jesus himself is called in Rev 3:14 the "Amen, the faithful Witness," and he frequently uses the expression for emphasis and assurance: "Amen, amen I say to you . . ." (The expression "Alleluia" means "Praise to you, Yahweh!" and along with "Amen" happily continues to be an important part of the liturgy of the Church.)

12. We have no information about Luke's family, but I have chosen to speak of his father as deceased and of himself as being an only son in order

to explain his tender love for his mother (pictured in our story about Luke) and, in turn, his special reverence for women in general and for the Blessed Virgin Mary in particular.

13. We also have no indication that Luke was not only a physician but also a *presbýteros* (elder, presbyter, or priest, used interchangeably by Paul with *epískopos*, overseer, bishop, as we see in Acts 20:17, 28, NIV, and Phil 1:1, etc.) and the spiritual head of the Church at Philippi. In the assumption that Paul appointed Luke as the spiritual leader of Philippi, it is most likely that he would also have ordained him a presbyter as indicated in Acts 14:23, NAB. Why then no mention of Luke in Philippians? My guess would be that Paul was aware that Luke was away at the time. Anyway, silence is no argument.

Luke's spiritual leadership of the Church at Philippi would help to explain why, when Paul was under house arrest in Rome (some think Ephesus or Caesarea), the Church of Philippi was the one most sensitive to his needs and, according to Phil 4:10-19, most faithful in caring for him with great solicitude. Was it not natural (and supernatural!) for the local Church to imitate the compassion of its leader, the gentle, tender-hearted Luke?

14. As we read at the beginning of the first "we section" (Acts 16:8-12), it was evidently at Troas that Luke first encountered Paul and then traveled with him to Philippi. What was Troas and why was Luke there? Located south of ancient Troy but in the same general area on the northwest coast of Asia Minor (now Turkey), its name derives from a combination and contraction of the Greek words for Troy and Alexander. During the first century A.D., Troas was a flourishing seaport with a vibrant Christian community (see Acts 20:4-12), possibly founded either by Paul or one of his companions.

It was here at Troas that, according to the first "we section," Luke initially joined Paul and his companions, then accompanied them to Philippi where he evidently remained (see Acts 16:10). Since there is no previous mention of his encountering Paul, the evidence seems to indicate that it was here at Troas that they first met, perhaps even that Luke was converted by Paul (though that could have occurred earlier at Antioch of Syria). What brought Luke to Troas is not mentioned, but the simplest explanation is either that he lived and worked there or that he was returning from Antioch to Philippi, where he already lived and practiced medicine. For more on Troas *see* E. M. Blaiklock, *Cities of the New Testament* (London: Fleming Revell, 1965) 35–38.

15. This is a quotation from one of Jesus' short parables, found only in Luke 17:7-10, NIV, in which Jesus requires the basic virtue of humility from those who serve him, a virtue beautifully exemplified in Luke himself.

16. This is a quotation from 1 Cor 3:7, NIV, also inculcating humility on the part of God's servants, in this instance Christ's preachers, who labor (like Paul and Apollos) at planting and watering in God's field, but only God "makes things grow." Hence, let there be no disunity among Christians because of allegiance to particular preachers. Luke had learned humility well from Paul.

17. The Egnatian Way, which also formed the main street of Philippi, was one of the famous Roman roads that linked the Empire with the Eternal City.

Still perfectly visible today complete with ruts from chariot wheels, it stretched east and west between Neapolis in Italy (today's Kavalla), the port of Philippi on the Aegean Sea, to Dyrrhachium on the Adriatic Sea opposite Brundisium in Italy (today's Brindisi), whence the famous Appian Way continued on to Rome.

From ancient times and in both Testaments, the words "way," "path," "road" (Hebrew *derek*, Greek *hodós*), have carried a special symbolism because of the general absence of roads and road signs, which meant that travelers were always at risk of losing their way. In Luke's case it may have been his many travels, often on Roman roads, that influenced him to put such emphasis in both of his works on this symbolism.

18. Just to the west of Philippi on the Egnatian Way were discovered the foundations of a great monumental arch. It is, of course, untitled because only the bases remain, but I have chosen to call it the "Arch of Augustus" because it is well known that in twenty-seven B.C., four years after the Battle of Actium, Octavian was honored by the Roman senate with the title of Augustus, which he then added to the official name of Philippi along with other endowments. It is believed by archaeologists that the construction of the arch dates from immediately after the Battle of Philippi or the Battle of Actium. In any case, the arch may have been given the name of Augustus in 27 B.C.

19. In Acts 16:13, NAB, we read, "Once, on the sabbath, we went outside the city gate to the bank of the river, where we thought there would be a place of prayer. We sat down and spoke to the women who were gathered there." The city gate indicated here was probably the monumental arch just mentioned, and the river in question could only have been the Ganga or Gangites, the only one in the area, located about a mile to the west of Philippi. Since there were not enough Jews at Philippi to build and support a synagogue, they (mostly women) did the next best thing by gathering for hymns, prayers, and readings of Scripture at the riverbank, where they could perform their ritual purifications.

20. We read in Luke 16:14-15, NAB, "One who listened was a woman named Lydia, a dealer in purple goods from the town of Thyatira. She already reverenced God, and the Lord opened her heart to accept what Paul was saying. After she and her household had been baptized, she extended us an invitation: 'If you are convinced that I believe in the Lord, come and stay at my house.' She managed to prevail on us." Thus, Paul's first convert in Europe was a woman and the first church, her home. I like to refer to her as Lady Lydia, not that there is any hint of aristocracy but that she was obviously a person of substance and initiative, being a representative of the well-known purple-dye industry of Thyatira (now *Akhisar)*, then as now a thriving industrial city in Asia Minor, known in Scripture as one of the seven Churches of (the Roman province of) Asia addressed in Rev 2:18-29. Possibly she was a widow carrying on her late husband's business, but at any rate she had shown the initiative needed first to embrace the worship of Yahweh as a proselyte (i.e., a Gentile who accepts Judaism) and then to embrace Christianity as the

fulfillment of Judaism. Of course, she was also one of those many women featured by Luke both in his Gospel and in his Acts of Apostles.

21. The literal translation of the Latin expression *Quid Nunc?* is "What now?" and so popular was its usage that it was later accepted into the English language as a synonym for "a gossip" or "busybody" *Webster's Ninth New Collegiate Dictionary,* s.v. "quidnunc").

22. The Greek word *acrópolis* simply means high city, and almost every Greek city of any importance sported one, at least as a natural defense against invasion. Hence it was usually fortified as was the case at Philippi, but only a few were also used for the worship of the gods as was exemplified at Athens, Corinth, Pergamum, etc.

23. The plain around Philippi seems to have been known both as the Plain of Philippi and as the Plain of Drama, but which nomenclature came first is not clear. It may be that the former was the earlier name, but that the latter became popular after the dramatic event of the famous Battle of Philippi.

24. To anyone who has visited them both, the similarity between Mount Orbelos rising out of the Plain of Philippi in Macedonia and Mount Tabor rising out of the Plain of Esdraelon in Galilee is quite striking. But how would Luke have become familiar with Mount Tabor? Probably from his accompaniment of Paul in his two-year imprisonment at Caesarea Maritima (Caesarea by the Sea) in Acts 23:23–26:32, though it is unclear whether Luke was with Paul or even in Palestine the whole time. In any case, I have drawn the comparison largely to highlight the mystical experiences of Moses, Elijah, and Jesus, which will receive greater attention later in these notes. Let me just add here that the touching miracle of Jesus' raising to life on his own compassionate initiative the only son of the widow of Naim in Luke 7:11-17 occurred just south of Mount Tabor, where the ruins of Naim remain to this day.

25. As we have already seen in treating "Matthew," the reference here is to the famous St. Ignatius, bishop of Antioch, one of the Fathers of the Church (especially because of his celebrated seven letters en route to his martyrdom in Rome) whom we have already described in treating the so-called Gospel according to Matthew.

26. It is presumed that the reader has already read the story of how "Matthew" came to be written and therefore needs no further explanation of Jewish Christians, Pharisees, Jamnia (the Greek form of "Jabneh"), *minim* (Jewish heretics), etc.

27. Before and even after the followers of Jesus came to be called Christians at Antioch in Acts 11:26, they were referred to as "followers of the way" (Acts 9:2), and Christianity was designated as "the way" in various instances: Acts 16:17; 18:25-26; 19:9,23; 22:4; 24:14, 22. This must have struck Luke, with his penchant for journeys, as particularly appropriate and meaningful.

28. The reader may recall from my treatment of Mark that I proposed the thought of Luke himself acting as a reconciler between Mark and Paul, who then became fast friends as indicated in Col 4:10-14; Phlm 24; 2 Tim 4:11.

29. Luke, as a master of both classical and Common Greek, would certainly have noticed the lack of refinement in Mark's Gospel, but he charitably attributes it to the haste with which Mark is forced to complete the work, gently passing over its inherent lack of refinement as owing to the fact that Aramaic was his native tongue. Besides, like "Matthew," Luke finds it necessary to ameliorate various of Mark's expressions in order to avoid possible misunderstandings. It is amusing that being a physician, he omits altogether the pejorative note about doctors in Mark 5:26.

30. Ancient tradition, mainly in the form of the anti-Marcionite prologue to Luke's Gospel dated from the end of the second century, testifies that Luke "served the Lord without distraction, without a wife, and without children." And perhaps this is obliquely confirmed when Luke has Jesus not once but twice (see Luke 14:26; 18:29) commend those who leave a wife for his sake.

Luke's reasons for celibacy are quite valid, namely, his two demanding vocations and the extraordinary example both of his friend Paul (see 1 Cor 7) and above all of Jesus himself. At the heart of his celibacy, however, I believe that there was still another motive entirely too private to be shared even with Theophilus, namely his personal love for and spiritual union with Jesus Christ, Incarnate Love.

31. This is a statement from Paul's motivation to celibacy in 1 Cor 7:34, NAB.

32. The *ágora*, or forum, of Philippi is still very well preserved today in its ruins, just to the right or south of the Egnatian Way as one proceeds eastward. Its size is estimated at 300 feet in length and 150 in width, or approximately the size of an American football field without the end zones. There once were temples at each end, east and west, and later, very prominently on the south side, a basilica whose ruins are still impressive.

33. The *bêma*, or tribunal, is at the foot of Mount Orbelos just left or north of the Egnatian Way, (facing east) and opposite the forum. It was probably here that Paul and his companions were brought before the magistrates and scourged, illegally at least in Paul's case, since he was a Roman citizen. To the right of the tribunal as one faces Mount Orbelos is what appears to be a jail or prison, quite possibly the very one where Paul and his companions were kept in chains and then freed by an earthquake.

34. At the extreme east end of Philippi, built into the base of Mount Orbelos, are the ruins of a theater typical of such structures in Greece, western Turkey, and southern Italy, all of which were inhabited or colonized by Greeks. Of course, since the jewel known as Philippi was so much smaller than many ancient Greek cities and also was not famous for many visitors as were the healing centers of Epidaurus and Pergamum, its theater was not much larger than an *ódeon*, a miniature theater used for recitals.

35. With his polished Greek language and style, his preoccupation with historicity, and the brilliance of his storytelling especially in the parables, Luke's writing would certainly appeal to cultured, well-educated people, while at the same time would be readable and understandable enough for the less-cultured common people who were the special object of his love and concern.

36. This, of course, is a prime emphasis in Luke's writings, namely, the universal salvation wrought by Jesus, the universal call to be members of his Church, and the special invitation to the neglected and rejected of the world. These are basic characteristics of the thinking and writing of Luke. He alone carries those challenging statements of Jesus: "I came to cast fire upon the earth, and would that it were already kindled!" (Luke 12:49, RSV); "Then he opened their minds to understand the scriptures, and said to them, 'Thus it is written that the Christ should suffer and on the third day rise from the dead, and that repentance and forgiveness of sins should be preached in his name to all nations, beginning from Jerusalem' " (Luke 24:45-47, RSV); "You shall receive power when the Holy Spirit comes upon you; and you shall be my witnesses in Jerusalem and in all Judea and Samaria and to the end of the earth" (Acts 1:8, RSV).

37. That part of his parallel Gospels in which Luke shows the greatest understanding of the Eastern mentality is his Infancy Gospel, which not only betrays a Semitic source but also Luke's intelligent and effective use of it.

38. By common consent among Scripture scholars, Luke is the most refined writer in the New Testament, with the possible exception of the author of the Epistle to the Hebrews, which many attribute (correctly, I believe) to the great Alexandrian orator Apollos, who is mentioned in Acts 18:24-28; 1 Cor 1-4; Titus 3:13. Perhaps his name was not attached to the Epistle because, as we see in 1 Cor 1-4, his spellbinding preaching at Corinth had occasioned disunity among the faithful according to their personal allegiance to various preachers.

39. Many if not most Scripture scholars deny that Luke was in possession of Paul's writings because he never cites them in his own works, but to me this argument seems to be outweighed by (1) Luke's personal devotion to Paul, on account of which he would have done everything possible to obtain a copy of Paul's letters; and (2) the differences in purpose and characteristics between Luke's writings and those of Paul. The latter were genuine letters written to particular Churches and persons on particular questions and problems, concerned not with Jesus in his lifetime or even so much with the Church as a whole but with the risen Christ, the local Churches, and the needs of individuals. In contrast, Luke's Gospel is primarily the story of Jesus in his earthly life, death, resurrection, and ascension, while his Acts of Apostles presents the first history of the Church as a whole. (3) While it is a truism in literary criticism that one cannot argue safely from silence, a comparison of Pauline and Lukan thought reveals a great amount of similarity, especially in the area of universalism and rejection of racial, sexual, and social distinctions as we find, for example, in Rom 1:16; Gal 3:28; Eph 2:11-22; Titus 2:11, and all through Luke-Acts.

40. There has been for some time a general consensus among Scripture scholars that Mark's Gospel is one of the major sources of the narrative order and content of both "Matthew" and Luke. In fact, when Luke deliberately omits material that depicts Jesus and the apostles in a ministry outside Israel (see Mark 6:44–8:27), which Luke prefers to hold for his Acts of Apostles, that

section is normally referred to as Luke's "great Markan omission." And when we refer to Mark's Gospel, we must bear in mind, as I have tried to clarify in treating Mark, that his Gospel in turn depended on the *kérygma* (the public proclamation of the Church about Jesus, comprising his baptism and witness by John the Baptist, his Galilean ministry, his journey to Jerusalem, and his saving events in Jerusalem) but also on the eyewitnessing of Peter the apostle as well as on segments of tradition (some gathered in collections) which had been developed in the Church largely as reminiscences about Jesus in response to later questions and problems.

41. As Mark's Gospel is generally accepted as the principal source of the narrative order and content in both "Matthew" and Luke, so the mysterious Sayings of Jesus, or Q (for the German word *Quelle* meaning "source"), a hypothetical written source, is generally accepted as a common tradition underlying the discourse material shared by "Matthew" and Luke but not contained in Mark. A good example would be the threefold temptations of Jesus in Matt 4:1-11 and Luke 4:1-13. Mark's Gospel simply says: "He [Jesus] stayed in the wasteland forty days, put to the test there by Satan. He was with the wild beasts, and angels waited on him" (Mark 1:13, NAB). John, probably more accurately, recounts the temptations of Jesus as recurring in the midst of Jesus' life and ministry, e.g., in John 6:14-15, 34-35; 7:2-9.

The threefold temptations common to "Matthew" and Luke and stemming from the Sayings of Jesus, or Q, obviously constitute a dramatization of the incarnational fact that Jesus, being truly human, was tempted. "The word became flesh" (John 1:14, NAB), that is, human in all our human weakness including temptations: "one who was tempted in every way that we are, yet never sinned" (Heb 4:15).

Why the dramatization? To emphasize the humanity of Jesus. And indeed the dramatization was effective because, as a matter of fact, it is the threefold dramatization of the temptations that remains in our memory. Why do I call it a dramatization rather than a detailed factual account? Well, who was there? Only Satan and Jesus. Now Satan would no more tell of his defeats than did the pharaohs of ancient Egypt. Nor can I picture Jesus, one evening around the apostolic campfire, asking, "Did I ever tell you about my temptations?" Note, however, that Luke has decided to reverse the order of the second and third temptations as we see them in "Matthew." Why? Evidently to have Jesus end up at the Temple just as the Lukan Gospel begins and ends at the Temple (see Luke 1:9; 24:53). Another clear example of Q material in "Matthew" and Luke is the Sermon on the Mount in Matt 5–7 and the Sermon on the Plain in Luke 6:17-49, which time does not permit me to expand on.

42. A key question regarding Luke's Gospel is this: Where did Luke obtain the material of Jesus' story parables, also called "action parables" and "reversal parables"? I am referring to such unforgettable stories as those of the good Samaritan (see Luke 10:25-37), the greedy farmer (see 12:13-21), the prodigal son (see 15:11-32), the unjust steward (see 16:1-8), the rich man and Lazarus (see 16:19-31), the Pharisee and the publican (see 18:9-14), and the parable-life Zacchaeus the publican (see 19:1-10).

It should be noted, first of all, that these wonderful stories are found only in Luke and only in Luke's journey account, which comprises the ten chapters (Luke 9:51–19:27) in which Luke gathers together those teachings of Jesus which seem to spell out the requirements or characteristics of those who follow Jesus on the "way" to the heavenly Jerusalem.

Where did Luke find these parables? We shall probably never know for sure, but there are several possibilities: (1) from the Sayings of Jesus, or Q which Luke shared with "Matthew," who apparently omitted them because they were teachings for individual Christians rather than for or about the Church as a whole, with which he was preoccupied; (2) from another source or sources generally listed as L and hinted at in the prologue under the heading of "eyewitnesses and ministers of the word" (Luke 1:2, NAB), including the seventy-two additional preachers found only in Luke 10:1-20, whom along with others Luke may have contacted during Paul's imprisonment at Caesarea Maritima; (3) from John, whom Luke visited in Ephesus according to my speculative account, though it is less likely that Luke derived these parables from John (who uses only two nature parables in his Gospel: the good shepherd and the sheep in John 10:1-18 and the true vine and the branches in John 15:1-8) than that he gained material for his Infancy Gospel, for stories about people whose names appear in both Gospels; e.g., Lazarus, Martha, and Mary (see Luke 10:38-42; 16:19-31; and John 11:1-44; 12:1-11); and for other stories common to both, e.g., the miraculous catch of fish (see Luke 5:1-11 and John 21:1-14) and other Lukan-Johannine material listed in Fitzmyer, *The Gospel According to Luke* 2:87-88; (4) from Luke's own creative imagination, taking teachings of Jesus and putting them into story parable form for greater effect. All of these theories are legitimate and possible, but in my own opinion the most plausible would be a combination of (1) and (4), namely that these action parables are from Q or the Sayings of Jesus, omitted by "Matthew" for his own reasons but rewritten by Luke in his own inimitable dramatic style.

43. The statement that Theophilus had "shot all his arrows" employs an expression which I and many others have used to indicate that we have acted or spoken to the best of our ability with nothing more to offer. I have not been able to identify its origin but have included it because, like the next expression, to "win the battle," it fits so well with the military role of Theophilus at Philippi.

44. There is no hard evidence that Theophilus, now *strategós* (general) of the Roman military colony of Philippi, is to be identified with the nameless jailer who, together with his entire household, was converted and baptized when Paul and his companions were miraculously freed from jail but chose to remain. But while there is no evidence for this connection neither is there evidence against it, so why not entertain the possibility?

45. As an important example of the Greek use of different words with diverse meanings, where other languages, ancient and modern, are content to use the same word equivocally, there are two different words for time in Greek: *chrónos* meaning "chronological time" and *kairós* meaning "event or eventful time, useful or meaningful time, occasion, or opportunity." Both expressions

are used carefully and extensively in Luke-Acts, sometimes in the same context, e.g., "And leading him [Jesus] up, he [Satan] showed him all the kingdoms of the world in a moment of time [*chrónos*] . . ." (Luke 4:5, WFD); "And, having completed every temptation, the devil departed from him [Jesus] for a while [or until a favorable occasion, *kairós*]" (Luke 4:13, WFD).

46. *Kaleméra* (a combination of the adjective *kalós,é,on* meaning "beautiful" or "good" and the noun *heméra* meaning "day") was and is a common greeting or farewell, "Good day!"

47. Luke's Gospel is often called the "Gospel of prayer" because it shows Jesus at prayer before or at the most important events of his public life, e.g., his baptism (see 3:21), his choice of the Twelve (see 6:12), his transfiguration (see 9:28-29), and of course his passion and death (see 22:39-46), and it also emphasizes his teachings on prayer (see 10:38–11:13).

48. There is an ancient tradition that Luke was not only a physician and an evangelist but even an artist of note. A venerable painting of Mary in the Sistine Chapel of Saint Mary Major Basilica in Rome purports to have been painted by him, but this is only a pious tradition; the painting in question dates from many centuries later. It is certainly true, however, that Luke was *an artist*, and a great one, in the medium of the written word, the inspired and inspiring Word of God.

49. The reference here is to the mystical experiences of Moses at Mount Sinai in Exod 33:19-23; Elijah at Mount Horeb (generally identified with Mount Sinai) in 1 Kgs 19:9-13; and of course Jesus in his transfiguration (accompanied by Moses and Elijah) on a mountain, traditionally identified with Mount Tabor, in Luke 9:28-36.

50. This is a quotation from the dramatic revelation to the child Samuel at the sanctuary of the ark of the covenant at Shiloh in 1 Sam 3:9-10, NAB.

51. See 1 Kgs 19:11-12.

52. Mark 10:38, WFD.

53. A rather free summary of and reflection on Ps 139.

54. 1 Kgs 19:11-12.

55. Idem.

56. Luke's surrender in my story is reminiscent of Mary's fiat in his account of the annunciation (see Luke 1:38).

57. Phil 4:13, WFD. As leader of the Philippian Church, Luke may have made his own this statement of Paul.

58. Epidaurus in southern Greece and Pergamum in western Asia Minor were the two main centers of the worship of the god of healing, Aesculapius, symbolized by a serpent as we still see on a doctor's caduceus today. Possibly the symbolism of the serpent was chosen because in the ancient world serpents were thought to be immortal, since they were able to slough off their old skin and thus renew their life, a belief which is probably referred to in the prebiblical epic of Gilgamesh. *See* James Pritchard, *Ancient Near Eastern Texts Relating to the Old Testament* (Princeton, N.J.: Princeton University Press, 1955) 96.

The methods of the physicians at these two famous health centers involved fasts, sleeping in the temple of Aesculapius, and dream analysis as the principal means of diagnosis and cure, apparently a mixture of religion and primitive psychiatry *(Encyclopaedia Britannica,* 1964, s.v. "Asclepius").

59. Hippocrates, the father of medicine, whose name still remains in the famous Hippocratic oath taken by all physicians, was born on Cos, a beautiful Greek island off the coast of southwestern Asia Minor, in 460 B.C., traveled widely, wrote profusely, and established a school of medicine which revolutionized the science by taking it out of the realm of religious superstition. *(Encyclopedia Britannica* s.v. "Hippocrates," also "Psychiatry"). Paul, Luke, and companions visited Cos overnight in Acts 21:1.

60. The perfect example of Jesus' compassionate initiative is that of Jesus' raising to life the only son of the widow of Naim in Luke 7:11-17.

61. The perfect example of Jesus' compassion for the most neglected and rejected is that of Jesus' cure of the ten lepers in Luke 17:11-19.

62. An allusion to Isa 55:8.

63. Two things in particular point up this profoundly mystical idea of the Church as the continuation of Christ's life, ministry, and suffering, namely (1) the first verse of Acts in which Luke states that Jesus only began to do and teach in his lifetime (the content of the Gospel), the clear inference being that he continues in the Church (the content of Acts) and (2) the running parallel between Jesus' life in Luke and his life in the Church in Acts, which will be clearer when spelled out in the outlines.

64. Paul's conversion by the risen Christ on the Damascus Road, like Peter's triple vision at Joppa and consequent conversion of Cornelius at Caesarea, is so important that it is told three times: in Acts 9:1-19; 22:1-16; 26:1-18.

65. *See* Matt 28:20.

66. This understanding of Luke's theology of salvation history as comprising three epochs was first popularized by Hans Conzelmann, *Die Mitte der Zeit* (The Middle of Time) (Tübingen, West Germany: J. C. B. Mohr, 1953), especially after translation into English by Geoffrey Buswell under the title of *The Theology of St. Luke* (New York: Harper & Row, 1961).

67. The reference is particularly to Eph 1:22-23, NAB, "He has put all things under Christ's feet and has made him, thus exalted, head of the church, which is his body, the fullness of him who fills the universe in all its parts."

68. *See* Matt 13:24-30, 47-50; 18:5-9.

69. Described by John in 1 John 2:16, RSV, as "the lust of the flesh, the lust of the eyes, and the pride of life."

70. At Luke 9:17, his "great omission," *see* Mark 6:45–8:26.

71. If Jesus' action parables in Luke are not from the Q tradition and simply omitted by Matthew as beyond his scope, then Luke must have collected these on his own, perhaps over a period of some time and especially during the two-year imprisonment of Paul at Caesarea Maritima.

72. Caesarea Maritima (Caesarea by the Sea) was built by Herod the Great between 22 and 9 B.C. to serve as an adequate seaport on the Mediterranean

coast of Judea. As we see in other Herodian construction (e.g., the temple area), Caesarea's artificial harbor and public buildings (among them an aqueduct, amphitheater, theater, and hippodrome) were constructed of massive stones, many of which are still in place today. Caesarea also included an ingenious sewer system, whereby the Great Sea tides washed the refuse from beneath the city's streets. When Judea became a Roman province in A.D. 6 with the deposition of Herod's son Archelaus, the Roman governors or procurators including Pilate, Felix, and Festus (all mentioned in the New Testament) resided at Caesarea. Also residing at Caesarea were Cornelius, the centurion received into the Church by Peter as the first gentile convert (see Acts 10) and Philip the deacon with his four prophetess daughters (see Acts 8:40; 21:8-9), from whom Luke may have gathered valuable information during Paul's Caesarean imprisonment. *See* Bruce, *Jesus and Paul: Places They Knew*, 111-15.

73. Ephesus, one of the four great cities of the ancient world, is now totally in ruins, but what ruins! Thanks to annual excavations and restorations by Austrian archaeologists, this magnificent city continues to grow into a semblance of what it must have been in the first century A.D. More detailed description of it, however, will be reserved until later in this work when we take up the writings of John the apostle and evangelist. For now, let us remember that according to Scripture and tradition, after John had to leave Palestine he took up residence at Ephesus, first with Mary whom Jesus had entrusted to his care as we read in John 19:26-27, then for some time—after her assumption until his death around the end of the century. *See* Bruce, *Jesus and Paul: Places They Knew*, 106-10.

74. These parallels comprise three in particular: (1) between John the Baptist and Jesus in the Infancy Gospel, (2) between the life of Jesus in the Gospel and of Jesus in the Church in Acts, and (3) between Peter and Paul in Acts. These will become more evident in the following segment when we consider outlines of the twin Gospels of Luke.

75. There are rather clear inclusion-conclusions in both of Luke's works: the Temple at Jerusalem at the beginning and end of Luke's Gospel (see Luke 1:9; 24:53) and the kingdom of God at the beginning and end of his Acts (see 1:6; 28:31).

76. Some of the triplets in Luke's writings are (1) three teachings on prayer (see Luke 10:38–11:13); three parables on sin and reconciliation (see Luke 15:1-32); three prophecies of coming death and resurrection (see Luke 9:22, 44; 18:31-33); and three accounts each of the visions of Peter (see Acts 10:9-48; 11:1-18; 15:7-12) and Paul (see Acts 9:1-19; 22:1-16; 26:9-18).

77. The structure of concentric circles is best seen in the outline I have drawn up of Acts as the unfolding of Jesus' directive to the apostles in Acts 1:8, WFD: "You will be my witnesses in Jerusalem and in all Judea and Samaria and to the end of the earth," an unfolding that shows the Church beginning in Jerusalem, then spreading in Judea and Samaria, and then, especially with Paul, expanding even to Rome, the capital of the entire Roman Empire, whose boundaries represented "the ends of the earth."

78. Chiasmus is not as evident in Luke as in "Matthew" and John, but in an outline of Luke's unique material in his Gospel, I do show an apparent chiasmus both in the Galilean ministry and in the journey account.

79. The journey structure is evident in both of Luke's works: in the great journey account of Luke 9:51–19:27 and in the journeys of Philip, Peter, and Paul and his companions in Acts 8–28.

80. The idea of making "a virtue of necessity" is common to almost all literature, being found most notably in both Chaucer's "Knight's Tale" and "Squire's Tales" and in Shakespeare's *Two Gentlemen of Verona*, act 4, scene 1. *See* Burton Stevenson, *The Home Book of Quotations* 10th ed. (New York: Dodd, Mead, 1967) 1393.

81. This idea of our pilgrimage on the way is found above all in Heb 4:1-11; 12:1-2, etc. as well as in the third Eucharistic Prayer of the liturgy of the Mass.

82. The concept of life with its difficulties as a journey makes a very appropriate symbol, especially for those who are required to journey often, as was the case with Paul, Luke, and other early Christian leaders. What made journeys notably difficult in biblical times and still to some extent in today's Third World was and is the lack of adequate roads and road signs. With the exception of the famous Roman roads, which were built for military, commercial, and communication purposes, what passed for roads were simply human and animal paths that followed the convolutions of the terrain. Just one false turn could cause one to miss a destination by miles. It is easy to understand, then, why a good road was much appreciated and became the symbol of a good way of life. The earliest designation of Christians was "those who are of the way" (Acts 9:2, WFD). Along with the parallels, the journeys are the principal structures of Luke's works. In his Gospel, he expands the journey segment of the *kerygma*, which takes only one chapter in Mark, to ten chapters (Luke 9:51–19:27) containing the epitome of all that should characterize those who follow Jesus to the heavenly Jerusalem. And of course, Luke's Acts is almost entirely an account of journeys, particularly those of St. Paul.

83. This is a quotation from Acts 1:8, which actually contains a summary of the entire book: the witness to Jesus in ever greater extension from Jerusalem to Judea, Samaria, and the ends of the earth.

84. The internal growth of Christianity consisted predominantly of the integraton of Jews and Gentiles on an equal footing without the latter having to become Jews in order to be Christians, according to the decision or *dógma* (the noun form of the impersonal Greek verb *dokeî* meaning "it seems good"), which was settled at the Council of Jerusalem around A.D. 49 or 50 (see Acts 15). Of course, the description of the Church as the "body of Christ" is from Paul, who uses it extensively in Romans, First Corinthians, Ephesians, and Colossians, as we will see more in detail when we study him.

85. In Luke as in "Matthew," there is a continuity between Israel and the Church which is seen especially in the early chapters of Acts, but there is less of a polemic against Pharisaic Judaism as pseudo-Israel because, as a Gentile who writes for Gentiles, that is not Luke's preoccupation.

86. The word "enthusiasm" is carefully used here because in its composite significance (from *en* meaning "in" and *theós* meaning "God") it speaks not just of excitement but of inspiration, that of Theophilus as well as of Luke.

87. Inspired or not, writing is never an easy task. Since even the inspired authors wrote in a human fashion, they needed to research, reflect, write, and revise in the same way as any noninspired writer. This, of course, was far more taxing when the materials were stylus and wax tablets, reed or feather pen and papyrus or parchment. What they would have given for pencil or pen and paper, still more for typewriters, and incredibly more for word processors and computers! Nevertheless, in spite of primitive materials, poor lighting, and many other inconveniences, even hardships, they wrote impelled by their love and zeal in a selfless exercise of God's gifts that seldom receives the recognition and gratitude it deserves.

88. Neapolis means in Greek "New City," the same name as Naples in Italy, which was originally a Greek colony. Ironically, while Naples is an Italian corruption of Neapolis, the current name of ancient Neapolis is Kavalla, a Greek corruption of the Italian word *cavallo* meaning "horse." In the first century A.D. it was both the seaport and suburb of Philippi, even though it lay a dozen miles distant by the Egnatian Way, which passes over Mount Symbolum, then terminates at Kavalla. The beautiful, thriving little city also boasted a three-level aqueduct as well as an acropolis with a fortress still in respectable condition. *See* Jack Finegan, *Light from the Ancient Past* (Princeton, N.J.: Princeton University Press, 1946) 209–10.

89. In fear of storms, ships usually sailed in sight of land.

90. This journey of Luke to visit John at Ephesus is fiction, for we have no evidence that it ever occurred. I like to imagine that it did, both because of Luke's curiosity as an historian and because of his desire to learn more about Mary and the early years of Jesus. Not that it would have been absolutely necessary, for it is generally agreed among Scripture scholars that his Infancy Gospel is largely his own composition. This, of course, could still be the case even if he did learn the main content from John.

91. To land at Ephesus, ships (or large boats) had to sail or row up the narrow Cayster River from the sea, then turn into an inland harbor. Since the river was constantly conveying silt to its mouth, a continuing process of dredging had to be employed to keep Ephesus a seaport. In time, as the city lost its importance, this process was neglected, so that today Ephesus is no longer a seaport and can be approached by sea only by landing at Kushadasi and traveling seven miles inland by car or bus.

92. The Arcadian Way, the colonnaded road that stretched from the inland harbor to the great theater, the heart of ancient Ephesus, is now quite visible but shortened. As one walks upon it toward the theater, a glance to the left reveals the ruins of the double Church of St. Mary, which held the Council of Ephesus in A.D. 431 that declared her to be *theotókos* (Mother of God), for she gave birth to the divine person, Jesus, according to his human nature.

93. As mentioned above, the Arcadian Way leads to the great theater where

the riot of the silversmiths, occasioned by the success of Paul's preaching, was quietly dismissed by a *grammateús* (scribe or clerk) of Ephesus. Luke would turn right here and proceed past the agora and the library of Celsus to the more inhabited area of the city in search of John the apostle.

94. *See* John 19:26-27. More on this when we study John.

95. Apparently, while Mary was alive John considered his care of her too important to be endangered by active involvement in administration. Even after his sacred charge was fulfilled, John seems to have left to others the distracting task of administration to devote himself to continued contemplation, preaching, teaching, instructing, and counseling. This would explain why Paul appointed his disciple Timothy as his delegated bishop of Ephesus, according to indications in his two Letters to Timothy.

96. This ancient Hebrew greeting (Ruth 2:4) must have been cherished and continued by Christians, for it is still a part of the liturgy today. In Ruth the response is "The Lord bless you!" which may have been changed in time to the current "And also with you" used in the liturgy now.

97. Traditionally, and I believe, still, according to a majority of scholars, the beloved disciple in John's Gospel is none other than John himself, who certainly was one of Jesus' three favorites, the other two being his brother James and his fishing partner, Peter.

98. It should not be surprising that John's innocence and his years of close association with Jesus and Mary as well as his years of deep contemplation could have given him a spiritual instinct which enabled him to "read" the minds and hearts of others.

99. Just as "Matthew" needed an Infancy Gospel for three reasons, (1) to show the fulfillment of messianic prophecy with the coming of Jesus, (2) to preview what Jesus would be like in the Gospel at large, and (3) to balance the eschatological discourse in his chiasmic arrangement, so Luke also needed an Infancy Gospel at least for the second reason and also to balance the "infancy gospel of the Church" in his Acts of Apostles.

100. As with "Matthew," so also with Luke, it is extremely important to keep always in mind that the Infancy Gospel is not part of the kerygma, the eyewitness-based story of Jesus in his public ministry and saving events. Hence, we are not only justified but well advised not to seek literal history in it but rather a theological and spiritual overture to the Gospel as a whole.

101. Just as Luke's visit to John, as I have said above, is drawn from my imagination and, to some extent, reasoning, so also this kind of advice from John to Luke is purely imaginary. Nonetheless, it would have been comforting and strengthening for Luke to hear such assurances, which would certainly be reflected in the freedom with which John later on will treat the life and teachings of Jesus in his Gospel.

102. Quotations are exact or almost exact word-for-word references, in this instance to the Old, or Hebrew, Testament. Allusions are descriptions or narratives which are so worded that the reader is led by the writer to think of some teaching, happening, or personage in the Hebrew Testament and thereby

derive greater fruit from what is said or written. One great difference between "Matthew" and Luke is that the former usually quotes from the Old Testament while the latter only alludes to it. Each is very effective in fulfilling the author's purpose.

103. This is an allusion to Paul's insightful description of *agápe* or Christian love, as patient and kind, etc. (see 1 Cor 13:4-7).

104. The great reverence shown to John the apostle in no way detracts from the respect and authority for the successor of Peter as bishop of Rome, who was what we now refer to as the "pope," a word derived from "papa," the Italian word for "Father." It is well known that while John was still alive at Ephesus, it was Clement of Rome, the third successor of Peter, who lovingly but authoritatively settled problems at Corinth by letter in much the same way as Paul had done in his lifetime. *See* St. Clement of Rome, "The Letter to the Corinthians," trans. Francis Glimm *The Apostolic Fathers*, The Fathers of the Church (New York: Cima, 1947) 9-58.

105. The title of Luke's second book is not "The Acts of the Apostles" *(hai práxeis tôn apostólon)* but just "Acts of Apostles" *(práxeis apostólon)*, i.e., of Peter and Paul.

106. One of the misdirected attempts to help people read and understand the Bible is that of weaving the four Gospels into one continuous Gospel story, thereby losing the distinctive portrait of Christ and the Church characteristic of each. Nor is this a new phenomenon in the Church, for the earliest such harmony, the famous *Diatésseron* of Tatian, meaning "[one] through four," was published in Greek and Syriac (updated Aramaic) in the second half of the first century. Afterward, there were harmonies in Latin, Persian, Arabic, Italian, Dutch, and modern languages. *See* Patrick Skehan: "Texts and Versions," The Jerome Biblical Commentary (Englewood Cliffs, N.J.: Prentice-Hall, 1968) 2:576. Today, this is no longer done very often except for the Christmas story, in which the disparate Infancy Gospels of "Matthew" and Luke are somehow woven together into one story, thereby missing the unique contribution of each.

107. As an example of Luke's impeccable Greek, he alone (except for Paul, rarely) seems to use the optative mood, which had been employed to express softer shades of verbal meaning (may or might, should or would) but which had largely disappeared from Koiné (Common) Greek by the time of Christ. A good example is in Luke 1:29, WFD: "At the word [of the angel], she [Mary] was deeply troubled and wondered what kind of greeting this might be."

108. These subthemes of Luke will be treated, at least in brief, when we consider theological and spiritual matters in the third part of this study of Luke-Acts.

109. *See* Acts 16:10-40; 20:5 ff.

110. Such a title as "Your Excellency" (Luke 1:4) applied to Theophilus (Luke 1:3; Acts 1:1) would seem to identify Theophilus as a magistrate, and in the hypothesis that Luke wrote at Philippi, Theophilus would most probably be one of the *strategoí* (generals) who governed that Roman military col-

ony, perhaps even the chief of staff, so to speak. A strong bond of friendship between the leader of the local Christian Church and the Christian leader of the military colony would not have been very surprising.

111. I am calling attention once again to the basic fourpart kerygma, or public proclamation of the Church about Jesus Christ, not to belabor the point or to provide an exegesis of the obvious but rather to call attention to the fact that it also enters into the discourses in Acts, particularly those of Peter in Acts 2 and 10, and that of Paul in Acts 13.

112. These are the forms that we have already examined, primarily when studying Mark and, to some extent, "Matthew," forms which are the special subject matter of form critics such as Bultmann and Dibelius, while their students and successors such as Marxsen, Bornkamm, and Conzelmann were more concerned to see how the evangelists reworked the forms to suit their purposes and theologies.

113. Among the most attractive features of Luke's Gospel is his marvelous collection of what I like to call "story" or "action" or "reversal" parables. Unique to Luke, they are found exclusively in his journey narrative which, as we have already noted, is not so much a geographical journey as a theological and spiritual one containing all the virtues that should characterize those who truly set out to follow Christ to the heavenly Jerusalem. Even more than most parables because they are clothed in real flesh and blood, these dramatic parables challenge us in the depth of our being as no others in Scripture or rabbinical literature.

114. For an adequate treatment of Luke's use of inclusion-conclusion, concentric circles, and chiasmus, please see above nn. 75, 77, and 78. I would just add to n. 75 two other and lesser inclusion-conclusions, namely those in which both the Infancy Gospel and the temptation account in Luke virtually end at the Temple of Jerusalem (see Luke 2:46, 49; 4:9).

115. For a previous treatment on parallels, journeys, and triplets, please refer to nn. 74, 76, 79, and 81–83. Besides the major journeys in Luke-Acts which are listed there I would like to add some lesser but important ones: (1) in the Infancy Gospel, those of Mary's visitation (see Luke 1:39-56); Jesus' nativity and presentation (2:1-39); and the finding of Jesus in the Temple (see 2:41-51); as well as (2) the very symbolic journey of Jesus with the two disciples of Emmaus (see Luke 24:13-35) in which Jesus first enlightens them from the Scriptures, then reveals himself to them in the breaking of the bread, reflecting in dramatic story form the Liturgy of the Word and Liturgy of the Eucharist, which comprise the Holy Sacrifice of the Mass, complete with the desired aftermath of sharing with others what the disciples (and we too) receive (see Luke 24:33-35).

116. This prophecy (or pseudoprophecy) of Dan 9:24 seems to refer to seventy weeks of years (490 years), from the time of Jeremiah until Israel's deliverance from oppression under Antiochus Epiphanes. The Fathers of the Church, however, generally understood the 490 years as the time between the supposed prophecy of Daniel until the messianic salvation by Jesus. *See* Louis Hart-

man, "Daniel," *JBC*, 1:457. Luke, for his part, supplies indications of time (see Luke 1:26, 56; 2:6, 22) which add up to 490 days from the annunciation about John to Zechariah in the Temple about John until the presentation of Jesus at the Temple (and purification of Mary) exactly forty days after birth (see Lev 12:1-12). Is this coincidence, God's providential design, or Luke's arrangement? It is difficult to say, but this is only one of many symbolic allusions characteristic of Luke's Infancy Gospel.

117. The symbolic riches contained in the annunciation to Mary will be taken up in the third part of our treatment.

118. Likewise, the symbolism of Mary's visitation to her cousin Elizabeth, since it is so closely associated with the annunciation, will be treated in the third part.

119. In Luke's description of Jesus' birth, note his typical emphasis on poverty, especially in the fact that with no room (for privacy?) in the caravansery (where animals were kept in the square courtyard, while people rested on or under the roof surrounding it), the birth of God's Son took place in a stable, as indicated by the manger or crib for feeding animals. Moreover, in Luke's Gospel the first to welcome the Messiah were poor and lowly shepherds, who then "made known" (the proper meaning of *gnorízo*, not "understood" as in the NAB), thus anticipating the evangelizing of Luke-Acts (see Luke 2:20).

120. Jesus, being the firstborn son, had to be presented to Yahweh for his service because of the sparing of Israel's firstborn sons in the tenth plague of Egypt (see Exod 13:1-2, 11-16), but then he could be "bought back" from that service in view of Yahweh's choice of the tribe of Levi for his special service (see Num 3:44-51). As we see in the next episode, Jesus, in spite of being bought back from the service of Yahweh's house, came to realize that as Son of God in a unique way, he was still consecrated to and somehow responsible for the Temple service and worship of his true Father.

121. The finding of Jesus in the Temple, whether it really happened or not, is important because of the symbolism of the young and human Jesus beginning to recognize and accept his divine sonship, yet continuing to be obedient to Mary and Joseph and growing (as he had to in his human nature) "in wisdom, age [or height], and grace [or graciousness] before God and men [humans]" (Luke 41-52, WFD). We may wonder if it was at this time or earlier that Mary and Joseph chose to inform Jesus of his extraordinary birth.

Note that I said, "whether it really happened," because the Infancy Gospel of Luke, like that of "Matthew," is not part of the kerygma and therefore not necessarily based on eyewitness history, but rather, somewhat like the first eleven chapters of Genesis, it forms a theologico-spiritual preview, or overture, of the portrait of Jesus in his public life, death, and resurrection. All we can logically regard as historical is what the "infancy gospels" of "Matthew" and Luke have in common, primarily that Jesus of Nazareth was born at Bethlehem, the ancestral home of David, of a virgin mother named Mary, who was married to a descendant of David named Joseph, that he was the Messiah of Israel and Son of God, and that he grew up in the lowly village of Nazareth.

The important thing to remember is that (1) history is not the only kind of truth and in fact not the principal concern of the inspired writers; (2) there are many kinds of truth in the Bible: that of metaphors, similes, parables, Infancy Gospels, etc.; and (3) in Luke's (and ''Matthew's'') Infancy Gospel we should look primarily not for history as we know it but for the rich treasures of theological and spiritual meaning intended by the inspired and inspiring author and brought out by his matchless use of allusions to (or quotations from, in ''Matthew's'' case) the Old Testament.

122. Note the historical emphasis in Luke's Gospel as he takes pains to situate the story of John the Baptist and, of course, Jesus himself in a brief but accurate and comprehensive historical setting.

123. Note the social dimension of John's teaching, found only in Luke's Gospel (see 3:7-18) and already anticipated by the Canticles of Mary and Zechariah (1:46-55, 67-79).

124. Note Luke's emphasis on Jesus' praying at the time of his baptism as also at all the principal times of his life in Luke's Gospel. Note also that as in Mark, the voice from heaven is directed to Jesus himself rather than about him as in ''Matthew'' and that it identifies him at the same time as Son of God (see Ps 2:7) and Servant of Yahweh (see Isa 42:1).

125. One can easily note important differences between the genealogy of Jesus in Luke 3:23-38 and Matt 1:1-17. These are due not, as is often thought, to his genealogy being traced through Mary by Luke and through Joseph by ''Matthew.'' Jewish genealogies were never traced through the mother. Mary may not even have been of the tribe of Judah. It was the legal descent from David through Joseph that counted, and both genealogies are traced through him, not for the sake of history but of teaching. As we have seen, that of ''Matthew's'' Gospel teaches that Jesus, the descendant of Abraham through David, is the expected Messiah of the Jews. Luke's genealogy, in keeping with his Gospel, teaches that Jesus (Yahweh is salvation) is the Savior of the whole human race, a truth which is elucidated by Luke's tracing his roots all the way back to Adam (man), whom he pointedly refers to as ''son of god'' (see Luke 3:38).

126. Luke has taken Jesus' disappointing return to his hometown of Nazareth, which appears later in Mark (6:1-6) and even later in ''Matthew'' (13:54-58), and made it an opening messianic manifesto for his public ministry. For this purpose he reads the beautiful messianic passage from Isa 61:1-2, which portrays the expected Messiah not as a conquering national leader but as a compassionate figure who is anointed by the Lord (the word ''Messiah'' in Hebrew and *Christós* in Greek means ''Anointed'') to bring good news (the gospel) to the poor, to heal the brokenhearted, to proclaim liberty to captives and release to prisoners. Then to his hearers' astonishment, he identifies himself as that Messiah. The end result, of course, is that his ''friends'' of Nazareth attempt to cast him over the precipice, which is not at the highest point north of the town but rather to the south where extended Nazareth overhangs the great Valley of Esdraelon in what is now called in Arabic *Jebel Qafzeh* (Moun-

tain of the Leap). What a perfect and prophetic opening for Jesus' public ministry!

127. The story of the miraculous catch of fish, which in our Gospel sets the stage for the call of Jesus' first disciples, is apparently used by the supplementary author of John's Gospel after that apostle's death to introduce the conferring on Peter of the primacy promised in Matt 16:13-20 and also to lay to rest the mistaken belief that John would not die (cf. Luke 5:1-11 with John 21:1-23).

128. In Matt 5–7 we have seen Jesus' Sermon on the Mount in allusion to Moses' mediation of the covenant and Law on Mount Sinai in Exod 19–20 ff. Now, in a shorter borrowing from *Q*, we have in Luke 6:17-49 Jesus' Sermon on the Plain, which portrays the Lord not as a distant mediator on a mountan like Moses but as an easily accessible leader on a plain, not only showing compassion but demanding it of all his followers.

129. It should be noted that the middle section of our outline about Jesus' Galilean ministry is all about women (Luke 7:11–8:21), at least in those parts unique to Luke. This is important, for along with other passages in Luke it clearly shows his predilection for the role of women in Jesus' life and the life of the Church. If the times and culture had been different, would he have chosen women also to be apostles and priests? We may never know for sure, but one fact is clear, namely that in Luke's Gospel and indeed in all the Scriptures God certainly chooses women for an inspirational leadership role, such as that of Sarah and Rebekah; Miriam and Rahab; Deborah and Jahel; Ruth, Judith, and Esther; Mary of Nazareth and Mary of Magdala; Martha and Mary of Bethany; Mary of Jerusalem and Tabitha, Lydia and Priscilla; etc. Is it not a pity that some (perhaps many) of our Catholic women are so desirous of the institutional leadership of priests and bishops that they overlook the precious God-given opportunities to exercise inspirational leadership?

130. What follows in Luke 9:51-19:27 is not so much a geographical journey, as evidenced by the fact that it jumps back and forth among places, but rather a theological and spiritual journey, a way of life, a portrayal of discipleship, the "followship" of Jesus en route to "Jerusalem." As such, it is of major importance in Luke's thought and Gospel, containing as it does Jesus' peripatetic (walking) instructions for our journey with him to the new, or heavenly, Jerusalem, the kingdom of God to which we are called.

131. Nowhere else is this "sending of the seventy-two" mentioned, so it is a moot point whether it occurred or whether it was simply a literary device of Luke's creation to distinguish between the apostles' (and bishops') more authoritative mission in Luke 9:1-6 (involving exorcisms as well) and the less authoritative but broader role of other Church leaders (priests, deacons, lay ministers) in spreading the good news of God's kingdom. The expression "Greet no one along the way" (Luke 10:4) sounds terribly uncharitable unless we have some idea of the amount of time an Oriental greeting can consume, time which Jesus' disciples cannot spare in their preaching mission.

132. The parable of the lost or prodigal son is a masterpiece in its description of sin, repentance or conversion, confession, and reconciliation, whose

Greek terms can be very helpful in our spiritual life. For this purpose *see* my book *To Live the Word, Inspired and Incarnate* (New York: Alba House, 1988) 330ff.

133. Note that the greetings to Jesus on his messianic entry into Jerusalem are rather different in all four Gospels (see Mark 11:9-10; Matt 21:5; Luke 19:38; John 12:13-15) and that in Luke they clearly recall the angelic greeting at his birth in Bethlehem (see Luke 2:14). Inclusion-conclusion?

134. Almost out of the blue in the account of the Last Supper, Luke's Gospel portrays the unique (though less explicit) leadership role that Jesus confers on Simon Peter: "Simon, Simon, Satan has asked to sift you [plural] like wheat, but I have prayed for you [singular] that your faith may not fail, and you [singular], when you have turned back, strengthen your brothers" (Luke 22:31-32, WFD). When Peter then boasts his willingness to die with Jesus, the Lord sadly predicts his triple denial before cockcrow.

135. See the brief treatment of the Emmaus event at the end of my remarks on journeys in Luke, n. 115.

136. Luke very cleverly couples his twin Gospels not only by his dedication of both to Theophilus but also by ending his Gospel and beginning his Acts with the same events: his worldwide commission, promise of the empowering Spirit, and ascension into heaven (see Luke 24:46-51; Acts 1:6-11).

137. When properly translated, Luke's prologue to his Acts provides us with the key not only to Acts but to the very Church and all of Church history. In contrast to the translation in the New American Bible (which fails to render an entire Greek verb into English) and even the Jerusalem Bible (which fails to render that verb in its most natural sense), the all-important first verse should read, "I wrote my former account, O Theophilus, about all the things which Jesus began to do and to teach until the day when, having enjoined his chosen apostles through the Holy Spirit [or having enjoined his apostles whom he had chosen through the Holy Spirit], he was taken up [into Heaven]" (Acts 1:1-2, WFD). The key word is "began" (*érxato*, the aorist, or past definite, of *árchomai*, "I begin." What Luke is saying, then, is that in his lifetime Jesus only began to do and teach; he continues to do so but now through his Church and its members, especially Peter and Paul. That is why Luke omits from his Gospel any sojourn of Jesus among the Gentiles, so that he can show him going to the gentiles through his followers in Acts. That is also why in John's Gospel Jesus can make that enigmatic statement, "Amen, amen I say to you, the one who believes in me will also do the works that I do, and will do even greater works than these because I am going to the Father" (John 14:12, WFD). When Peter, for example, does miracles by his very shadow (see Acts 5:15-16), something never recorded of Jesus, it is not Peter but Jesus doing it.

138. While the parallel outlines of Jesus in himself and in the Church are in chronological sequence, this is not so in the parallels between Peter and Paul in Acts. A quick glance at the biblical references will confirm this.

139. The so-called cloth cures described in Acts 19:12 can be described as the first mention of the use of relics in the Church.

140. At first glance it would appear that Luke's Acts of Apostles concludes with Paul under house arrest in Rome because he was shortly afterward beheaded for the faith, but the common (and evidently correct) consensus today is that after two years Paul was released from captivity in Rome because his Jewish accusers never appeared to press their charges, undoubtedly because they knew they had no case that would be honored in Rome. This would have been around A.D. 62 or 63, at least a year before the Great Fire and the Neronian persecution of the Church in Rome. Luke closes his Acts at this point since he has finished his story, that of following the Church "to the end of the earth."

Once released from his Roman captivity, Paul seems to have returned to Greece and even Asia Minor, at least as far as Troas, whence he asks Timothy in his final Letter (see 2 Tim 4:13) to bring his cloak and books, especially the parchments. It would have been during this period of some five years that Paul wrote his First Letter to Timothy in Ephesus and his Letter to Titus in Crete.

What then? Was Paul arrested again, possibly at Troas as some contend, taken back to Rome, tried and beheaded there? I think not, for the simple reason that the Neronian persecution was confined to the city of Rome. It seems more likely that around A.D. 67 or 68 Paul may have concluded that it was safe for him to return to the Eternal City, possibly to strengthen the Christians who had been decimated by martyrdom or defection since the Great Fire and its cruel aftermath. Or perhaps he was well aware that the persecution was still continuing but felt strongly moved to return and do what he could for the embattled Christian community in Rome. In either case, he was arrested and crowned his life with a glorious martyrdom.

141. *See* Charlton Lewis and Charles Short, *A Latin Dictionary* (Oxford: Clarendon, 1958) 387.

142. *Theological Dictionary of the New Testament, s.v. "páscho."*

143. *See* Francis Brown, S.R. Driver, and Charles Briggs, *A Hebrew and English Lexicon of the Old Testament* (Oxford: Clarendon, 1939) 933.

144. *See* St. Thomas Aquinas, *Summa Theologica,* trans. English Dominicans (New York: Benziger, 1947) vol. 1, pt. 1, quest. 6, ans. to obj. 1, p. 29.

145. *See* W. Norman Pittenger, "Bernard F. Meland, Process Thought, and the Significance of Christ," from *Religion in Life,* vol. 37, (1968), ed. Ewert Cousins in *Process Theology* (New York: Newman/Paulist, 1971) 205–06.

146. "El evangelio de Lucas presenta a Cristo como liberación del pecado, del demonio, de la ley farisaica, del mal en el mundo . . . incluyendo una verdadera denuncia contra la situación de opresión." (The Gospel of Luke presents Christ as liberation from sin, from the devil, from the Pharisaic Law, from evil in the world . . . including a veritable denunciation against the situation of oppression) Antonio Alonso, *Iglesia y Praxis de Liberacion* (Salamanca, Spain: Ediciones Sigueme, 1974) 124. *See also* Arturo Paoli, *Meditations on Saint Luke* (New York: Orbis, 1977).

147. Recall in particular the angelic announcements in regard to the birth of Isaac (see Gen 18:1-15), the call of Moses to rescue Israel from Egypt (see

Exod 3:2 ff.), the call of Gideon as liberator (see Judg 6:1-38), and the birth of Samson (see Judg 13:1-25).

148. In actuality, it is only through Jesus Christ that the promise to David is being fulfilled because it is a fact of history that the earthly Davidic dynasty ceased at the time of the Babylonian Captivity, which occurred in 587 or 586 B.C.

149. *The Birth of the Messiah* 307-09.

150. There is a further meaning possible in the angel's words which may or may not have been intended by Luke. In the second part of Luke 1:35 the expression *diò kaì tò gennómenon hágion klethésetai huiòs theoû*, in addition to the translation already given and accepted in substance by most translators today, is also able to mean "therefore the holy to be born will be called Son of God."

I can say that because the term *tò hágion* (the holy) happens to be the technical expression for that part of the tabernacle or Temple containing the altar of incense, the loaves of proposition, and the seven-branched lampstand. And what would it mean in this translation? That Jesus is to be the living temple of God, referred to in John 2:18-22 and Rev 21:22.

151. *Theological Dictionary of the New Testament*, 1967, s.v. "episkiázo."

152. See Brown, Driver, and Briggs, *A Hebrew and English Lexicon of the Old Testament* 1014-15.

153. Notice the passive voice of the optative mood used in Mary's response, *génoitó moi katà tò rhêmá sou*. Where we, especially we Americans, would be more inclined to say "Let me do . . . ," Mary shows complete dependence on God, complete abandonment to Divine Providence, by saying "Let it be done to me according to your word."

154. The Feast of the Annunciation and Incarnation is celebrated very solemnly on March 25 of each year nine months before December 25, the traditional date of Christmas, chosen to supplant the "Birthday of the Sun." No one seems to know the actual birthday of Jesus, so what could be more appropriate than choosing the day of the Birthday of the Sun to celebrate the birthday of the Sun of Justice, the very Son of God?

155. In a way, this traditional site of the incarnation is even more sacred than the famous altar of the star in the Church of the Nativity at Bethlehem, for it was here that the divine took on human nature when Jesus was miraculously conceived in Mary's womb. *See* Bruce, *Jesus and Paul: Places They Knew* 5-17.

156. From time immemorial the hometown of Zechariah and Elizabeth has been identified with picturesque Ain-Karim, once west of Jerusalem but now one of its suburbs. There, two beautiful churches supposedly mark the locations of the visitation and the birth of John respectively.

157. Beth-Shemesh (House of the Sun) was located some fifteen miles southwest of Jerusalem and is identified with Tell er Rumeileh near the modern Ain Shems. *See* John McKenzie, "Beth-Shemesh," *Dictionary of the Bible* (New York: Macmillan, 1965) 94-95. However, the geography of the area may outweigh any remaining artifacts, because it is the perfect setting for the return of the ark, as described in 1 Sam 6:10-16.

158. Kiriath-jearim was a Gibeonite city allied by covenant with Israel (Josh 9–10) and identified today with Tell el Azhar, a few miles west of Jerusalem. *See* McKenzie, *Dictionary of the Bible* 484.

159. According to 1 Sam 7:2, the ark of the covenant seems to have remained at Kiriath-jearim about twenty years, until David retrieved it for Jerusalem.

160. When one compares the exclamatory question of David in 2 Sam 6:9 with that of Elizabeth in Luke 1:43, there appear to be some distinct differences, but these are more apparent than real because David's *pôs* and Elizabeth's *póthen* are quite capable of being translated the same way: "How can it be that . . . ?" or "How can it happen that . . . ?" That leaves as the only real difference, but with what seems clearly to be a play on words, David's *he kibotòs kuríou?* (the ark of the Lord) and Elizabeth's *he méter toû kuríou mou* (the mother of my Lord)! *See* Joseph Thayer, *A Greek Lexicon of the New Testament* (New York: American Book, 1889) 524, 559. (Note that I have compared the Greek of the New Testament with the Greek Septuagint translation of the Old Testament rather than with the original Hebrew because in the vast majority of references the New Testament cites the Septuagint.)

161. Jean Paul Richter, *Levana,* quoted in *A New Dictionary of Quotations,* ed. H. L. Mencken (New York: Knopf, 1942) 332.

162. Some have maintained that the followers of Jesus were called Christians in a pejorative sense because the word *Christianoí* is a combination of Greek and Latin, but this conclusion is unwarranted because there are other instances of such combinations without any demeaning sense, *(New Catholic Encyclopedia,* 1967, s.v. "Christian [The Term]").

163. *The Woman Who Was Poor: A Contemporary Novel of the French "Eighties,"* trans. I. J. Collins (New York: Sheed and Ward, 1947) 356.

164. Solomon's Porch, more properly called a portico, was a covered walkway about fifteen hundred feet long with two rows of stone columns along the east side of the Temple area overlooking the Kedron Valley, which separates Jerusalem from the Mount of Olives. Like everything but the Temple proper, which was preserved intact since the time of Zerubabel (after the return from the Babylonian Captivity in the sixth century B.C.), Solomon's Porch was constructed by Herod the Great and his successors in typical massive Herodian style. *See* Gonzalo Baez-Camargo, *Archaeological Commentary on the Bible* (Garden City, N.Y.: Doubleday, 1986) 230–31.

165. The performance of miracles through Peter's mere shadow is something never reported even of Jesus, which to me is a confirmation of the truth of his statement in John 14:12 that one who has faith in him will do even greater things than he has done, the explanation being that it continues to be Jesus doing them but now through his followers, in fulfillment of Acts 1:1 that he only began in his lifetime.

166. Recall how this was predicted by Jesus in his parabolic and ecclesial discourses (Matt 13:24-29; 18:5-9) and hinted at in that enigmatic question in Luke 18:8, WFD, "Yet the Son of Man, when he comes, will he [even] find faith on the earth?"

167. *NCE,* s.v. ''Hellenist.''

168. Notice how the apostles authorized the first deacons to take care of material concerns such as food and clothing, but the Holy Spirit had other plans. Without delay the Spirit moved deacons like Stephen and Philip to engage in such spiritual works as preaching, teaching, baptizing.

169. In the biblical anthropology symbolically described in Gen 2:7 we are flesh, person, and spirit. As flesh our whole being is naturally inclined to temptation and sin, but as spirit we naturally aspire to relationship and union with God. As St. Augustine has stated it so lyrically, God has made us for himself, and our hearts are restless until they rest in him. (*The Confessions of St. Augustine,* trans. F. J. Sheed [New York: Sheed and Ward, 1941] 1, 1, 3).

170. This passage (see Rom 8:26-27) is frequently interpreted in terms of speaking in tongues and used as a warrant for employing the gift of tongues as one's regular personal prayer. I for one question such an interpretation. In the entire ch. 8, which so carefully describes life in the Spirit, there is no emphasis at all on the charismatic gifts of the Spirit with the possible exception of this text. Even in Paul's list of charismatic gifts in ch. 12, there is no mention of tongues. No, I believe the reference here is rather to that deep, mystical prayer of contemplation of and union with God in the depths of our spirit, beyond words, yes, even beyond ideas and certainly beyond dependence on emotions. This kind of prayer truly unites us with God in a way that goes far beyond ecstatic utterances. Besides, it is quite clear in both Eph 4:11-13 and 1 Pet 4:10-11 that the gift of tongues, like all the charismatic gifts, is given not for our own sanctification but for the good of others, to build up the Church of God. On these matters, please consult *NCE,* ''Charism'' and ''Gift of Tongues,'' and ''Charismatic Prayer,'' *NCE* supp. ''Change in the Church.''

171. Paul's treatment on life in the Spirit in the eighth chapter of Romans concludes, very appropriately, with the question ''Who will separate us from the love of Christ?'' (8:35, NAB), which he answers completely in 8:37-39.

RECOMMENDED READING LIST

Anchor Bible, vols 1 and 2, Joseph Fitzmyer, *The Gospel According to Luke: Introduction, Translation, and Notes.* Garden City, N.Y.: Doubleday, 1981, 1985.

Brown, Raymond. *The Birth of the Messiah: A Commentary on the Infancy Narratives in Matthew and Luke.* Garden City, N.Y.: Doubleday, 1977.

Bruce, F. F. ''The Book of the Acts,'' *The New International Commentary on the New Testament,* rev. ed. Grand Rapids: Eerdmans, 1988.

Keck, Leander, and Martyn, Louis eds. *Studies in Luke-Acts.* Philadelphia: Fortress, 1980.

McBride, Denis. *The Gospel of Luke: A Reflective Commentary.* Dublin: Dominican Publications, 1982.

QUESTIONS FOR REFLECTION AND DISCUSSION

1. What do we know about the authorship of the Gospel of Luke and his Acts of Apostles?

2. What seem to have been the circumstances and purposes that led to the writing of these parallel works?

3. What are some of the principal characteristics of these twin writings?

4. What are the principal parallels and journeys in Luke-Acts, and why are they important?

5. What are some of the most helpful lessons that we can draw from Luke-Acts for our Christian living today?

Index

REMARKS: This subject index is at the same time selective and comprehensive; selective because an index of each and every subject touched on in this volume, let alone proper names and scripture references, would be far too unwieldy; but comprehensive because, unlike many indices, references are also made to the endnotes, where subjects are expanded for the sake of greater clarification and explanation, not to mention documentation, without burdening the main text, especially the story part. For economy of time and space, all references are to page numbers, including the endnotes.